Walking the Border

A JOURNEY BETWEEN SCOTLAND AND ENGLAND

Ian Crofton

With photographs by the author and
additional photography by Joyce Nicholls

BIRLINN

This edition first published in 2015 by
Birlinn Limited
West Newington House
10 Newington Road
Edinburgh
EH9 1QS

www.birlinn.co.uk

ISBN: 978 1 78027 308 2

British Library Cataloguing-in-Publication Data
A catalogue record for this book is available from the
British Library

Typeset by Iolaire Typesetting, Newtonmore
Printed and bound by Grafica Veneta
www.graficaveneta.com

CONTENTS

Contents

ILLUSTRATIONS

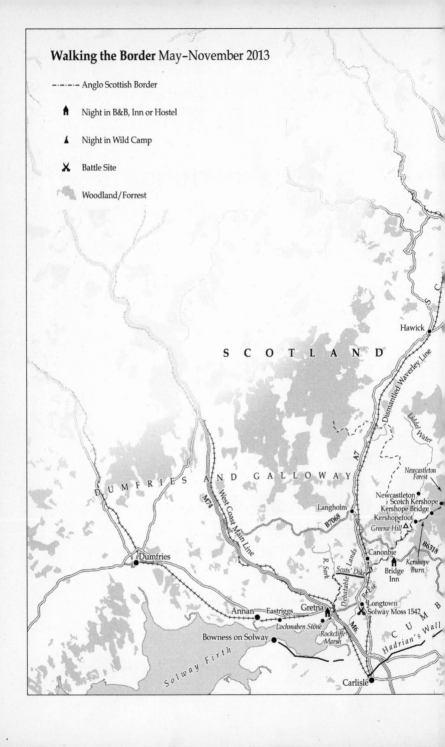

Walking the Border May–November 2013

–·–·– Anglo Scottish Border

🏠 Night in B&B, Inn or Hostel

▲ Night in Wild Camp

✕ Battle Site

Woodland/Forrest

SCOTLAND

Hawick

DUMFRIES AND GALLOWAY

Dismantled Waverley Line

Liddel Water

A7

Newcastleton Forest

Newcastleton
Scotch Kershope
Kershope Bridge
Kershopefoot
Greena Hill △

B6318

Langholm

B7068

Canonbie

Kershope Burn

Bridge Inn

West Coast Main Line

M74

R. Sark

Scots' Dike

Debatable Lands

R. Esk

Dumfries

Annan   Eastriggs   Gretna

Lochmaben Stone

Longtown
✕ Solway Moss 1542

M6

CUMB

Hadrian's Wall

Bowness on Solway

Rockcliffe Marsh

Solway Firth

Carlisle

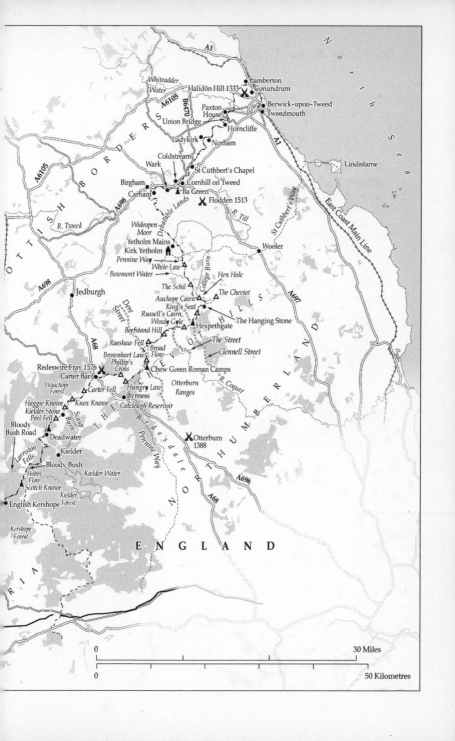

ONE

CONUNDRUM

Borders, barbed wire and bonny bairns

It's, well, a more or less borderless world. And that's as it should be.
   Except for the borders where they check your passport for hours, the child's small voice says from the other end of the table.

– Ali Smith, There But For The (2011)

I don't know how many times I've crossed the Border. Maybe a few score times, maybe several hundred. I never counted. Sometimes I've known the moment, sometimes not. No one's ever stamped my passport.

The first crossing would have been some cold spring night in 1955 or 1956. Every year my mother would take us south from Edinburgh to spend Easter with our grandparents in the Isle of Wight.

In what felt like the middle of the night we'd be stirred out of bed with low lights and whispers. Still in our pyjamas we'd be bundled into jumpers and coats and a taxi, and drive off into the urgent dark.

Waverley Station in the steam age was a cavern of black walls, black girders, blackened glass. Even the locomotives were soot black, not the red, blue or green of engines in picture books. Yellow lights glared through smoke and steam. Everything was in motion, nothing certain. The air shook with shouts, whistles, hisses, the din and clang of metal on metal.

Tottering along the platform half asleep, one hand in my mother's, my other hand let go its burden. Panda slipped between train and platform. The loss was incomprehensible, irrecoverable, complete. I was too tired to cry.

Once in the tiny sleeping compartment, my mother pulled down the blinds, lowered the cover over the basin, tucked me and my sister toe-to-toe in the bottom bunk, our heads at either end. Foot-fighting soon gave way to half sleep, rocked by the jerk and rattle of the train. And so, sideways, we travelled southward. And somewhere, at some point in the dreamlike dream of sleeping and waking and sleeping through a night punctuated by the rhythm of rails, sleepers, points – somewhere, at some point, I crossed the Border for the first time.

When the sleeper attendant knocked in the early morning with

2

tea and biscuits, he told us we would soon arrive in London. I had no idea what that meant.

Other crossings have followed: by rail on the East Coast Line or the West Coast Line; by road on the A1 north of Berwick, or by Coldstream Bridge over the Tweed or the hill pass of Carter Bar, or the A7 south of Canonbie, or over the Sark on the M74 as it flows imperceptibly into the M6. In the days I worked for Collins Publishers in Glasgow, I would sometimes take the early morning shuttle to Heathrow, changing countries somewhere high above the Solway Firth or the Irish Sea. 'Anything to drink, sir?' a flight attendant would ask. 'Coffee, please. Black.' I'd've been up too early for breakfast, could only cope with a coffee. Some businessmen on the flight would order a double vodka.

Hurtling towards Edinburgh on the East Coast Line, you've got to have your wits about you to spot the England–Scotland Border. There is a sign, but it flashes past in an instant. The guard makes no remark, the passengers remain unmoved. North of here you won't pay for your prescriptions or your university education or your care in old age. You can walk where you want without fear of prosecution. And if you find yourself in court for some other misdemeanour, a jury may judge you neither innocent nor guilty, but conclude instead that the case against you is merely 'not proven'.

In contrast to the rail routes, all the main road crossings have enormous signs welcoming you to either Scotland or England, the former streaked with the Blue Saltire, the latter adorned with the Cross of St George. 'Welcome to Scotland', the former says. 'Fàilte gu Alba'. No one has spoken Gaelic in these Border regions since the Dark Ages – if then. In the west it might have been Welsh, in the east Pictish or Anglo-Saxon.

The summer of my walk, as the temperature rose in the independence debate, small posters began to appear on the back of road signs on the English side. They bore a Cross of St George and the slogan 'HOME RULE'. The local authorities were incensed. They'd have to pay taxpayers' money scraping them off. The English Defence

League was suspected, but did not claim responsibility. Nothing they'd like better, one suspects, than to cut off the Celtic Fringe.

On smaller roads, the Scots keep up the national welcome, but on the English side you're more likely to be welcomed to Northumberland or Cumbria, with no mention of the country you're entering. The only place there's any real fuss is at Carter Bar, where there's a magnificent view north over Scotland, a snack bar in a caravan, and a man in a kilt who stops picking up the litter when a coach party appears, hoists his bagpipes aloft and bursts into a medley of popular tunes. He has a sign:

> This is my livelihood
> Please leave a tip.

The Italians and the Americans and the Chinese queue up to have their photograph taken with him. His face is as stony as the Border Stone beside him. Only the tourists smile.

One of the last walks I had with my father, in his nineties, was up the path from Holyrood to Salisbury Crags. It was a grey, damp winter day. I kept my eye on the old man as he negotiated the wet paving stones, stick in hand. We slowly rose above the newly-opened Parliament. He was a fan of the building, I was not. It was too fussy for me, with too many unnecessary ornamentations, though it sat well in its setting. But my father was always thrilled with 'modern architecture'. In the 1960s he'd drive us out to see Livingstone New Town when it was still being built, show us the new Napier College, its glass and steel and concrete enveloping the old stones of Merchiston Tower. He'd taken us to see Basil Spence's new Coventry Cathedral, built next to the charred ruins of the medieval cathedral that had been blitzed in November 1940. It was a symbol of postwar reconciliation, he told us. His sister had married a German just after the war, and he'd introduced his German nephew to mountain-climbing. He was of the generation of 1945, the generation that looked forward to a new and better world, a world in which the modernist, collectivist, internationalist project in architecture was to play its part. He shared in the vision of a united Europe, one that would succeed the old empires and prevent the 'balkanisation' of the continent, in which smaller and smaller groups of shriller and shriller nationalists would insist on their separation from (and superiority to) their neighbours.

And yet – if it is an 'and yet' – he was very much in favour of Scottish devolution, and of the Scottish Parliament as an institution as well as a building. Scotland was not his country, but it was the country he and my mother adopted before I was born. They loved Scotland – its landscapes, its people, the richness of its past – and saw the Scottish Parliament as a revitalisation of a country that had been demoralised and impoverished under Thatcher. But at the end of the day, if he had still been alive, he would have voted for maintaining the Union come September 2014. Complete independence would have been a balkanisation too far. Had he lived, he would have had the opportunity to vote. His son, exiled in London for a quarter of a century, won't need to make that difficult decision.

I have never been prevented from crossing a border. The nearest I've come to it was in 1970. I was fifteen and driving with my older brother into Derry/Londonderry at the end of a family holiday in Donegal. At the edge of the city, just inside the border between the Republic and the North, there was an army roadblock. The barrier was down. Soldiers armed with FN automatic rifles ordered us out of the car. We stood at the roadside half-thrilled, half-terrified, under the watchful gaze of a lance-corporal up on a grass embankment. He was shielded behind sandbags and had his finger on the trigger of a Browning medium machine gun. The soldiers searched the car. Boot, bonnet and glove compartment were opened, door-pockets rifled, seats lifted. Even my brother's spectacle case was opened. Then they waved us on. No smiles, no thank-yous. I'm not sure if they said a single word. It was all done by gestures. Now I knew what it was like to be under armed occupation.

In the past, borders right across Europe were manned by armed guards. They still are if you are arriving from outside Europe. The combination of uniforms and guns, or even uniforms on their own, can be intimidating. It is dehumanising for anybody who comes under scrutiny. Are you who you say you are? And even if you are, will we allow you to pass? Or will we put you in handcuffs, hold you uncharged in a cell, send you back to where you don't want to go?

Five years after my visit to Northern Ireland I was travelling alone on the overnight train from Munich to Belgrade. I shared the small old-fashioned compartment with an elderly peasant couple. He wore a black suit, white shirt and no tie. She was also dressed in black, and kept her hair wrapped in a red headscarf. In those days many Yugoslavs worked as *Gastarbeiter* in West Germany, so I guessed this elderly couple had been visiting their children, maybe even their grandchildren. The separation must have been painful, but no doubt the money sent home was welcome.

Though I had no Serbo-Croat and they had no English, we understood each other well enough. The man cut chunks off a cold leg of lamb with a fierce-looking knife and offered them to me. I passed round the bottle of Swabian red my aunt had given me for the journey.

The old couple were canny enough, when darkness fell, to stretch out on the banquette seats facing forward and facing back. I'd been out in the corridor, a daft laddie peering up at the mountains as the moon rose. So I was left with the option of either sitting upright on one end of a banquette, or the floor. I chose the latter, and so spent the night sideways, in and out of sleep, rattling through the Alps and into what was then communist Yugoslavia.

I woke in bright early morning light with a boot pressed on my head. 'Bassbort,' a mouth way above the boot demanded. Between the boot and the mouth there was a shiny brown leather pistol hol-ster. Careful not to make a sudden move, I extracted my head from under the boot and dug out my passport. In those days I had long hair. The guard looked at my photograph, then at me, then at the photograph. My hair had grown several decadent Western hippy inches since the photograph had been taken. He looked like he'd just found something deeply unpleasant on the sole of his boot.

Although in those days all the ports and roads and railway lines between European countries had border and customs controls, there were still places you could cross frontiers without anyone paying you any attention. In the Alps the borders often follow the crests of high ridges, and on mountaineering trips I have often crossed between France and Switzerland, or France and Italy, or Italy and Switzerland without noticing. On occasion, when climbing a ridge, I have followed the actual border for hundreds of metres with one foot in one country and warm sunshine, and the other foot in another country and icy shade. The only marks of man are metal crosses on summits, or, lower down, cairns and flashes of paint marking a path. In those days, when there were still border controls on the roads, if you descended to a mountain refuge or a village in a different country from the one where you'd started your climb, no one asked to see your passport, no one asked whether you had anything to declare.

Since the creation of the single EU market in 1993 and the borderless Schengen Area in 1995 you can travel from Spain to Finland, from Norway to Sicily, without being stopped at a single frontier. In the whole of western and central Europe, only Fortress UK (bound together in this instance with the Republic of Ireland in the 'Common Travel Area') maintains border controls with its continental neighbours.

Perhaps it's living on an island that makes Britons so untrusting of outsiders. Ironically, we were all once outsiders. We think of the Celts – ancient Britons, Welsh, Gaels, Picts – as the aboriginal inhabitants of these islands, but there were people here long before they arrived, some of whose languages may survive in certain ancient river names, including that of the River Tweed. After the Celts came the Romans, then the Angles, Saxons and Jutes, the Vikings, the Normans. In later centuries there were French Huguenots and Central European Jews, Italians, Irish, Germans and Poles, Jamaicans, Barbadians and Guyanese, Indians and Pakistanis, Bangladeshis and Cantonese.

There's always been resentment of the incomer, fear of the other, emotions that politicians the world over have been quick to exploit.

There's nothing like wrapping yourself in the flag of nation or race or ethnicity to whip up support, gain power and make a few quid on the side.

In the UK today, few in the political and media establishments are prepared to depict immigration as anything other than a problem. A huge apparatus of state bureaucracy has been assembled to close the door; a state bureaucracy that, in obeisance to the fetish of the free market, has handed over the power to deprive individuals of their liberty to the likes of Serco and G4S. Such private corporations profit from running a series of 'Immigration Removal Centres', where people who are not EU citizens and who do not have the right paperwork can be held indefinitely without trial, wondering every day if this is the day they are going to be deported – to face uncertainty, or impoverishment, or shame, or persecution, or even death.

Too few people pause to ponder the ethics involved. What moral justification can there be for treating somebody differently just because he or she was born on the other side of a border? To attempt to justify such discriminatory treatment would involve lending an arbitrary line on a map some kind of moral authority: on this side of the border live the deserving; on the other, the undeserving.

This is not just an idle philosophical question. There are thousands of human beings – men, women and children – who have come to the UK to escape poverty or persecution, to make a better life for themselves. All too often they find their dream goes sour. They cannot – for one reason or another – go back to the place they came from. But if they stay they become non-persons. With no papers, no recognised status, no right to work and, in the official phrase, 'no recourse to public funds', they cease to be officially human. They are rendered invisible.

While I was researching this book, I was anxious to find out what borders meant to a range of different people. A friend suggested I come along to the migrant drop-in centre she was involved in. I'd hear some stories from the visitors there, she said, that'd tell me all about what borders can do to people.

The centre sets up its stall in a church hall one day a week. The hall is filled with tables spread with brightly-patterned cloths and laid for lunch. At the far end of the hall a few volunteers are working in the kitchen, chopping up fruit and vegetables donated by local shops. There is a smell of garlic and cooking oil, onion and spices. Someone's bashing a halved pomegranate with a wooden spoon to extract the sweet seeds. The volunteers range in age from students to retired professionals. Some are migrants themselves.

The visitors come from all over: Eastern Europe, North Africa, the Middle East, the Horn of Africa, West Africa, Congo, Latin America – even as far as Mongolia and China.

As well as lunch, the centre offers advice both on immigration and on welfare. Volunteers try to identify in what ways the centre might be able to help. Do they have somewhere to live? Do they have a GP? Do they have family here? Are they homeless, destitute? Difficult welfare issues are dealt with by a highly-trained adviser, while immigration questions are referred to one or other of the lawyers who work at the centre pro bono.

There is an atmosphere of warmth and welcome, quiet calm and efficiency, sometimes livened up by a toddler on the rampage. Some of the visitors are cheery, but many are at the end of their tether – stressed, anxious, depressed. Some are in 'regular' accommodation, though this can mean the only bathroom they have access to is three floors away, a problem for a mother with a young child. Many are sleeping at a friend's house, often in overcrowded conditions. Too many are street homeless. You can tell the ones who're sleeping rough from the acrid smell of unwashed clothes.

Fear makes many withhold key details of their stories. Sometimes they change their accounts as they begin to trust you. They've had enough of what officials will do to you if you tell them too much of the truth. They'd been made to feel they didn't belong where they'd come from. And once they'd got to the UK – some of them smuggled, some trafficked, some on temporary visas – they'd been made to feel that they didn't belong here either. If they did claim asylum, the whole system is geared to finding any chink of a reason to refuse them.

So these borders, these arbitrary lines that we invest with moral agency – where are they? What are they?

The world's longest land border between two countries is that between the USA and Canada. It runs for 5,500 miles and is marked by a twenty-foot-wide strip or 'no-touching zone' cleared through the forest and prairie. For a considerable proportion of this distance the Border is dead straight, following the 49th Parallel, ignoring topography and traditional tribal lands. It is technically illegal to cross the border anywhere there isn't a border control – but there is nothing to stop you. Unlike the 'Demilitarized Zone' between the two Koreas, the no-touching zone doesn't have a minefield. There are no guard towers with machine guns, backed by heavy artillery and tanks. There isn't even a fence.

In contrast, the USA's southern border with Mexico is guarded by 17,000 members of the United States Border Patrol. There are nearly seven hundred miles of double chain-link and barbed-wire fences and solid steel walls. In places the fences run through the middle of towns. The remaining 1,300 miles of border – much of it wild and tractless – is monitored by towers, cameras, sensors and aerial drones. Many would-be migrants now avoid the fence by seeking out remote trails through the desert mountains. Unprepared, hundreds die of thirst or sunstroke. Their bodies sometimes lie undiscovered for months. Some have hanged themselves from trees to hasten the inevitable end.

Similar barriers have appeared over the centuries wherever the rich world has found itself cheek to cheek with the dispossessed. The Chinese protected their 'civilisation' from the 'barbarians' beyond the gates with the Great Wall. The Romans built Hadrian's Wall to mark the edge of the Pax Romana. The Warsaw Pact ostensibly built the Berlin Wall to keep socialism safe from destruction at the hands of the Western capitalist marauders – although the real reason was to stem the haemorrhage of skilled workers to the consumer utopia of the German Federal Republic.

The Israelis claim the West Bank Barrier protects their citizens from Palestinian suicide bombers. The Palestinians see the invasive and disruptive maze of fencing and concrete as just one more move in an expansionist land-grab. In 2004 the International Court of Justice issued an advisory opinion stating that 'the construction of the wall, and its associated régime, are contrary to international law'.

While Fortress UK refuses to become part of the Schengen Area, some EU member states seem set on constructing a Fortress Europe. Spain, for example, has separated its wealthy North African enclave of Melilla from neighbouring non-EU Morocco with razor wire. This has inflicted hideous injuries – or even death – on numerous migrants from Sub-Saharan Africa who have tried to cross it.

Some don't make it this far. In October 2013, while I was writing this book, the bodies of ninety-two people, mostly women and children, were found in the Sahara Desert in northern Niger. It is thought they were being trafficked to Algeria and that their lorry had broken down. They were found scattered over a large area – sometimes a mother with her children, sometimes children alone. What motivated these people to attempt such a dangerous journey is not difficult to fathom. Niger comes at or near the bottom of a range of indices of development, including life expectancy, education and income. Save the Children have declared that Niger is the worst country in the world to be a mother.

At the other end of the Mediterranean from Melilla, Greece has built a four-metre-high wall along its land border with non-EU Turkey. Towards the end of 2013 Turkey itself started to build a wall along its border with Syria. Refugees from the conflict in Syria, and other conflicts in Afghanistan, Somalia and Eritrea, have tried to get round such barriers by boat. Those landing on Greek islands are kept in conditions that Amnesty International has condemned as 'shocking'.

Some boats don't make it. A popular route across the Mediterranean traverses the straits between North Africa and the tiny Italian island of Lampedusa, south of Sicily. In October 2013, the same month as those 92 corpses were found in the Sahara, at least 359 people were drowned when the 20-metre boat carrying them from Libya to Lampedusa capsized. They'd paid at least $3,000 per head to get a place on board.

There are increasing numbers of reports of EU states on the Mediterranean ordering illegal 'push-back' operations. These involve naval or coastguard vessels intercepting migrant boats in international waters and towing them back to where they came from without finding out whether any of the passengers are entitled to protection under international law.

For too many Britons the sea is also, as Shakespeare wrote, a wall or moat 'Against the envy of less happier lands'. At ports such as Dover sniffer dogs and carbon-dioxide detectors surround disembarked lorries, looking for stowaways from those 'less happier lands'. International airports also serve as borders. Huge queues develop, especially at Heathrow, as each individual arriving on a flight from outside the UK is subjected to close scrutiny by tight-lipped, inscrutable officials. Even for UK and EU nationals it feels like a place where your identity might be doubted, even taken away from you. For most people, going through passport control is the only time they are aware of being put under suspicion by the state.

Britain also has internal borders. Back in the eighth century, Offa of Mercia marked the frontier between his kingdom and the Welsh with his eponymous dyke. Between the Welsh and the English the physical barrier of the dyke – whose course is still broadly followed by the Anglo-Welsh border – was reinforced by difference in language.

The same could not – and still cannot – be said of the inhabitants of southern Scotland and those of northern England. In the Middle Ages they all spoke the same northern variety of Anglo-Saxon, and even today they share many dialect words ('bonny bairns' are to be found as far afield as Edinburgh and Newcastle). The accents are broadly distinct, although, as I was to find as I walked along the Border, they sometimes mingle. Throughout the Middle Ages the Anglo-Scottish Border continually shifted. The question of the division of the Debatable Lands between Sark and Esk was only settled in 1552 with the construction of Scots' Dike, and in some remote parts the Border was not clearly defined until the nineteenth century. Loyalties were often stronger to relatives and allies across the Border than to the notional authorities in either London or Edinburgh.

It is thus more a matter of historical accident, diplomatic fixing and legal wheeler-dealing that the people of Northumbria and Cumbria find themselves in England, and the people of Berwickshire and Roxburghshire find themselves in Scotland. Berwick itself changed hands thirteen times between 1147 and 1482, finally ending up in England.

On the A1 just north of Berwick, still within England, there is a farm called Conundrum. I'm not sure of the significance of the name (the origin of the word itself is a conundrum), but for me it sums up the whole oddity of the Anglo-Scottish Border – and of borders more generally.

I myself am uncertain about where I belong. Although I was born and schooled in Edinburgh, and then spent the first ten years of my working life in Glasgow, my parents weren't Scottish. They had moved north from London two years before I was born. My father was Anglo-Irish, from Dublin, and my mother born in Liverpool of a Lancastrian father and a Scottish mother. I myself have lived for the last quarter century in London.

So I have my own conundrums, out of which the idea of walking the Border emerged and became something of an obsession. I studied maps in greater and greater detail, fascinated by the wandering course of this random line, and of the names along its way: Sarkfoot Point, Solway Moss, Scotland Gate, Liddel Strength, Skurrlywarble Wood, Harelawslack, Hobbs' Flow, Bloody Bush, Foulmire Heights, Deadwater Rigg, Butter Bog, the Hearts Toe, Wideopen Moor, Gallows Hill, Folly Farm, Meg's Dub . . . I traced the line of the Border along rivers, across fields, through thick conifer plantations, over remote and tractless hills and moors. I could tell from the map that much of the route was far from picturesque. There were surprisingly few paths. It wasn't an established walking route, like the Southern Upland Way or the Hadrian's Wall Walk. That was part of the attraction. It would be a journey of discovery, of unexpected meetings with strangers, of encounters with the past, whether historical or legendary. It would also be an inward journey, as my intention was to walk much of the way alone.

My original plan had been to walk the entire length of the Border in a single push of seven days. But as the going turned out to be much tougher than I had expected, and the weather as unkind as I *should* have expected, I ended up by doing the walk in three stages – at the end of May, in mid-July, and in November. I also ended up walking in company – good company – for three out of the ten days I eventually took to complete the distance.

In between these trips, back home in London, I continued to visit the migrant centre, collecting stories of what borders can mean to those who are told they are on the wrong side of one of these arbitrary lines.

Many break under the strain. Those lines on the map can turn into mental whips, chains, snares, depriving those caught up in them of freedom and dignity – even sanity.

One failed asylum seeker from the war-ravaged Democratic Republic of Congo was so far deep in depression he could not even remember the age of his young daughter. She was in care in Manchester. Her mother was in a psychiatric ward. He himself was broken by months of living rough on the streets. He'd spent time in jail for trying to leave the UK on a stolen passport to join the Congolese community in France. When the UK tried to deport him to the DRC, he was refused entry. He had to be flown back to Heathrow.

Then there was the birdlike nurse from Iran. The first thing you noticed about her was her huge, frightened eyes. Some weeks after she'd arrived in the UK to study English she'd been told by friends back home that the security forces were looking for her. They'd heard she'd treated an anti-government protestor at her hospital.

Her asylum request was refused on the standard grounds that she hadn't claimed immediately on arrival in the UK.

I spent many months talking to a West African mother of two. She was living in a garage. Her local social services refused to take any responsibility for her baby and toddler, even though their health was suffering and her accommodation had been condemned as not fit for human habitation. Eventually she confided in me that her fare to London on a visitor's visa had been paid by a woman friend of her father whom she knew only as 'Nana'. When she arrived in London Nana took her passport, made her swear a juju oath, locked her in the house and forced her into prostitution. She was told that if she went to the police she'd be put in prison. After three years she managed to escape. She is now in a safe house.

One of the biggest characters at the centre is a small but forceful old man from Belarus, who was born in a labour camp in Siberia. Eventually he and his mother found their way back to Belarus, where he became active in the opposition, first against the Soviet authorities, and then, after independence, against 'the last dictator in Europe'. His activities cost him his front teeth and his family, whom he had to leave behind when he fled. It took the UK authorities ten years to grant him asylum.

These are just a few of the stories I gleaned the year I walked the Border. It has indeed been a journey of discovery. As I zigzagged between Scotland and England, only thwarted by the roughness of the ground, I sought to find what makes us different. I'm not sure I found any kind of answer. Back in the city, though, the city of migrants, I found what makes us the same.

TWO

RUMOURS OF WAR

Gretna and the Solway

We don't sound very Scottish, do we?

– Barmaid in Gretna

Day Zero: Thursday, 23rd May 2013   The two-carriage train south from Glasgow Central to Gretna Green is in no hurry. It's one of those few rambling lines that Dr Beeching forgot to close. At first your track is one of many running in parallel, but as the city sprawls south through Crossmyloof, Pollokshaws and Nitshill into Renfrewshire, the tracks diverge. You soon leave the Virgin expresses to hurtle down the main West Coast Line, and your little wandering train is on its own, heading for Ayrshire. People get on, people get off. No one has much luggage. They're just doing the stuff they need to do – shopping, visiting relatives meeting friends.

The names of the stations resonate: Barrhead, Dunlop, Stewarton, Kilmaurs, Kilmarnock, Auchinleck. And so on past the coal bings of New Cumnock and Kirkconnel, into the valley of the Nith.

This is wilder country, with woods of twisted oaks showing only a hint of yellow leaf, even at the end of May. Above sheep-filled green fields the hills are still winter brown. It's been a long, hard spring. Not much more than a month before, in mid-April, many lambs died in snowdrifts.

We pass through the market towns of Sanquhar and Dumfries before coming to Annan, a royal burgh and former port. Daniel Defoe, visiting in the 1720s, thought the place to be 'in a state of irrevocable decay'. A century or so later Thomas Carlyle, who was born at nearby Ecclefechan, considered Annan 'a fine, bright, self-confident little town'. Annan was more recently synonymous with its nuclear power station, commissioned in 1959 and known as Chapelcross. For years its four mighty cooling towers dominated the flat lands along the shores of the Solway. Their sinuously curved shapes looming on the horizon imprinted themselves on my memories of childhood holidays in Dumfriesshire. To me, with their plumes of steam billowing eastward on the wind, they represented a glimpse of the future. What I didn't know then was that the primary purpose of Chapelcross was to produce weapons-grade plutonium.

Chapelcross was decommissioned in 2004. Three years later the towers were demolished in a controlled explosion. Within ten seconds the horizon was cleared. Only heaps of rubble remained.

If you were to float one of the old hulks rotting in what's left of Annan's harbour and sail it down the river to its mouth, and then let the ebbing tide take you out into the Solway Firth, you'd find yourself in the channel of the River Eden. At low tide there'd be bird-rich mudflats on either side. Drifting a mile or two westward, between Howgarth Scar and Cardurnock Flatts, you'd come to a point – a seemingly arbitrary point, at grid reference NY 152 631 – where the Ordnance Survey has marked the western end of the Anglo-Scottish Border.

Whoever decided the Border should start here – in an uncertain, chill seascape of shifting quicksands and treacherous currents, home to nothing but crabs and gulls and flounders – must have had a heightened sense of the ridiculous.

If, still aboard your hulk, you then dropped anchor and waited to weigh it until the tide turned, you'd float back up the channel of the River Eden for three or four miles until you could just make out, on the English shore, the small settlement of Bowness-on-Solway. This was the western terminus of Hadrian's Wall, and is the closest the line of the ancient Roman frontier comes to the modern Border. Just north of the Border, on the edge of the mudflat called Gowkesk Rig, the Ordnance Survey marks an 'Altar Stone'. But the OS does not specify to which god – Olympian or Christian or Druidic – this altar was dedicated.

Beyond Bowness, through the reach called Bowness Wath, the Border makes its way eastward up the Solway, abandoning – so the OS informs us – the 'Channel of the River Eden' for the 'Channel of the River Esk'. On the south shore the settlements are few and far between. Port Carlisle, despite its grand name, is now little more than a pub. Then there's the hamlet of Burgh by Sands, where in

1307 – in a medieval version of paper, scissors, stone – Edward I, Hammer of the Scots, finally succumbed to the scythe of the Grim Reaper. He was seen off, not by a sword on the field of battle, as he might have wished, but by the bloody flux.

To the north of Burgh by Sands lies Rockcliffe Marsh, a maze of channels and pools and salt sward whose features are so transient that only two have names: Near Gulf and its remoter neighbour Far Gulf. It is no place for humans, but a haven for gulls, waders and wildfowl. The northern tip of Rockcliffe Marsh is Sarkfoot Point. Just across the mud and water from here the Border is sucked inland by the mouth of the River Sark into the peatlands of Solway Moss.

Long before Chapelcross began its nuclear alchemy, the north shore of the Solway east of Annan was the site of another sinister industrial installation, a massive munitions plant that extended some nine miles from Dornock and Eastriggs in the west to Longtown, just over the Border, in the east. It was built in the wake of the crisis in 1915 when the British Expeditionary Force in France ran short of shells. The scandal almost toppled the government, and the immediate physical consequence was HM Factory Gretna, said to be the most extensive factory complex ever built. It was serviced by 125 miles of narrow-gauge railway lines, a water-treatment plant, a laundry that cleaned 6,000 items every day and catering facilities that produced 14,000 meals daily. Some 20,000 workers – the majority of them women – were brought in to labour here. They followed in the wake of the 10,000 navvies who had built the site – which included a number of new towns such as Eastriggs and Gretna to house the workers. To keep the workforce sober, the government nationalised all the pubs and breweries in the neighbourhood, as far as Carlisle. The site, codenamed Moorside, was carefully chosen, far from centres of population and out of reach of German raiders, whether coming by sea or by air.

HM Factory Gretna was built to make cordite, the propellant used to fire shells from big guns. Cordite is made by kneading nitroglycerine and gun-cotton together. The result was dubbed 'the Devil's porridge'*. This 'low explosive', produced in unprecedented quantities

---

* Coined by Sir Arthur Conan Doyle when he visited the plant in 1917.

at Gretna, helped to industrialise death all along that most transient of borders, the shifting trench networks of the Western Front. There, in the mud of Flanders and Picardy, Lorraine and Champagne, Englishmen and Frenchmen and Scotsmen and Germans all mixed their blood and guts and bones together to make another kind of porridge, a shambles of meat in which it was impossible to allocate a national identity to any one cut.

Today, at Eastriggs and at Longtown, the OS marks neat row after neat row of buildings, set far apart from each other. These are the explosive stores – some of them still in use by the MoD. The world is, after all, still at war with itself.

When I went to see what I could see on the ground, it proved tricky to get even a glimpse. I drove close to the gates of both Longtown and Eastriggs, parked up, then approached on foot and pressed my face against the barbed-wire-topped perimeter fence. There were signs saying 'MOD Property – Keep Out' and 'Guard Dogs on Patrol'. I dare say there was a camera somewhere that noted my registration number. I'll no doubt be on a GCHQ database by now.

It was a fresh spring afternoon when I stepped off the train. The sun was shining, the wind blowing gently – ideal weather for a walk. With the rumple and whoosh of the M74 in the background, I followed signs for 'Famous Blacksmith's Shop Attractions'. I popped into the Gretna Hall Hotel and tried to engage the tartan-jacketed receptionist in conversation. I was going to ask him about the Border, and how he felt about it. He looked very uncomfortable. I suspect he didn't like the look of my rucksack and boots. When some real guests turned up, he had the perfect excuse to attend to more pressing matters. I left him to it.

I needed to refine my approach, I realised. Not scare people.

I'm not sure I did much better in the Tourist Information Office. The uniformed young woman with a Cumbrian accent was friendly and helpful. But she found herself tongue-tied when I asked her what was the stupidest question she'd ever been asked. (Probably because she had, at that moment, just been asked it.) However, after a long pause and some blushing, the answer came: 'Does the Loch Ness Monster live in Loch Lomond?'

I asked her what it was like travelling across the Border to work.
'I don't really notice,' she said.
Had anyone ever told her to go back to England?
'Not yet,' she said.

I asked about the campsite marked on the map by the Old Toll House, just next to the motorway. She told me that the site no longer existed. When I passed by the Old Toll House later that afternoon there was a sign in the window saying 'Site closed'. Behind, there was a field with a few abandoned caravans, tipped up at jaunty angles. The site was derelict. It looked like a tornado'd hit it. I was all for wild camping on the Solway shore, but the young woman in the Tourist Information Office told me that the tide'd likely take me away. But she gave me the address of a nearby guest house.

What Detroit once was for automobiles and Sheffield was for steel, Gretna is for weddings. The nuptial industry here predates plutonium, predates cordite, and has survived both. Gretna thrives on the wedding business. The signs say it all:

OVER 10000 MARRIAGES
PERFORMED IN THIS
MARRIAGE ROOM
EST^D 1830

GRETNA HALL HOTEL
& BLACKSMITH SHOP
"THE ORIGINAL MARRIAGE HOUSE"

Gretna
Registration
Office

GRETNA ONE STOP WEDDINGS

The Complete
Wedding Flower Service

The
Gretna Wedding Bureau

ROLLS ROYCE
WEDDING CAR
HIRE

The sign to the Courtship Maze (where getting together has never been harder) was placed next to another pointing to the Gretna Parish Cemetery.

It all started with an Act of Parliament of 1753 that was intended to put a stop to the clandestine marriage of minors in England – especially the marriages of young heiresses to unscrupulous rogues. Scotland had no such legislation, and a couple could marry there without a licence, banns or a presiding minister. All that was required to make a marriage legal was a declaration by the couple in front of witnesses. This latter role was taken on with enthusiasm by various worthies in the village of Gretna and nearby Gretna Green, who would receive a handsome reward for their services. The blacksmith at Gretna Green appears to have pretty much abandoned the shoeing of horses for the tying of nuptial knots – the ceremony being performed over the smith's anvil.

You might have thought the Marriage (Scotland) Act of 1939, with its abolition of marriage by declaration, would have put a stop to all these 'owre-the-march marriages'. But in fact young English couples continued to elope north of the Border, as minors over the age of sixteen could still marry there without parental consent. This went on until 1969, when the legal age of majority was reduced from twenty-one to eighteen. Even this seems not to have done too much damage to the Gretna wedding industry, and couples with an appetite for such things still flock to Gretna to get hitched. There is much big hair and big frocks in evidence, trimmed out in tartan and lace.

In addition to attracting wedding business, Gretna has also cashed in on its history to bring in a wider range of tourists, whatever their marital status. In 1886 a local farmer called Hugh Mackie opened the 'Famous Blacksmith's Shop', said to be one of Scotland's first visitor attractions. The business has stayed in the family ever since. Expansion has been steady, and there is now a wide range of enticing retail offers, from whisky tastings in the Wee Big Shop (with its porcelain cats in kilts and its miniature brass anvils) to the Gretna Green Story Exhibition and the recently opened Courtship Maze.

Most of the visiting couples are middle-aged or older. I watched them in the open-air cafe, sipping coffee from plastic mugs, chewing on scones, few talking, most seemingly resigned to their lot. Perhaps they'd hoped the visit would kindle memories of tender kisses in the back row of the Scala. There was little evidence of this. Not even the large but perfunctorily executed sculpture of a naked couple chastely embracing appeared to elicit a response. Most preferred to avert their eyes. In the plaza there's another sculpture, two giant forearms forming an arch as they clench their hands together. It reminded me of the crossed scimitars of Saddam Hussein's triumphal arch in Baghdad.

If the Famous Blacksmith's Shop doesn't satisfy your appetite for shopping, then there's always the Gretna Gateway Outlet Village. They've got a Costa.

In the early evening, dumping my rucksack in the guest house, I set out to explore. I found a little footpath leading through a small park on the south side of town. The path seemed to be heading towards the Solway. I was hoping it would take me to the Lochmaben Stone, the traditional marker of the western end of the Border, but soon I found the path was leading me east, in exactly the wrong direction. Through the hawthorn hedge on my right I caught glimpses of Skidaw and the northern Lakeland Fells. On the other side there was a deep ditch full of dead reeds.

In its own time the path turned south, and I came out onto the salt marsh on the edge of the estuary. Sheep were grazing on the grass above the mudflats. It's said that lamb reared on salt marsh is particularly sweet. In the distance I could just make out lorries roaring north on the M6. Here, where the motorway crosses the Border on its causeway, there's nothing to see but flat expanses. The peat bogs of Solway Moss extend far inland on one side, while the salt marshes and mudflats of the estuary spread out on the other. In this watery realm, one cannot believe that the Border could be anything but mutable.

A martin darted low over the water, after insects. I walked westward along the edge of the salt marsh dodging brackish pools. The greensward was dotted with sea pinks still in bud, waiting for the spring to warm up. The sea had washed some old tree trunks into twisted shapes, the wood swirled with yellows, blacks and greys. To the west, where the Solway widened out towards the Irish Sea, the skies were huge. Great balloons of cloud scudded overhead on the chill wind. There was a hint of blue on the far horizon, but most of the sea and the sky and the land I could see was grey. In the distance a curlew let out a plaintive *crwee*. It is a lonely spot, with barely a sign of the hand of man beyond a ragged barbed-wire fence. The sea and the sky dominate, the land just an afterthought.

These unfrequented reaches were once the haunt of smugglers. One of the most infamous was a Dutchman called Captain Yawkins, a man possessed of considerable daring and brilliant seamanship. On one occasion, it was said, he sailed his vessel directly between two Revenue cutters, so close that he could toss his hat onto the deck of one and his wig onto the deck of the other. Walter Scott fictionalised Yawkins as Dirk Hatteraick in *Guy Mannering*, while he appears under his own name in *The Raiders*, S.R. Crockett's 1894 tale of smuggling and slit throats.

There is another literary connection with the Solway smugglers. In 1792 Robert Burns, realising that he could not make a living out of verse, joined the Dumfries or Third Port Division of the Revenue. Early that same spring, he was involved in a dramatic incident, as related by the *Edinburgh Evening Courant* on 8th March. The previous Wednesday, the *Courant* reported: 'The revenue officers of Dumfries, assisted by a strong party of the Third Regiment of Dragoons, seized a large smuggling vessel at Sark Foot.' Sarkfoot Point was just over the water from where I was standing, though it's so flat there on the edge of Rockcliffe Marsh that it's almost impossible to distinguish it from the sea. 'Upon the officers and the military proceeding towards the vessel,' the *Courant* continued, 'which they did in martial and determined manner, over a broad space of deep water, the smugglers had the audacity to fire upon them from their swivel guns, loaded with grapeshot; but the vessel lay in such a situation as prevented their having a direction with effect.'

A more detailed account of the incident was left by another Revenue officer present that day, one Walter Crawford. A strong flowing current, Crawford reports, lay between the dragoons and the vessel, so they decided they needed boats in order to board her. But the locals had more sympathy with the smugglers than with the forces of law and order, and had holed every available boat along the coast. All the while there was constant fire of grapeshot and musketry from the vessel. With the tide ebbing, the Revenue officers decided to risk the quicksands on foot, Crawford leading one detachment of Dragoons, Quartermaster Manly a second, and Burns a third.

> Our orders to the Military were to reserve their fire till within eight yards of the vessel, then to pour a volley and board her with sword and pistol. The vessel kept on firing, tho without any damage to us, as from the situation of the ship, they could not bring their great guns to bear on us, we in the mean time wading breast high, and in justice to the party under my command I must say with great alacrity; by the time we were within one hundred yards of the vessel, the crew gave up the cause, got over [the] side towards England, which shore was for a long, long way dry sand. As I still supposed that there were only country people they were putting ashore, and that the crew was keeping under cover to make a more vigorous immediate resistance, we marched up as first concerted, but found the vessel completely evacuated both of crew and every moveable on board, expect [*sic*] as

per inventory, the smugglers as their last instance of vengeance having poured a six-pounder Carronade through her broadside. She proved to be the *Rosamond* of Plymouth, Alexander Patty Master, and about one hundred tons burthern, schooner rigged.

After repairs, the ship and what remained of its contents were put up for sale, and the proceeds divided among the excise officers. It is said that Burns dispatched four carronades from the *Rosamond* to the French Convention as an expression of his democratic sympathies.

Getting to the Lochmaben Stone was not as easy as I had anticipated. Although there is a signpost directing you along the shore, when you actually come to the field where the Stone squats there's a barbed-wire entanglement in your way. But I managed to scramble over it and made my way up the field edge to the Stone itself.

The Lochmaben Stone is a ten-ton lump of granite over six feet high. It is pretty much all that is left of what was once supposed to be a 'Druidical Stone Circle' – although it's actually much older than that, dating to 3000 BC, long before the Celts and their druid-priests arrived in Britain. There were originally nine standing stones, arranged in an oval covering half an acre. But in the nineteenth century the tenant farmer at Old Graitney, intent on improving his land, had his men bury the stones in deep pits so they would no longer get in the way of ploughing and harvesting. The operation was inter-rupted by the arrival of Lord Mansfield, the landowner, who ordered them to stop work. Presumably he was something of an antiquary. And so the Lochmaben Stone itself was saved from an ignominious fate.

The Stone has long been a significant landmark. It was used as a navigation aid by Viking seamen – indeed, the name Solway is from Norse *sula*, 'pillar', and *vath*, 'ford' (while the word 'firth' itself is from *fjord*). The *Loch* element in Lochmaben Stone may be a corrup-tion of *cloch*, Gaelic for 'stone'. Indeed, the earliest recorded form of the name (from 1398) is *Clochmabenstane*, and the later 'Loch-'

version may be borrowed from the small town of Lochmaben, between Lockerbie and Dumfries. The *maben* element is from the Celtic fertility god Mabon, whom the Romans called Maponus and made into a sort of British Apollo.

In the Middle Ages and early modern period the Stone was taken to mark the western end of the Border and so became a meeting place for the Wardens of the Western March from both the Scottish and English sides. Here on truce days the Wardens would discuss matters of mutual interest, exchange prisoners and attempt to control the endemic Border bloodletting. This was not always successful. In 1448, for example, an invading English army under Henry Percy, Second Earl of Northumberland, was resoundingly defeated between the Lochmaben Stone and the mouth of the Sark. The victorious Scots were commanded by Hugh Douglas, Earl of Ormonde, and Sir John Wallace of Craigie, Sheriff of Ayr. The English had made the mistake of making camp by the Lochmaben Stone, which was then in a tidal area. Some fifteen hundred Englishmen were killed in the battle, and a further five hundred drowned as they tried to flee. The encounter became known as the Battle of Lochmaben Stone, or the Battle of Sark. There is now nothing to mark the site of the battle, the first significant victory of the Scots over the English since Otterburn in 1388.

As I made my way back east along the Solway shore, I came across a couple of men mending a fence. I asked them whether they were trying to keep the English out or the sheep in. Good-humouredly, they told me that dogwalkers kept cutting the wire.

'I'll step over here, if that's ok,' I said, and did so.

'Och, look, you've broken it,' one man said. He had a big grin on his ruddy face.

'Yup,' I said. 'I seem to have left some of my wool behind.'

They asked what I was doing. When I told them I was walking the Border, all they could say was 'Christ!' I said I was planning to get to Berwick in seven days' time. They thought that would all depend on how many pubs I encountered. I told them that the following night I'd be at the Bridge Inn at Penton.

'You'll be heading for Pen*ton*, that's where you'll be heading.' They clearly didn't think much of my pronunciation.

After Pen*ton*, I said, there was a singular scarcity of pubs for quite some miles. I would have to rely on the malt whisky in my rucksack. They offered to share my bottle with me. I apologised, confessing I'd left it back at the guest house. They laughed. We left each other to it.

After a while I came to the mouth of the Sark, where the Border turns inland.

The tide was low, the river a dingy ditch about twenty yards wide, banked by mudflats stuck with pebbles. Along the middle of the dingy ditch ran the Border line. I was at the end of Scotland – the southwest edge of it, as far as England and Scotland are concerned. The wind was channelling down the ditch, setting up ripples that made the water look like it was flowing faster than it was. Upstream a line of pylons crossed the Border. I could hear the distant rumble of the motorway above the roar of the wind. The wind was cutting down from the northeast, so cold I could have done with gloves. And this was late May.

When I started to look, I found that even this bleak place had hints of beauty. Below the high-tide mark there was a striking edge to a sandbank. The sand had formed into the thinnest of strata, like mudstone, forming flakes and scallops, layer upon layer. Then a few yards further on an old tree trunk jutted out of the sand. It might once have been an ash, but now it was more like some prehistoric monster lurching from its lair, a knot hole for an eye, a root for a snout, the body scaly and green with algae.

A little further up the Sark, on the other side, a land drain trickled into the river. Next to it were piles of broken concrete, shoring up the sandy edge, tightly canalising the Sark to stop it flooding. Zigzagging across the river swam a goosander and her two chicks, oblivious of the Border. The mother was making a grunty noise that sounded like satisfaction. It was probably an alarm call. The boundaries between species was more important to her than the borders between nations.

A couple of hundred yards upriver stood the brick piers that once carried the narrow-gauge railway linking the different parts of HM Factory Gretna. Beyond I passed by the edge of Gretna itself, with rows and rows of bungalows and small council houses dating from the decades after 1945. There was no sign on this side of the village of the workers' housing built in the First War.

My riverside path shortly turned away from Gretna towards Sark Bridge, an elegant structure of dressed red sandstone built by Thomas Telford in 1814 as part of the turnpike road running from Glasgow to Carlisle. Willows, teasels, butterbur, giant comfrey and wild roses lined the banks. The roses weren't yet in bloom. I scrambled up some steps to the road and a large brown sign saying: 'Scotland Welcomes You'. On the other side, a white sign said: 'Welcome to England, Cumbria'.

In between was the Old Toll House, which claims in the past to have been the venue for some 10,000 weddings. Over the door there were two signs, one facing north, the other south:

LAST HOUSE
IN
SCOTLAND
MARRIAGE ROOM

FIRST HOUSE
IN
SCOTLAND
MARRIAGE ROOM

It's now empty and lifeless, with that uniquely desperate feel of a tourist attraction that's shut up shop. It'd maybe be happier if a bulldozer put it out of its misery.

At the 'Scotland Welcomes You' sign I met a couple of identically equipped, super-fit middle-aged cyclists who'd stopped to take photographs of each other. I asked them what it felt like to be in Scotland. The woman said she was 'rather relieved'. They'd been cycling from Land's End against headwinds all the way, and that day had been over Shap, the long high pass between the Pennines and the Lakeland

Fells. 'It's a massive milestone,' her partner added, clearly familiar with the tropes expected of interviewed sportsmen. 'Lovely, fantastic to be out of England and into Scotland.' They'd been on the go six days and were just halfway.

As they headed off to their B&B, a Ugandan couple emerged from a car to have their photograph taken by the Border sign. I hoped that Scotland would welcome them.

This evening amble, on Day Zero of my walk, was partly intended as a reconnoitre. I wasn't sure whether I could walk under the motorway, or whether I'd have to make a diversion north and take the minor road that cuts under the M74 to Springfield. As it turned out, there was a good path under the motorway bridge, beside the Sark.

Stopping underneath the bridge, where the M6 transmutes into the M74, I was surrounded by sounds: muffled, echoing clangy roaring rumbling noises from above, as juggernaut after juggernaut crossed in either direction; and then below me, in contrast, the tinkling and clattering of the Sark as it runs across pebbled shallows. It was a strange experience, standing where the modern motorway cuts at right angles across the timeless river, where one country butts up against another. The river will go on tinkling and clattering towards the sea long after the motorway has shattered into sand, long after the very notion of borders has faded from human memory.

I ate that evening in the half-timbered Gretna Inn. It's a friendly place, with a beautiful art nouveau stained-glass window in one of the interior doors, with the word TOILETS elegantly reversed in white out of a red background.

I sat in the lounge bar along with a scattering of other tourists, chatting with the barmaid about accents hereabouts. 'Yeah, we don't sound very Scottish, do we?' she said. I'd certainly heard a lot of Cumbrian accents in Gretna, I said, and plenty of Geordie. But hers wasn't either, it was something I couldn't put my finger on – a touch of Scots, a touch of something more southern. I'd heard a similar accent in nearby Newcastleton, amidst other, more distinctively

Scottish voices. My barmaid was aware of the nuances. 'Yeah, my friend lives ten minutes away, over the Border,' she told me. 'She's in England, I'm in Scotland, and our accents are *totally* different.'

When I told her I was walking the Border, her reaction was similar to that of the men mending the fence down by the shore. 'God!' she said. 'Very good,' she added.

I was oddly happy I had her approval.

From the public bar at the back I could hear the unlikely sounds of reggae and R&B. As the evening progressed the volume of the conversation back there increased, interspersed with shouts and yelps. That was where the locals drank. I should have joined them, it sounded good humoured enough, but I was tired, not sure my patter would be up to the mark.

Instead, I cast my eyes along the bookcase next to my table. I picked out *The Charm of Birds*, by Viscount Grey of Fallodon. Turning to the chapter on 'May, the Month of Full Song', I read: 'In May we passed definitively from the bareness of winter to the luxury of summer.' With a bitter northeast wind biting down the Sark, I wasn't at all sure whether the luxury of summer was coming anytime soon.

As I sat reading, I recalled that Viscount Grey of Fallodon was none other than Sir Edward Grey, the British Foreign Secretary on the outbreak of the First World War. 'The lamps are going out all over Europe,' he said on 3rd August 1914, as he looked out of his window at the Foreign Office. 'We shall not see them lit again in our lifetime.' He knew by then his diplomacy had failed. The next day, Britain declared war on Germany.

And here I was, sitting in the middle of one of that conflict's greatest factories of death, the vast munitions complex that was HM Factory Gretna.

On leaving office in 1916 Grey was elevated to the peerage and spent more and more time at his farm at Fallodon, in the Border county of Northumberland. There he indulged in his greatest passion, ornithology. The best-known photograph of him shows him with a robin sitting on his hat.

As I left the Gretna Inn, I was greeted by a forty-something Englishman with short-cropped hair. He was having a smoke at the door. He had a story to tell me, the one about the Englishman, the Asian and the Scottish pound note. 'I almost got arrested in Mansfield,' he said. 'I was out drinking, wanted some cigarettes. Been working in Scotland, had Scottish pound notes. Went to a Paki shop. The man wouldn't accept Scottish notes.'

He paused for effect.

'*You'll take 'em*, I said.' It was clear from his tone of voice this had been no idle threat. 'The police were called,' he said. He gave a short, hoarse laugh. I wasn't sure there was any good humour in it.

'Oh, dear,' he said, as if suddenly dismayed at his own behaviour. Then he crushed the stub of his filter tip under his heel and returned to his pint and his wife at the bar.

THREE

NO ONE BOTHERS ABOUT THE BORDER

Sark, Scots' Dike and the Waverley Line

No one bothers about the Border, do they, eh? A load of nonsense.

— Builder at Corries Mill

Day One: Friday, 24th May 2013   Over breakfast I asked my land-lady Christine about the range of English accents in Gretna. She attributed it to the workers brought in for the munitions factory in the First World War. 'They came from all over the country,' she told me. 'I know it's nearly a hundred years ago, but a lot of them stayed.'

I asked her whether any parts of the installation were still in use. She said they still stored munitions at Longtown. Eastriggs was closed three or four years ago. There was talk now about closing Longtown, maybe turning it into a mega-prison.

'That's nice,' I said.

'Yeah, isn't it?' she said. 'But if it gives folk in the area jobs . . . Cos Longtown employs an awful lot of people.'

I asked what they did there.

'To be honest, I don't know,' she said. 'My ex-brother-in-law and my ex-father-in-law both used to work there, but I never asked them what they did.'

'Well, you're not allowed to ask,' I suggested.

'No.'

It turned out Christine comes from Penton – pronounced, as I was quickly discovering, Pen*ton*. There's no actual village called Penton, it's the name of an area on the English side of the Liddel Water, but everyone round here knows it. Her grandfather bought a farm there in the 1930s, and when he died he left it to her brother, missing out her father, though her father owned the stock and still farmed it. 'It's strange,' she said. 'Strange.' It's not good arable land, she told me, but the pasture's not bad.

She'd been to junior school at Shank Hill, had to walk a mile and a half there in the morning and a mile and a half home in the afternoon. At the age of five. Nowadays, she says, parents take the car to pick up their kids from the junior school in Gretna, even if they live in the village.

As I hoisted my rucksack onto my back, I asked Christine what she thought the day would bring. I'd heard on the radio that the A1 had been closed, with eighty-mile-an-hour winds blowing lorries over. She hadn't heard that but said she'd been wondering whether to put the washing out. Then she'd decided it would get wet before it got dry.

Whatever the weather, it was time to step out and begin my walk.

The wind was brisk and chill. Clouds scudded westward. As I made my way to the edge of the village I passed a billboard advertising a Rod Stewart Tribute Night the following evening at the 'Blacksmiths Functions Venue Opposite Smiths Hotel'. I thought I'd give it a miss and walked on, alongside a ditch with a smell of dead animal. Ahead of me lay a field full of buttercups and ladysmock, and then the motorway.

Before long I rejoined the Sark where I'd left it the previous evening, babbling happily over little rapids and stones, one bank in England, the other in Scotland. The morning sun was bright, the wind so strong I had to put my head down into it – not something you often have to do at sea level. If this keeps up, I thought, it's going to be a hard day's walk. The wind was even stronger where it funnelled under the railway bridge carrying the West Coast Line north over the Sark to Glasgow. Spray blew off the surface of the water. Waves were racing faster than the current towards the sea. A grey wagtail squeaked in panic when it saw me. The bridge was built of sandstone, patched with grey brick. Shortly after I passed it, the Euston express hurtled by. I wondered what it would have sounded like underneath the arch.

At Quintinshill, just up the line from here, an accident took place that in the scale of the First World War was only a footnote to the larger tragedy. It was nevertheless Britain's worst ever rail disaster. On 22nd May 1915 a train carrying soldiers of the Royal Scots south to embark for Gallipoli crashed into a stationary local train. One minute later a northbound express hit the wreckage. Fire broke out, and many who survived the initial impacts died in the subsequent blaze. In all, 226 people were killed and 246 injured. Following an inquiry and a court case, two signalmen were jailed for culpable homicide. The dead are buried in Rosebank Cemetery in Edinburgh. The Grim Reaper had gathered in his harvest early.

A little further on, a small road crosses the Sark, linking the peat works by Solway Moss to the sewage works at Springfield. I scrambled up a bank of stitchwort and wild roses to gain the road, and made a brief incursion into England. The welcome sign was fortified, flanked by castellated towers.

Back in Scotland I dropped down the other side of the road to join a farm track running parallel to the river. At first I walked by areas of hard standing and piles of gravel before emerging into a field. Along one side there was a barbed-wire fence strung with the desiccated bodies of thirty-two dead moles. I counted them. I wondered whether it was a warning to other moles not to cross this farmland. Or a warning to English people to keep away. Or to English moles who might think of resettling across the Border. Just look what we do to our own moles. Imagine what we might do to you.

The river meanders aimlessly through this flat land. Even with a map it's difficult to know where you are, unless you pay very close attention. At one point I thought I was following up one of the Sark's tributaries, the Black Sark, but it turned out to be a giant loop of the Sark itself. Where I could, I cut corners – after all, to stick precisely to the Border line here would mean wading up the middle of the river, which was never part of my plan.

At one point on my wild goose chase I trod in something brown and unpleasant. I wasn't certain what it was, but it was deeply agricultural. I hoped it would dry up and the smell dissipate before I reached the Bridge Inn.

The river here has sandy banks. Sand martins were flying low over the water – although how they could catch any insects with that wind blowing I have no idea. Then the sandbanks gave way to tips of rubble, broken concrete, scattered plastic bags. The land I was walking through, though notionally agricultural, was more brownfield than greenfield. All around lay the detritus of human activity, although it was rarely clear what these activities might have been.

When I got to the Black Sark, I didn't realise that I had. Then I came to a bridge. The only bridge near here goes over the Black Sark rather than the main stream, so I found myself again. The Black Sark lives up to its name. It's dark and still, with the occasional lazy eddy.

I left the riverbank and strode north along the minor road with Newton Flow on one side and Black Brows on the other, to the pebble-dashed farm cottage of Westgillsyke and its big black slurry tanks, then on to the larger farm at Campingholm, between Cowgarth Flow and Drownedcow Moss.

The hedgerows were full of bluebells, red campion, ferns, lady's mantle and water avens. Over on the English side the green of pastoral farmland gave way to the brown of the peat cuttings of Solway Moss, extending for miles and miles to distant woodland. I'd heard that the peat workings were going to be abandoned. Good news for the local wildlife, no doubt, but bad news for local employment.

Somewhere beyond the peat workings and the distant woodland, near St Michael's Well and Arthuret House, lay the site of the Battle of Solway Moss, fought on 24th November 1542. It was a disaster for the Scots.

There had been skirmishes along the Eastern March earlier in the year, and in October Henry VIII determined to 'pacify' the Border by sending an army to burn Kelso and destroy all the surrounding agricultural land. In November the Scots tried to relieve the pressure on them in the east by mounting an invasion of Cumberland in the west. They crossed the Border but were quickly routed at Solway Moss. Although few Scots were killed in battle, many drowned in the Moss, and many more were taken prisoner. As the remains of the Scottish army retreated up the wilds of Liddesdale, the inhabitants – famously unawed by royal authority – fell upon the stragglers, seized what goods they could and killed any man who resisted.

James V, aware of the fate of his father at Flodden, watched the battle from a safe distance – perhaps from Burnswark Hill north of Ecclefechan. The king fell into despair, a despair that deepened a few days later. The contemporary chronicler Robert Lindsay of Pitscottie picks up the story:

> Be this, the post cam out of Linlighgow, showing the king good tidings, that the queen was deliverit. The king inquired whedder it was a man or woman. The messenger said it was ane fair dochter. He answered and said, 'Fairwell, it cam with ane lass and it will pass with ane lass.'

James was referring to the Stewart dynasty, which had come to the throne through the marriage of Walter Stewart to Marjorie, daughter of Robert the Bruce. He was right about the way the dynasty would come to an end, but wrong about the chronology. His daughter grew up to be Mary, Queen of Scots, and her Stewart descendants continued to rule Scotland, and then the whole of Great Britain, until the death of Queen Anne in 1714. Ironically, the last Stuart monarch was the first monarch of the United Kingdom, the Scottish Parliament having voted itself out of existence seven years before. After Anne, the UK was to be ruled by the man the Scots called 'the wee wee German lairdie': the lacklustre Georg Ludwig, Elector of Hanover and Duke of Brunswick-Lüneburg. We're still stuck with his descendants.

James's despair sapped the life out of him. On 14th December 1542, at Falkland Palace, he died. He was only thirty.

Back on the road, next to a plantation of young willow, a man drove past in a tractor, the first person I'd seen since leaving Gretna. I gave a wave. I didn't get a wave back. Maybe it was the farmer who'd strung up the dead moles on the barbed wire.

At Corries Mill there was a man working in the garden of a bungalow. I asked him if he was a landscape gardener.

'I'm not,' he said. 'I'm a builder. I'm just tidying up after the job like.' His accent was Scottish, but that 'like' was pure Geordie. His face was weather-worn, his smile infectious. 'I'm just tidying up, lad, like.'

I asked him what he felt about the Border, just along the road.

'No one bothers about the Border, do they, eh?' he said. 'A load of nonsense.'

I asked him whether he considered himself Scottish or English, or just a Borderer.

'A reiver,' he said. 'We're reivers in this area.'

The reivers (from *reive*, 'to carry off by force') were the armed and mounted raiders who until the early seventeenth century preyed upon their neighbours, no matter which side of the Border, stealing cattle and sheep, burning houses and slaughtering any who resisted them. When the larder was low, it was said, the womenfolk would serve up a dish of spurs, hinting to their menfolk that it was time once more to saddle their horses and ride off into the night.

It wasn't war. War is the exception to peace. The reiving went on all the time, whatever the state of relations between the kingdoms of Scotland and England. It was just the way life was. If you lived on the Borders, you were a reiver. There was no other choice. You took what you could get. You took what was coming to you. There was an old rhyme that summed it up:

> The good old rule sufficeth them,
> The simple plan,
> That they should take, who have the power
> And they should keep who can.

There were reiving families on both sides of the Border, often allied to each other by blood or marriage, their loyalty being more to kin than crown. Many Borderers to this day have a similar suspicion of those in power in London or Edinburgh.

'James VI of Scotland, James I of England,' my friend continued, 'he upset it all, like.' James, who presided over the Union of the Crowns in 1603, set about 'pacifying' the area by force. Whole groups of clansmen were tried as one, and hanged as one. 'Before that it was ok,' said my friend. 'That's all gone now, of course.'

I mentioned that James had renamed the Borders the Middle Shires of his new country of Britain.

'Aye, that's the way it bloody worked,' my man said.

I told him what I was doing, walking to Berwick, and remarked on what good walking weather it was.

'Aye, it's quite nice. Nice to be here in the country, innit? Once you get to town, everybody gets their head down.'

I mentioned that I'd been chatting with my landlady in the guest house. He knew at once where I'd been staying. He knew Christine. I said it turned out she was from Penton, where I was heading. 'She is, aye, she is,' he said. I said I was going to be staying at the Bridge Inn at Penton, and he knew the people there too, Linda and her husband from Australia, where she'd lived for some years.

I told him about my project, explained that although brought up in Scotland my parents weren't Scottish and I'd been living in England for a long time.

'You sound just like Tony Blair,' he laughed.

'I didn't go to Fettes,' I protested.

'Aye, godsake, eh?' he laughed. 'That's bloody awful.'

Then we got on to the serious business of a weather conversation.

'There's a wee shower coomin',' he said. 'Won't be much, I don't think. Too much wind blowin'.'

I knew my cue. 'There were a few spots earlier,' I offered. 'Not worth bothering about. This amount of wind is nice cos it keeps you cool for walking.'

I told him of the days walking ahead of me. I said it was ok so far, my feet were standing up to it. But there was a long way to go.

'Godsake, eh?' he laughed. 'Eh man, aye ye'll get the knack of it as you're going. That's the main thing, the feet.'

We happily got back on to the weather. 'I was sitting there yesterday,' he said, 'and there was bloody sleet and snow. Just enough to say how cold it was. It's funny, last year we had two really hot weeks, you know, all the blossom came out on the trees, the fruit trees. The bloody frost came, and of course, that was them gone.'

Some road menders came by. It was time for me to be gone too.

'I'll step on my way now,' I said. 'Good luck.'

'Good journey,' he said.

I crossed the Sark by the bridge below Corries Mill. There were no signs on either side to indicate I'd swapped countries. The man was right, the Border – in these parts at least – was an irrelevance. People just got on with their lives.

Just across the river, the people at Sark Hall had other concerns. They'd put up several printed signs saying 'NO TO WINDFARM'. One of the children had even produced a hand-painted version.

The long straight road north to Englishtown, cutting off a corner of the Sark, palled after a while. I cheered myself up with a song:

> Forty dead moles on a barbed-wire fence
> Yo ho ho and a bottle of rum.

After the long trudge on tarmac, I was relieved to come at last to Scots' Dike. Though, as it turned out, relief was not the appropriate emotion.

Scots' Dike was built to end the long-standing and bloody disputes over the Debatable Lands. The term Debatable Lands was applied to various regions along the Border, but particularly the area between the Rivers Sark and Esk, bounded on the north by Tarras Moor, on the south by the sea, and encompassing the wastes of Solway Moss. Why anyone should want this wilderness is unclear. It was poor land, the abode of outlaws and brigands, who, according to a contemporary complaint, 'makis quotidiane reiffis [forcible seizures, as in 'reivers'] and oppressionis upon the pur'. In 1551 the Wardens of both countries made a chilling proclamation: 'All English men and Scottish men are, and shall be, free to burn, spoil, slay, murder and destroy all and every such person or persons, their bodies, buildings, goods and cattle as do remain or shall inhabit upon any part of the said Debatable Land, without any redress to be made for same.'

Open season had been declared. That same year Lord Maxwell burnt every single dwelling-place in the Debatable Land, right down to the ground.

The following year, 1552, the dispute over sovereignty was submitted to Monsieur D'Oysel, the French ambassador to Scotland. With Gallic rigour, D'Oysel drew a straight line on the map, from Craw's Knowe on the Sark more or less due east to the Esk. In its uncompromising geometry, and its disregard for human geography, it was reminiscent of the European carve-up of Africa three centuries later. The three-mile line of the new frontier was marked by the Scots' Dike, an earthwork consisting of two parallel ditches with the dug-out earth piled up in between. It was the first artificially created frontier in Europe since the time of the Romans.

Not everything went smoothly during the construction. Two teams worked on the project, starting at either end. When they met in the middle, they found they hadn't met at all. They were out of line with each other by twenty-one feet.

It didn't really matter, as the Scots' Dike wasn't intended as a fortification like Hadrian's Wall, or a barrier like the Berlin Wall or the DMZ, but merely a marker. At each end there once stood a square stone bearing the arms of both Scotland and England, although these were long ago plundered for building material. I'd heard that there were a few surviving boundary stones along the length of the Dike, but that these were difficult to find in the undergrowth.

It wasn't quite the end of the debate over the Debatable Lands. A linguistic difference remained. The Scots called the line the Scots' *Dyke*, a 'dyke' being a wall, while the English called it the Scots' *Dike*, a 'dike' being, in England, a ditch. The Ordnance Survey opts for the English version.

For Walter Scott, the line retained a symbolic and unifying significance:

> Ye ken Highlander and Lowlander, and Border-men, are a' ae man's bairns when you are over the Scots Dyke.

In other words, once a Scot has gone south over the Border, all internal differences are forgotten.

Leaving the road, I plunged into the long strip of woodland that covers the Dike. There was just the faintest of paths through the new spring grass, but it didn't look like more than a couple of people had trodden it. There were primroses and ferns, some still curled up tight like a bishop's crozier. There were also bog pools, so I had to tread carefully. I was surrounded by the peace of birdsong and dappled deciduous woodland. On my left, on the Scottish side, there was a dense line of conifers. I caught a glimpse of a roe deer's scut as it darted into thicker woodland. Then I heard it bark.

The faint path would often disappear entirely. The going was getting tougher. Above me a buzzard called continually, a plaintive sound among the whispering of the treetops in the wind.

Every now and again I had to scramble over a barbed-wire fence. At one point I crossed a wide clearing dotted with sheep and trees. The clearing wasn't marked on the map. At another point I thought I'd actually found a remnant of the Dike. Leaning over some barbed wire, I could see a ditch parallel to the fence, and then a low ridge covered in grass and birch trees and reeds. Beyond that it looked like there was another ditch.

Much of the actual Dike was destroyed by forestry work a hundred years or so ago. A temporary railway line was built, partly along the line of the Dike, and a locomotive used to pull out the trees. As it pulled out the trees it pulled out the roots, and with the roots it pulled out a lot of the earth of the Dike.

Out of the wind I could enjoy the warmth of the sunshine. It actually felt like late May for once. Another deer flicked across my path before disappearing into the dark of the conifer plantation. Back in deciduous woodland I was faced with a mossy bog, so I made my way cautiously south to the field edge. I didn't want to be sucked into a quagmire. Nobody'd know where I'd gone. I began to sing again, 'Forty dead moles on a piece of barbed wire . . .' It was as well I was on my own – although the sheep in the field on the English side did give me a funny look. I asked them what they thought of it so far. Baa, one said.

The field edge proved to be no easier to negotiate. There was a line of old pollarded beeches, twisted into strange shapes. Once upon a time they'd been a hedge, I supposed. I had to scramble over the gnarled roots of one tree, jump across the marsh to the roots round the next tree, then jump over another bit of marsh to another bit of root. I recorded myself as I attempted this obstacle course: 'Oooh dear, squelch squelch, woo-er, oop, er, oooh. Whoo – up. Hip hop. Phew. Sigh.' In the field to the south four hares stood up and stared at me. And they call us mad, they said.

I came to a shallow stream, the Beck Burn. The name is something of a tautology, yoking the Scots and Cumbrian words for the same thing. I splashed towards the violets on the far side and crossed another barbed-wire fence, straight into a bog. So I cut back to the old beech hedge, jumping from tussock to tussock, swinging on gnarly branches. This was turning out to be not so much a walk as a replay of *Pirates of the Caribbean*. All I was missing was the bandana.

The bog was unremitting, and to add insult to injury some farmer had put a double line of barbed-wire fences in my way. Sometimes, I told my Dictaphone, I think the farmers are just trying to piss me off. Why on earth would they put barbed-wire fences through a bloody great bog?

My spirits rose a little when I found – at last – one of the rumoured boundary stones. It was barely two feet tall, with straight sides and a rounded top, covered in moss. There was something engraved on the Scottish side. It might have been a date, 1701? Or perhaps some letters . . . M, O, L possibly. The light was bad, the stone eroded, the meaning uncertain. Further along, I found more boundary stones. One stood by a ditch that must have been part of the Dike. It was bound in barbed wire. Another had been recruited as a gatepost, with two iron brackets hammered into it to serve as hinges. There was no sign of a gate, or even of the other gatepost. Nearby a scattering of feathers lay across the ground. Some bits of wing, a lot of down. Presumably a pigeon hit by a peregrine at speed.

After a while I came to a defile cutting across my route. This was the valley of the Glinger Burn, about 150 feet deep. I slithered down the steep slope, my rucksack catching on overhead branches.

It was worth the effort. The bottom of the valley through which the Glinger trickled was a carpet of bluebells dotted with moss-covered birches. And there was a wooden footbridge across the burn. Who knows when it had last been walked across, but at least it wasn't rotten. I leant against a birch tree, brewed myself a cup of tea and munched on oatcakes and cheese.

Ahead the woods became confused. So did I. I needed to check my compass to keep me right. I'd almost been lured off in the wrong direction, towards Daffystonerigg. That would never have done.

Passing through some geans in blossom, I came to a field full of reeds. The field turned out to be a very soft bog, so I clambered over another barbed-wire fence into the open woodland of what I presumed was Scotland. As I walked along I noticed there was a ditch on either side of me, green moss on the surface, black water underneath. I was on top of the Dike. For the first time on my walk, I was actually striding along with one foot in Scotland and the other in England.

As I neared the end of the Dike, a pair of orange-tipped butterflies danced in the sun. There was a stile over the next fence – unusually helpful. Then another stile. This last one dropped me straight into a bramble thicket.

As you emerge out of the woods, leaving Scots' Dike behind you, there's a kilted scarecrow in a garden with a Union Jack in each hand. Attached to the scarecrow there's a long pole, and from the top of the pole flapped a Blue Saltire. We may be Britons, yes, the scarecrow says, but above all else we're Scots.

At the eastern end of Scots' Dike the Border hits the A7, the main Edinburgh–Carlisle trunk road. After the green solitudes of the Dike I was ambushed by the stench of burnt petrol, black tarmac, white lines, the roar and whine of traffic.

If you want to follow the Border precisely, you'd have to scamper across the carriageway dodging the lorries. Then you'd stumble over a rough field and splash into the Esk – just like Young Lochinvar. For, Scott tells us,

> He stayed not for brake, and he stopped not for stone,
> He swam the Esk river where ford there was none.

Lochinvar took a short cut straight across the river, but if you wanted to follow the Border here you'd have to swim upstream with the salmon for half a mile or so. Then, like a faithless lover, the Border abandons the Esk and jinks eastward up the Liddel Water to Kershopefoot.

If you wanted to stay dry, you could risk annihilation at the hands of the juggernauts and walk parallel to the Border north up the A7. After about half a mile, past Todhillwood and Newstead, you'd enter a cutting. People speeding by in cars and coaches would never know it, but if you clambered up the eastern bank of the cutting, you'd see, between the road and the Esk, a faint mound in a field of rough grass. The place is known as Woodslee, or Withisleis, and is said to be the site of Kinmont Tower. Although the mound has never been excavated and the tower is long gone, the name lives on in the story of Kinmont Willie.

William Armstrong of Kinmont was, to his enemies, the most feared of the 'ryders and ill-doers upon the borders'. If there'd been charge sheets in those days, Armstrong would have had one as long as his arm. He was the hardman's hardman, descended from the notorious reiver Sandy 'Ill Will' Armstrong. The Armstrongs had originated in Cumbria, but now their power base was in Liddesdale, on the Scottish side of the Border. Following in the family tradition, William Armstrong would ride out at the head of several hundred men – nicknamed 'Kinmont's Bairns' – to seize great numbers of cattle and sheep, killing anyone who got in his way. He does not seem to have been too particular about which side of the Border he plundered.

48

Armstrong had powerful friends. He had married a Graham, so allying himself with one of the great local families whose influence extended across both sides of the Border. He was also a tenant of Lord Maxwell, who more than once stood surety for him when he got into trouble. Furthermore, Armstrong had married his daughter to Thomas Carleton, constable to the Warden of the English West March.

The powers-that-be in Scotland found they had their uses for this turbulent reiver, employing him in 1585 to ravage the town of Stirling, then in the hands of the upstart Earl of Arran. Such was Armstrong's reputation for savagery that King James himself considered inflicting Armstrong and his men on the citizenry of Edinburgh in retaliation for their riotous behaviour in December 1596.

But on the other side of the Border Armstrong's freebooting had exhausted the patience of Thomas, Lord Scrope, Warden of the English West March. These wardens – one from each side of the Border – were meant to keep the peace, meeting regularly on appointed Truce Days to discuss and resolve grievances and disputes. There was a long-standing Border convention that on a Truce Day all who attended were granted safe conduct:

> Upon paine of death all persons whatsoever that come to these meetings should be safe fra any proceeding or present occaisioun, from the time of meeting of the Wardens, or his deputies, until the next day at the sun rising.

Yet one fateful day in March 1596 Lord Scrope ignored the fact that a truce was in force and ordered his deputy, Thomas Salkeld, to apprehend William Armstrong. Armstrong was in the small retinue of Robert Scott of Hayning, deputy to Walter Scott of Buccleuch, Keeper of Liddesdale and Warden of the Scottish West March.

This particular Truce Day meeting was held at Dayholm of Kershope – a meadow adjacent to the confluence of the Kershope Burn and the Liddel Water, just west of the old Waverley Line at Kershopefoot. It seems that after this Truce Day meeting, Salkeld spotted Armstrong on the Scottish side of the Liddel, making his way home. Seeing that Armstrong was accompanied by no more than two or three men, he decided to take his chance. So he led his force of several hundred across the river and pursued Armstrong on horseback for three or four miles before seizing him and taking him in chains to Carlisle Castle.

Buccleuch was outraged when he heard the news. Whatever crimes Armstrong may have committed, he had at the time of his seizure been in Buccleuch's service, and the English had violated diplomatic conventions by taking him on a Truce Day. Furthermore, Armstrong had been seized on Buccleuch's own land, where only Buccleuch's word was law. In vain Buccleuch remonstrated with Scrope for Armstrong's release. Not even King James's requests to the English ambassador, or to Queen Elizabeth herself, bore fruit. So Buccleuch determined to mount an expedition to free Armstrong, 'in sae moderate ane fashion as was possible to him'.

An hour before sunset on 12th April the peace of the evening at the Tower of Morton on the River Sark was shaken by the arrival, from all points of the compass, of two hundred armed horsemen. Buccleuch had assembled a rescue party from among his followers, insisting that no heads of houses should take part, only their brothers or younger sons. If the raid ended in disaster, he calculated, the fabric of his following would not be entirely shredded. Three heads – Gibbie Elliot of Stobs, Auld Wat of Harden and the Laird of Commonside – ignored Buccleuch's order and insisted on taking part.

They rode out through the darkness. Some among them must have known secret ways through the treacherous marshes of Solway Moss. They'd no doubt chosen a moonlit night, when they could ride without torches or lanterns. Some two hours before dawn they crossed the River Eden, then in spate. And so, unsuspected and undetected, they came to Carlisle.

There may have been those who knew of their coming – Englishmen who owed more loyalty to their kin on the Scottish side than to their own crown. In particular it has been suggested that inside

Carlisle Castle there were certain Grahams and Carletons – to whom Armstrong was tied by marriage – who aided the rescue attempt.

Buccleuch selected fourscore men to break into the castle, leaving his main force in reserve. At first they tried to scale the walls, but their ladders turned out to be too short. Then a smaller force of two dozen men forced an entry through a postern gate on the western side of the castle – or perhaps the gate had been left unlocked? While six guarded the entry, the remainder, having had intelligence of Armstrong's whereabouts, made their way to the place where he was kept, bound in chains. The rescue party then gave an agreed signal, a blast on a trumpet. Hearing this, Buccleuch ordered his main force to let out a great roar, to frighten the garrison and the citizens of Carlisle into thinking a far vaster army had fallen upon them. With some satisfaction, a Scottish chronicler recorded that:

> The people were perturbit from their nocturnal sleep, then undigestit at that untimeous hour, with some cloudy weather and saft rain, whilk are noisome to the delicate persons of England, whaise bodies are given to quietness, rest, and delicate feeding, and consequently desirous of more sleep and repose in bed.

In the chaos, the chronicler continued:

> . . . the assaulters brought forth their countryman, and convoyit him to the court, where the Lord Scrope's chalmer [chamber] has a prospect unto, to whom he cried with a loud voice a familiar guid-nicht! and another guid-nicht to his constable Mr Saughell [Salkeld].

The rescuers quickly overcame what little resistance they met with, a few nightwatchmen being 'dung on their backs'. Meanwhile, 'both the Lord Scrope himself and his Warden Depute Salkeld, being there with the garrison and their own retinue, did keep themselves close'. So Armstrong was hustled away and, still in chains, put upon a horse.

Buccleuch was meticulous in his determination to limit the damage.

He knew that, in carrying out his obligations to his own retainer and the defence of his own honour, he had lit the fuse to a diplomatic time bomb. He thus did everything he could to avoid embarrassing his king, or offending the English queen. A few prisoners who had escaped in the chaos he returned to their cells, while any booty his men had taken he ordered to be returned. Apart from the breaking of the postern gate and the iron door to the room where Armstrong was kept, no damage was done. Buccleuch might have taken the whole castle – Warden, Deputy and all – but his single aim was the freeing of his man, which, he said, 'maun necessarily be esteimit lawful, gif the taking and deteining of him be unlawful, as without all question it was'.

By now the cat was out of the bag. Bells rang out, drummers beat their urgent tattoos, beacon fires were lit to warn the country of the danger. But Buccleuch made good his escape through the misty dawn. Coming to the Eden once more, he saw on the other side a small English force, alerted by the signal fires and bells from the city. Buccleuch urged his horse into the turbulent river, his men following and sounding trumpets. Seeing the determination of their opponents, the English force wisely gave way, and so, some two hours after sunrise, Buccleuch and his men returned to Scottish soil, and Kinmont Willie was a free man once more.

The general satisfaction on the Scottish side was reflected in the diary of Robert Birrel, a burgess of Edinburgh, who wrote 'the like of sic ane wassaledge [vassalage, i.e. feat of arms] wes nevir done since the memorie of man, no in Wallace dayis'. More memorably, the ballad 'Kinmont Willie', collected some two hundred years later by Buccleuch's descendant, Sir Walter Scott, celebrated the incident, with considerable poetic licence. The following verses recount Buccleuch's victorious return:

> Buccleuch has turn'd to Eden water,
> Even where it flowed frae bank to brim,
> And he has plunged in wi' a' his band,
> And safely swam then thro' the stream.

He turn'd him on the other side,
And at Lord Scrope his glove flung he;
'If ye like na my visit in merry England,
In fair Scotland come visit me!'

All sair astonished stood Lord Scrope,
He stood as still as rock of stane;
He scarcely dared tae trew his eyes,
When through the water they had gane.

'He is either himsel' a devil frae hell,
Or else his mother a witch maun be;
I wadna hae ridden that wan water,
For a' the gowd in Christendie.'

However punctilious Buccleuch might have been in his handling
of the operation, the diplomatic time bomb duly detonated. Scrope
sought to expunge his humiliation by leading a force into Scotland,
burning the towns of Annan and Dumfries, and herding some two
hundred prisoners back to England, 'naked, chained together on
leashes'.

From London, furious notes were dispatched northward. James
stood his ground, and suggested the affair be submitted to an international commission – knowing full well that the seizure of William
Armstrong had been a breach of international law and that any
commission would condone Buccleuch's actions. Queen Elizabeth
realised that if she acceded to such a commission the outcome would
go against her and she would lose face. So she wrote a lengthy letter
to her 'dear Brother' James, whom, she said, had been 'seduced by
evil information'. James's refusal to hand over Buccleuch might, she
said, be forgiven in a stripling prince, but was 'strange, and I dare say
without example' in 'a father's age'. Elizabeth could barely contain
herself. 'Shall any castle or habitation of mine,' she railed, 'be assailed
by a night larceny, and shall not my confederate send the offender to

his due punishment?' As for the idea of a commission: 'For other doubtful and litigious causes upon our Borders, I will be ready to permit commissioners, if I shall find it needful, but for this matter of so villainous a usage, I answer you I will never be so answered . . .'

James kept his nerve, despite risking his likely succession to the throne of England. In due course the furore died down, and good relations were restored between the two kingdoms.

Kinmont Willie does not appear to have found any reason to mend his ways, and his depredations continued in a sporadic fashion. The last we hear of him is in January 1603, when we find Lord Scrope writing to Lord Cecil in London, complaining that Armstrong has just wasted two villages in Cumberland. Armstrong himself died later that same year, apparently in his own bed. He was probably still in his forties.

As for 'the Bold Buccleuch', as he had become known, he had the temerity to pay Queen Elizabeth a personal visit in London, on the way back from founding a regiment in the Netherlands to help the Dutch fight their Spanish oppressors. The queen quizzed him why he had dared to undertake such a desperate and presumptuous enterprise. 'What is it,' Buccleuch replied, 'that a man dare not do?' Elizabeth was impressed. 'With ten thousand such men,' she said, 'our brother in Scotland might shake the firmest throne in Europe.'

Whatever his contemporary reputation, Bold Buccleuch does not appear to have appealed to posterity in the same way as the man he rescued. In addition to the ballad immortalised by Sir Walter Scott, there was in the last century a racehorse called Kinmount Wullie, which won the Scottish Grand National in 1960. As it happens, it was owned by George and Dorothy Mackie, proprietors of Gretna Green's Famous Blacksmith's Shop.

Today, there is an oatmeal stout brewed in the Scottish Borders by Broughton Ales Ltd called Kinmont Willie. The brewers make great claims for it: 'Indulging yourself with Death by Chocolate at a white tablecloth restaurant?' they purr. 'Slurping up oysters at a sawdust-floored raw bar?' they coo. 'In either case, savour your repast with the perfect malt beverage – Kinmont Willie Scottish Oatmeal Stout.'

Och aye. Broughton also produce a variety of other manly beers, such as Old Jock Ale, Black Douglas, The Ghillie, and Excisemans 80/- (with a picture of Rabbie B on the label). Hoots.

I was disinclined to join the salmon in the Esk, so from the end of Scots' Dike I settled on a deviation from the exact course of the Border. The closest place to cross the Esk dryshod was about half a mile to the south, across the Thistle Viaduct.

The short section south along the A7 was the most dangerous stretch of my entire walk. Although a major trunk road, the A7 is narrow and windy. There's no pavement, barely a verge, and the juggernauts and coaches rush by so close they force the unwitting pedestrian into the hedge.

With some relief I left the perils of the A7 and joined the course of the old Waverley Line, which once linked Edinburgh and Carlisle. At this spot the disused railway consisted of a narrow path between hawthorn and birch. I followed it northeast towards the Esk.

When I came to the river I found my deviationism was justified. 'Private Fishing', a notice firmly advised me. 'No Swimming.' So I couldn't have followed the Border exactly even if I'd wanted to. Swimming wasn't allowed.

The Esk here is a magnificent river, broad and easy, flowing gently to the sea. Above the water the air was full of birdlife: oystercatchers, swifts, martins, wagtails, all feeding on the river's riches. The water looks shallow, but this may be misleading. In the eighteenth century the Welsh traveller Thomas Pennant wrote of the Esk:

> The water was of the most colourless or crystalline clearness, no stream I've seen being comparable. So persons who ford the river are often led into distresses by being deceived as to its depth, for the great transparency gives it an unreal shallowness.

Just upriver from where I stood was the Thistle Pool, after which the viaduct got its name – or perhaps it was vice versa? The Esk is one of those rivers where the fishing's so good the names of the different pools are marked on the Ordnance Survey map. Further upriver there's the Willow Pool and the Mason's Stream. Downriver, there's Redbank Pool and Wax Pool.

Beyond Wax Pool, close to an old Roman fort, is the site of something that in medieval times was known as the Fish Garth. The Fish Garth was a great bone of contention between the Scots and the English hereabouts. A *garth* is a kind of enclosure – so the Fish Garth was a giant trap to catch the salmon swimming upriver to spawn. This far south the Esk was usually reckoned to be in English territory, and certainly it was the English who owned and operated the Fish Garth. However, the Scots upriver were not best pleased that all the salmon in the Esk were being trapped by the English before they could swim into Scottish territory. So every now and again the Scots would come in the night and destroy the Fish Garth. And then the English would build it again. Then it would be destroyed again. In the end the matter was settled by treaty.

These days there's no sign of a Fish Garth – probably because there's more money to be had letting out the fishing to wealthy anglers than in industrial-scale netting of diminishing stocks.

The viaduct came to an abrupt end as the track stopped at a gap. The ground fell away in front of me. Presumably there was once a bridge here. I had to clamber down a crumbling wall of brick and rubble to pick up the line on the other side.

The track on the far side degenerated. At one point it went through an old cutting. If the cutting had once been well drained, it certainly wasn't now. To escape the quagmires, I was forced up the thickly wooded side. I tried to make my way along the crest, but I couldn't get myself and my rucksack under the low branches, so had to hop over a barbed-wire fence and walk along a field edge.

At another point the old line was covered in pools of slurry. In an effort to dodge the noxious puddles I jumped onto a pile of straw on one side. Except it turned out not to be straw, but manure. Very soft manure, into which I sank. Up to my knees. What *were* they going to think of me at the Bridge Inn?

The going improved as the line approached the confluence of the Esk and the Liddel Water. The Liddel is a smaller version of the Esk – a wide, gentle river, trickling over beds of small stones. Between me and the Liddel there was an expanse of butterbur, cow parsley and wild garlic, the scent of the latter doing something to dull the excremental aura in which I was enveloped.

For some miles, as it winds through a wooded valley, the Liddel forms the Border. The steep overgrown sides, in places scarred by cliffs of soft red sandstone, are flanked by gentler fields – a landscape combining the pastoral with the picturesque in a way guaranteed to appeal to the polite sensibilities of the eighteenth century. One amateur poet of the period apostrophised it thus:

> Hail sacred flood
> May still thy hospitable swains be blest
> In rural innocence, thy mountains still team
> With the fleecy race, thy tuneful woods forever flourish
> And thy vales look gay with painted meadows and the golden grain.

These lines were penned by Dr John Armstrong, better known for his self-help manuals in verse, such as *The Art of Preserving Health* and *The Oeconomy of Love* (the latter offering advice on 'how / Best to improve the genial joy, how shun / The snakes that under rosy pleasure lurk'). There was nothing Armstrong liked better, it seems, than to fish the Liddel, something he recalled with a fervour as heightened as that with which, in *The Oeconomy of Love*, 'The madd'ning boy his bashful fetters bursts':

> In thy transparent eddies have I laved,
> Oft traced with patient steps thy fairy banks
> With the well-imitated fly to hook
> The eager trout, and with the slender line
> And yielding rod, solicit to the shore
> The struggling panting prey.

Fly-fishing, in Armstrong's hands, was a form of seduction. But though I scanned the waters of the Liddel closely, not a sign could I spy of the eager trout. This year, I was told, the water was running too low. In the fields above the defile, however, members of the fleecy race were everywhere apparent.

The charms of the lower Liddel also appealed to those of a more Romantic bent, such as the Tory MP Lord Ernest Hamilton. 'As I rode under the birken-clad heughs,' his lordship effused, 'golden now in the death of their summer glory, sniffing the sweet fresh smell of the moorland, I wondered whether anywhere on God's earth was to be found a fairer spot than this same Vale of Liddel.' Regrettably Lord Hamilton – younger son of the Duke of Hamilton – turned in the 1920s to fascism and anti-Semitism.

This being the Border, the Liddel has not always been such an idyllic place. Somewhere above me, beyond the steep, tree-covered escarpment, were the remains of an ancient motte and bailey called Liddel Strength. No pussyfooting about the name. Liddel Strength was built by the Anglo-Normans in the twelfth century as a bastion against the Scots. In 1346 David II invaded England and took the castle by assault. Its keeper, Sir Walter Selby, was put to death. Before he was killed, he was forced to watch his two sons being strangled. The castle was then razed to the ground.

As I sat resting on what appeared to be a floodplain, the map told me that I was actually in a little patch of Scotland, stranded on the south side of the Liddel. This aberration came about in 1861, during the construction of the Waverley Line. As they laid the track up the south side of the river, the engineers and navvies came to an impasse below Liddel Strength, where the river ran right up against a hundred-foot escarpment. The engineers had a choice. They could either move the river or move the cliff. They opted for the former, dumping great piles of sandstone blocks in the Liddel, so diverting its course away from the cliff and providing a causeway for the railway. The Border, however, remained where it was. But instead of running up the middle of the Liddel, it now – for a short stretch – ran along the south bank.

The anomaly came to light in 2002, when Riddings Farm, just up the line, came on the market. The English solicitors doing the conveyancing advised the purchaser that they would not be able to deal with the two-acre patch beneath Liddel Strength. And so a Scottish lawyer had to be engaged to complete the purchase. The anomaly also means that the owner of Riddings can fish his bank of the Liddel on a Sunday – except for this short stretch.

I continued on my way. The old line here must have been double track, for in front of me spread a wide lawn covered in daisies, with primroses lining either side. A roe deer bounded ahead of me, before darting into the woods. The pastoral here was matched with the post-industrial: metal posts alongside the track, broken drainage pipes, abandoned concrete shacks once used by railway workers.

Riddings turned out to be a rather grander affair than the average farmhouse. It was more of a Victorian suburban mansion, or perhaps a manse, with walls of dressed red sandstone. Nearby stood the remains of Riddings Station, which had become part of a cow byre. The platform was grown over with brambles.

The Waverley Line has been closed for the best part of half a century, so there has been plenty of time for nature to reclaim its territory. The last passenger train to pass through here was the Edinburgh Waverley to London St Pancras sleeper on the night of 5th January 1969. It was two hours late reaching Carlisle. Protestors objecting to the closure had blocked the line at Newcastleton. Among those arrested was the local minister, and it was only the intervention of Borders MP David Steel, who was travelling on the sleeper, that secured his release.

As I looked around the deserted station, a large tractor roared up beside me. The driver pulled on the brake and gave me a look. Was I on forbidden ground?

Always best to play the daft laddie in these circumstances, I find, so I asked him which was my best way ahead. He was glad to enlighten me, and so we fell into conversation. It turned out he'd just recently taken over Riddings Farm. I could tell by his accent that he was from the other side of the Border, so I asked him what it was like coming from the Scottish side and farming on the English side. He said he already had two farms on the Scottish side. But he'd always had his eye on Riddings. Its free drainage, he said, made it prime arable land. 'You can grow maize to the height of this tractor,' he assured me.

I said I'd never seen maize growing this far north in England – let alone in Scotland. Because I'd heard there was a wee bit of Scotland on this side of the Liddel, where they moved the river.

'That's right,' he said. 'God, you know more about it than I do.'

I told him I'd been researching. I was writing a book.

'*Are* ye?' he asked.

I said I'd read about the previous owner needing two sets of solicitors, one Scottish, one English, to do the conveyancing. He'd found the same thing. 'You'll never believe this,' he said, 'but it was absolute luck that this solicitor we went to, there was a girl there who might be thirty, thirty-five? But she can do both English and Scottish. She can tie people in knots. Absolutely right what you say, you need the English and Scottish law. Ye're well read up on the thing.'

I told him I'd been staying at a guest house in Gretna, and that the landlady used to live round Penton.

'Aye, that's right,' the farmer said. 'She did.' It seems everybody knows Christine.

I told him I was making for the Bridge Inn. He knew it, had just passed it. 'There's some big cars there,' he said. 'Moneyed people.' I became aware once more of the state of my trousers. Maybe I'd have to sleep in an outhouse.

'Ah, but you'll have a good place at the Bridge Inn, you'll be pleased with that,' he continued. 'Eat meat, don't eat fish. Do you like fish?'

I assured him I liked both. I wondered, was it his meat they served at the Bridge Inn?

'No, no, it isn't. But the meat *is* good. But you have what you want.'

It turned out he not only had three farms, but also half a dozen houses. And he'd just finished building a retirement bungalow for himself. I asked whether it had a good view. 'Depends whether you want to look at gravestones,' he said. The new bungalow was next to the churchyard.

'I've always admired this farm from over there,' he said. 'It's a helluva farm.' Then he started up his tractor. 'You've probably got another's hour's walking,' he said. 'Nice speaking to you.'

I could see it was time to go. Blether was all very well, but there was business to be done.

A little beyond Riddings Farm is Riddings Junction, where a branch line once cut north across the Liddel Viaduct up Liddesdale to Langholm. The Liddel Viaduct today represents the most impassable barrier between Scotland and England. Rivers you can swim, mountains and moors you can trudge over, but at the English end of the Liddel Viaduct there is a ten-foot-high fence made of spike-topped steel railings. The fence extends some way either side of the viaduct, over the drop.

It was at Riddings Junction, on 8th January 1969, that British Railways invited the press to a ceremonial track-lifting ceremony. The closure was final. Now, on the fence, there is a sign:

Highways Act 1980
The British Railways Board
hereby give notice that this way
is not dedicated to the public.

Just beyond the viaduct, a locked gate, topped by barbed wire, barred further progress up the old Waverley Line. There was another sign:

PRIVATE PROPERTY
NO RIGHT OF WAY
NO TRESPASSING

So near to Scotland, I felt the right to roam enshrined in Scottish law might extend a little across the Border. So I clambered over the gate and walked on. Trespassing always struck me as a very odd sort of concept. Keep out. We don't want your sort here. My land. Not yours.

The 'PRIVATE PROPERTY' was very pretty – open woodland, the ground carpeted in bluebells, wild garlic and dog's mercury. You'd think the landowner would want to show off the beauties of the place to a wider audience.

At one point I passed an old abandoned caravan. Green algae had begun to stain its white exterior.

It was getting late and the woods were growing gloomy. So I was relieved to clamber up the side of a cutting into the light of the evening and onto the road that leads up to the Bridge Inn. In the distance I heard the chimes of an ice-cream van. Then it roared past. Palozzi's Ice Cream. It was an out-of-the-way place for an ice-cream van. Mr Palozzi must have a vast territory in this sparsely populated area to sell enough ice-creams to make a living.

Down the road there's an attractive bridge over the Liddel that takes you into Scotland. Far below, as you stand directly above the Border, is Penton Linn, a dramatic stretch of the river that sent the authors of the *Ordnance Gazetteer of Scotland* (1882–5) into paroxysms of purple prose:

> Stupendous rocky precipices, which fall sheer down to the bed of the stream, and wall up the water within a narrow broken channel, along the Scottish side have a terrace-walk carried along a ledge, and affording a view of the vexed and foaming stream, lashed into foam among the obstructing rocks; and they are fringed with a rich variety of exuberant copsewood. In the middle of the cataract rises from the river's bed a solitary large rock crowned with shrubs, whose broken and wooded summit figures majestically in a conflict with the roaring waters during a high flood.

These days the place is celebrated not so much for its exuberant copsewood or its vexed and foaming stream, but rather for the challenge it throws down to the local youth. I was told all about it by a Geordie gentleman who lives in Penton House, just up the road. I chatted to him by his gate, as he tended to his garden.

'The locals, the young 'uns, I've seen them queuing up,' he told me. 'They jump off that bridge. Did you have a look over?'

'I did,' I said.

'It's quite steep,' he said. 'There was a lad killed there before we came here. But he didn't die with hitting. He drowned. The trouble is there's so much rubbish underwater – prams and so on. So you can get trapped. Especially when you've had a drink or two at the pub.'

Apparently the oldest bit of Penton House is a medieval keep. The bits I could see looked like they could be seventeenth century. My informant, Mr Thompson, had come to live here a few years previously, along with three or four other families, all related. Although a Geordie, his ancestors originally came from Dumfries.

'My grandfather moved to Newcastle to work,' he explained. 'His father did not like the English at all. They fell out arguing.' The father used the commoner Scottish spelling of the name, without the P. The son who'd gone to Newcastle put a P in his name.

'To annoy his dad?' I asked.

'To annoy his dad. Real animosity,' Mr Thompson laughed. 'He was a joiner by trade, and he stayed and settled in Newcastle. So we've been to Dumfries to have a look round, see the Thomsons on the graves.'

'There's quite a few there?' I asked.

'With a P and without it. Mostly without it. I suppose we're all related eventually.'

'We're a' Jock Tamson's bairns, as they say up there.'

'That's right.'

Mr Thompson also told me the story of his visitors from Peru. He'd found them wandering around outside the house. One of them presented his card. 'Pablo Penton', it said.

'Apparently his great-great-wayback-grandfather lived in this area,' Mr Thompson told me. 'And he got a baronetcy or whatever. When he came, I thought this was a con. He was with his lawyer.

Actually he was in oil. He'd done very well, he'd just come to see where his ancestors came from.'

Thankfully it was only a few hundred yards up the road to the Inn. I could see it glowing white in the evening sunshine.

As I stumbled heavily laden into the bar, a man said, 'That's one small rucksack, isn't it?'

'Luckily it's quite light,' I said.

'You've got to say that, haven't ye?' the man said.

Tony the publican was Australian. His wife Linda was the chef. She's originally from Ulverston, on the Cumbrian shore of Morecambe Bay, but now her father and brother farm the neighbouring farm in Penton.

I told him I'd got a room booked.

'You have,' he said.

I asked for directions to the outside tap. 'I had a close encounter with some slurry,' I explained.

'Round the back,' he said. 'There's a hose there.' I must have smelt that bad.

Refreshed, after a fashion, I returned to the bar. It being Friday night, it was in full swing. A local lady had had a disaster with her Aga. 'It's all gone and thingy blasted carboned it all up, so I can't light it. So I said, Well, I'm going down the pub. I've got no cooker. Eh, I says, what do you want for supper? He says, Oh well just get summit.'

'Two fish and chips for a tenner?' Tony suggested.

'Well, I might have lasagne,' she said.

'It looks absolutely delicious,' Tony said encouragingly.

A local at the bar was having none of it. 'Waste of good mince, that pasta shite.'

A younger man, also with a Cumbrian accent, was sporting a dark blue Scotland rugby strip. I asked him why. He told me he'd been to Dundee University. And before that his dad took him to see the rugby. 'It's a lot closer to Murrayfield to watch Scotland play than it is to Twickenham,' he explained.

I asked him whether it was not a bit dispiriting supporting Scotland, given their performance in recent years. 'Yeah, it's a very poor choice in that sense,' he said. 'But it's an easy choice in terms of getting there.' He was a dairy farmer's son. And now he too was a dairy farmer, working the farm next door.

My meal, I was told, was ready. I was ushered through to the west-facing conservatory, full of evening sun. Having taken advice along my journey, I decided against the fish, and the lasagne. But Linda's steak turned out to be all that it had been cracked up to be.

Later, in my room above, I lay on the bed staring through the window westward to the sunset. There were trees and then fields and then a low hill and then distant hills silhouetted in pink. Above them mauve-grey clouds streaked across a sheet of palest blue.

An owl flew past my window, telling me night was on its way. I drew the curtains, turned out the lamp. Outside the simmer dim slowly faded in the northern sky. Midsummer was less than a month away.

FOUR

WASTE GROUND WITHOUT HABITATION

Penton to Scotch Knowe

Kyrsopp is a small becke, and descendes from the wast grounde called Kyrsopeheade. It . . . is from head unto foote without habitacion.

— Thomas Musgrave, letter to Lord Burghley, 1583

Day Two: Saturday, 25th May 2013   It was a glorious sunny morning as I strode down the hill towards Penton Bridge. The wind had died, there was not a cloud in the sky. It promised to be hot later. As I turned right down a minor road parallel to the Liddel Water, all was quiet, apart from the birdsong.

I'd heard in the pub the night before that there were sheepdog trials taking place on Linda's brother's farm at Haithwaite. I'd be going right past it. I met two women walking in the opposite direction. I asked them if they were going to the sheepdog trials.

'Nope,' one said.

'You've had enough of sheepdog trials?' I asked.

'Yeah,' she said.

And they continued on their way.

The entrance to the sheepdog trials was through a gap in a hedge. I was greeted by a farmer. I asked him whether he was in charge. 'Well, I'm takin' yer money,' he said. It was only a pound. He pointed me to the marquee where refreshments were being served.

In front of the marquee I was greeted by a big man with a big smile and a big, bald head, leaning on a crook. He introduced himself. 'Welcome,' he said. 'I'm Ian Imrie, the chairman of this . . .' He waved his hand, taking in the marquee, the spectators, the course in the sloping field above us, where a woman was whistling and calling. A dog darted about. Three sheep seemed not to have much of a clue what was expected of them.

I asked Mr Imrie whether he was the judge. No, he said, the judge was sitting over there in a car. 'Have you seen a sheepdog trial before?' Mr Imrie asked me. I said I hadn't, so he explained the course in detail, what was expected of dog and handler.

When I looked at the programme of events for the day, I saw that the thing that Mr Imrie was chairman of was the 'Penton Discussion Group (Affiliated to the International Society)'. The judge was called Michael Peugniez, so perhaps that's where the 'International' bit came in. Or perhaps because the Group had members from both sides of the Border. Mr Imrie himself had a Scottish accent. His farm, he told me, was at Harelaw, on the Scottish side of the Liddel.

I asked Mr Imrie why it was called Penton Discussion Group. It all goes back to 1943, he told me, when the Ministry of Agriculture set up local groups of farmers so they could be shown how to grow more. Since then the Group, which meets at the Bridge Inn, has diversified and welcomes talks and discussions on all kinds of topics. 'Jolly friendly group,' Mr Imrie said.

He showed me the refreshment tent. I said I'd better not, I'd never get going again. 'Oh, go on. Never mind your walk,' he said. 'Just go back to the Bridge Inn the night.' I was tempted, but I had a schedule. I had to get to Carter Bar the day after tomorrow. I had a rendezvous with my sister. She had the food for the second part of my walk.

Another man took over the role of explaining the dog trials. He bemoaned the fact that working sheepdogs are dying out. It's all quad bikes these days, he said.

It was a regret I heard expressed on other occasions on my Border wanderings. A few months later I found myself at an agricultural fair at Dalston, a village near Carlisle. An old fellow with long grey sideburns, a sweeping grey moustache, a grey pullover and a flat grey cap leant on a table spread with ram's horns. He was a crook- and stick-maker. Hazel and blackthorn were his favoured woods.

'Do shepherds still use these to catch sheep?' I asked him.

He gave me a pitying look. 'No, they chess 'em wi' a quad bike,' he said, as if every fool knew that. 'Some of the old shepherds still use a crewook, though. You catch 'em wi' a crewook, yoo'uv got to have a dog bring 'em to it. And he's got to know exactly where to put that sheep. As it goes past ye, you've go like that.'

He suddenly shot out his arm.

'Cos when the sheep goes hurtling past ya with a dog after it, and the dog want to get it right till ya, and the sheep wants to get the hell out t'other way, yoo'uv got to be able to catch it with that hand and the force it's going it swings in behind, and yer six foot'll be short enough so that when it swings in behind, you grab the bloody wool on the sheep as well.'

It sounded extremely complex and skilful. I asked whether mastery of the crook featured in sheepdog trials.

'No, no, a lot of these fellows who do sheepdog trials only have three sheep,' the old crook-maker told me. 'I reckon in these world-class trials, that should be on the final day. The crewook. To see whether you can catch your sheep in an open field.'

Back at Penton the trials may not have been world class, but the spectators all took an expert interest in the proceedings. There was a constant quiet murmur as they marked the finer points of the performance. 'Mind over matter,' one said. 'The better dogs are showing 'em how to do it,' said another.

There was all to play for: the Robertson Cup for the Highest Pointed Lady Handler; the Joss Nixon Memorial Cup for Best Out-Bye Work; the Thomson McKnight Memorial Cup for Best Penning. 'All Trophies,' the programme declared, 'are Perpetual.' There was an Open Trial, a Local Trial and a Novice Trial.

And then the programme listed the names of the handlers and, more importantly, their dogs. Among the humans there were Marshalls, Mundells, Helliwells, Armstrongs, Tods, Grahams, Longtons, Billinghams, McDiarmids. And among the dogs were Sel, Jess, Cap, Craig, Jock, Rex, Tweed, Taff, Mirk, Lad, Meg, Dale, Spot, Flint, Tarn, Peg, Bess and Moss – names woven out of the Border landscape, its rock and moor.

I could have spent all day at the trials, the people there were so friendly and hospitable. But I'd barely started my day's walk, and there was far to go – past Peter's Crook and Hog Wash, Harelawslack and Hudd's Hole, Bendal Pool and Pudding Crook, up the river to Kershopefoot. And then up the Kershope Burn into the dark heart of the Kershope Forest. So I couldn't wait for the lunch break at the trials, when the programme promised that 'a stick, kindly donated by George Smithson, will be auctioned'.

I walked along the minor road for a while, parallel to the Liddel, and then rejoined the Waverley Line. There was a rotting broken gate with a rotting broken sign that said:

STRICTLY PRIVATE

NO   LIC

ACC SS

The next sign contradicted the first. 'Public Footpath' it said.

Then I was confronted with a gate across the line with yet another sign, this one hand-painted on an aluminium sheet:

PRIVATE PROPERTY

NO TRESPASSERS

BY OR

I climbed over the gate and went on my way. Apparently 'trespass' in English law means the 'unjustifiable interference with land which is in the immediate and exclusive possession of another'. I couldn't see how I was interfering with the land, either justifiably or unjustifiably. I was barely leaving a footprint, let alone mining for copper or coal, or building a retail outlet. I did think about holding a one-man all-night rave, but quickly abandoned the idea. That might open me up to criminal prosecution.

There was a good track along this private bit of the line. Young trees on either side gave me dappled shade. Again the only sound was birdsong. A woodpecker drummed. After a while, I heard distant bleating. Somewhere nearby, if I was not mistaken, the fleecy race was massing. Then, up on the hillside, I made out a farmer rounding up his flock on his quad bike. As my informant at the trials had lamented, gone were the hard-learnt whistles and calls, gone was the tight bond between human and dog, gone the fierce concentration of dog on sheep.

71

I wondered whether the quad-biker would come my way and ask me whether I was indulging in any unjustified interference. I was fairly sure I wasn't, but prepared my daft laddie defence just in case.

After a while the sense of property began to dissipate. The drystone wall by the side of the line relaxed then crumbled. Its flanks were grown over with moss. In one place, the limb of an old ash had crashed down and ruptured it. No one round here seemed too concerned with marking boundaries with barriers. The stones were, in their own time, reassuming their place in the earth.

As I walked northeastward above the wooded defile of the Liddel, past Fowlsnest Pool, Tom Bell's Linn, Atterson's Crook and Hagg Sike, the landscape began to change. The space around me was expanding. Now there were open vistas towards bare hills, the grass still winter-bleached. The sheep too were changing to match the landscape, and the lowland varieties were giving way to the black-faced hill breed.

A curlew called. It had left its winter shores and was now searching for a nest site up on the moors.

One sure sign that I was approaching the uplands was the fact that I was now walking through what the map marked as 'Access Land'. This is the label given in England to certain designated areas – such as hills, moors and heaths – where you are allowed to walk wherever you like, even where no rights of way are marked. In Scotland, of course, the default position is that you can walk pretty much anywhere you damn well please, as long as you're not trampling down a farmer's crops or taking a short cut across someone's garden. Or mounting some kind of protest inside the perimeter fence at Faslane, or any other 'prohibited place within the meaning of the Official Secrets Act'.

Although I was approaching the hills, I was still in the midst of a working landscape. Swathes of conifers draped the distant moors, and over the river the top of Greena Hill had been hacked away by the quarrymen. The map marked a disused kiln, so I suppose they were quarrying limestone – not a common rock in Scotland, but not unknown. That night, as it turned out, I was to camp beside a burn called Limy Sike.

I arrived quite suddenly at Kershopefoot. It's always pleasing to arrive somewhere before you expect to. Kershopefoot is more a scattering of houses than a village, although it does have a post office. There is a small road bridge over the Liddel into Scotland, and here the Border leaves the Liddel to follow the Kershope Burn for some miles into the hills. Next to the confluence, on the English side, there's a meadow of rough grasses and butterbur, dotted with alder and willow. It was here, at Dayholm of Kershope, that the Wardens of the Western March met on that fateful Truce Day in 1596 when the English seized Kinmont Willie. This meadow marked the eastern end of the Western March and the beginning of the Middle March. It was a common spot for meetings on Truce Days, and disputes between individuals on either side of the Border could be resolved here by single combat – hence the meadow's alternative name, the Tourney Holm (from Old French *tourneier*, 'tournament', and Old Norse *holmr*, 'river meadow'). The man who ended up dead on the ground at the end of the tourney was, according to popular opinion, clearly the guilty one. Everybody else seems to have enjoyed a good time, and pedlars and vendors would come from many miles around to sell their wares, turning the occasion into a sort of fair.

There were occasional outbreaks of unpleasantness, however, such as the Truce Day in 1508 at Tourney Holme when Sir Robert Kerr, the Scottish Warden of the Middle March, was murdered by three Englishmen called Lilburn, Starhead and John Heron of Ford, known as 'the Bastard'. After the murder they fled, but Lilburn was quickly taken, and the English handed over Heron's legitimate brother, Sir William Heron, to answer for the sins of the Bastard. Starhead, meanwhile, had ridden all the way south to York. Here, in the course of time, a party of Kerrs caught up with him. They took his severed head home as a trophy.

Close by to the Tourney Holm I came across the following curious sign on a gate:

> This site contains
> confined spaces
> Check register for
> confined spaces

It was another place I wasn't allowed to go, for reasons I failed to fathom.

A sign on another gate proclaimed:

> Thieves beware!
> You Are Now Entering
> A Cumbrian Farmwatch
> & Smartwater Area

It was clear that, although remote, Kershopefoot was still prone to lawlessness. The traditions of the reivers have not, apparently, entirely died out.

The name Kershope – as in Kershopefoot, Kershope Burn, Kershope Forest, Kershopebridge, Scotch Kershope, English Kershope and Kershopehead – is from Anglo-Saxon *coerse*, 'cress', and *hop*, 'secluded valley'. Inspired by the etymology, I hoped I might find some watercress along the banks of the burn to add to some fresh green to my evening meal.*

Just as you hardly notice you've arrived in Kershopefoot, you hardly notice that you've left it. It peters in, then peters out. There was a steep section of tarmac up past Kershope Mill, the steepest stretch of the walk so far, but as soon as you've climbed up the hill

---

* It was as well I didn't. I have since learnt that eating wild watercress is a good way of infecting yourself with liver flukes. These parasitic flatworms are deposited in water via the faeces of sheep and cattle. Once in the water they are taken up by water snails, which in turn feed on watercress. Thus humans feeding on the watercress may in turn find their livers and gallbladders riddled with blood-feeding worms. Even food for free may come with a cost.

you have to walk down the other side to pick up a forestry track – at first no more than a path – that leads up the English bank of the Kershope Burn, with Thief's Cleugh on one side and Battle Hill on the other – names, like so many along the Border, that hint at stories that have long been forgotten.

I was now embarking on one of the wilder stretches of the Border, still as deserted as when Thomas Musgrave wrote in 1583 to his master, Lord Burghley, Elizabeth I's chief minister:

> Kyrsopp is a small becke and descendes from the wast grounde called Kyrsopeheade. It devydes the realmes in a meare dyke untill it meat with Lyddall, and is from head unto foote without habitacion.

On the English side, row upon row of conifers marched southward and eastward, while on the Scottish side there was still open moorland. But just beyond Kershopebridge, where a minor road crosses the burn and the Border, the firs of the Newcastleton Forest crowd in from the Scottish side. This is the edge of one of the largest man-made conifer plantations in Europe, taking in not only the forests of Kershope and Newcastleton, but also those of Kielder, Wark and Wauchope.

I had feared that the next stretch up the track by the Kershope Burn would be unremittingly dull, hemmed in by tall walls of dark green monotony. But the Forestry Commission, conscious of their responsibilities towards public amenity (as they would no doubt put it), have cleared the ground for some way on either side of the track and the burn, and allowed the growth of scatterings of native woodland – birch, alder, willow and rowan. The amenity value of the place was attested by the tracks of horses and humans and mountain bikes, though after a car passed me at Kershopebridge I did not see another soul for the rest of the day.

After a while I crossed a concrete bridge into Scotland and came to a bifurcation in the track. One signpost said 'Kielder via Bloody Bush'. The other said 'Kielder via Scotch Knowe'. My route along the Border took in both Bloody Bush and Scotch Knowe, so this apparent paradox in the signage should perhaps have given me a warning. The signs pointed the sensible walker and cyclist along routes where there was a track, or at least a path. My route, I knew, dispensed with a path from this side of Scotch Knowe to Bloody Bush and beyond, and pitched me instead into the hell that is Hobbs' Flow. But that was for another day.

A heron, tall and elegant, stood peering into a pool. It had its back to me but must have had a sense of my presence. With slow beats of those massive wings, it rose into the air and flapped further up the burn. Perhaps it was just looking for a change of fishing ground. Perhaps my presence was entirely irrelevant to its purpose.

At another point I came across a lamb bleating pitifully for its mother. The lamb was on the English side of the burn, the mother in Scotland. Then the mother realised I was just behind her and panicked back across the burn to her offspring. After a brief reunion, the mother settled down to chomp on a clump of primroses.

As the track climbed slowly and steadily into the hills, there were fewer and fewer leaves on the trees, sometimes barely the sign of a bud. The long cold spring had chilled the sap to a standstill. But now there was a touch of warmth in the sun, maybe the leaves would begin to unfurl. A red admiral flicked past me, the first I'd seen that year.

I came to another split in the track. This time the choice was between Scotch Kershope and English Kershope. The track by the former would keep me close to the Border. The track passing the latter would come to an abrupt end at Lazy Knowe, stranding me in a wilderness of spruce.

If I had taken the way by English Kershope, I might have come across, between the Wythes and Skelton Pike, a lonely weathered pillar called Davidson's Monument. This was erected in 1852 to the memory of a 'gamewatcher' murdered by poachers on 8th November 1849. Thomas Davidson, father of eight children, had been 'a steady and honest servant' of Sir James Graham for some twenty years. That fatal morning he had set out from his home at Kettle Hall in the parish of Bewcastle on his usual rounds across the bleak moors. He never returned. A search was mounted, and two days later his body found. He had been strangled with his own neckerchief. There must have been some other injuries as well, as contemporary newspaper reports recount that he was found face down in a pool of his own blood. (After all, a Border murder without a pool of blood would hardly count as a Border murder.)

The inquest led to the arrest of three suspects. The first of these was James Hogg, who just three weeks prior to the murder had been fined for shooting without a game licence. Davidson had been the key witness against him. The poacher's cousin Nicholas Hogg was also arrested, as was a young man called Andrew Turnbull. Three days after his arrest Turnbull hanged himself in his cell in Carlisle jail. On the wall beneath the window he had scrawled a message. 'The two Hoggs are guilty. I am innocent. I will not come in the hands of man.' The Hoggs appeared the following spring before the Cumberland assizes, but after a lengthy trial they were found not guilty. Soon afterwards, both emigrated.

Tempting though it was to visit Davidson's Monument and pay my respects, it would take me on too big a diversion. So instead I took the track that led past Blaemount Rig and Thwartergill Head to Scotch Kershope.

There was no one in when I got there. A long, low, whitewashed cottage sits in a clearing, facing south over a pond surrounded by grass and scattered willows. There was a diving board. I might have been tempted had the day been a bit warmer. The only thing that spoilt the idyll was the dark line of conifers masking the near horizon. Somewhere on the other side of the conifers lay English Kershope.

When it was put on the market in 2012, the cottage had no mains electricity or gas. The estate agent made much of this, waxing lyrical about dinner by candlelight and Scrabble *à deux* by the open fire. 'With no game centres or computers,' the blurb continued, 'children can learn how to have fun as they did a century ago.' A year later, I noticed a satellite dish had been installed on the roof. There was, I assumed, a generator somewhere. I wondered whether the postman delivered here. Did the council come and pick up the rubbish? Or did the inhabitants make a weekly trip to Newcastleton or Canonbie, taking out their waste and bringing back their post?

Disappointed that I'd found no one at home, I continued on my way, quietly closing the gate behind me. I was tired and thirsty, and the dodgy vertebra in my neck was pinching on its nerve. As I plodded on, I kept an eye out for a slope or tree against which I could rest myself and my sack. But the ditches by the side of the track were freshly dug, slick with moist peat, filled with rust-patched water. Beyond them lay bog and scrubby willows.

I passed a line of poplars, about a hundred feet high. They looked out of place in the middle of this wilderness. The wind whispered through them the way the wind whispers through poplars the world over. Just beyond I found a big tussocky divot of earth by some dried-out moss. I gratefully sat down with my back against it. Up here the Kershope Burn had narrowed to no more than a few feet across. A couple of wary steps from stone to stone would take you from Scotland into England, and a couple more would take you back.

The burn burbled quietly as the shadows lengthened. A faint gossipy honking drew my eyes upward. There, overhead, flying in V-formation, two or three hundred geese beat northward to Svalbard. There they'd breed and feed and fatten through the end-to-end daylight of the short Arctic summer. I too was heading northward to feed, if not to breed or fatten. Luckily I only had to go as far as Scotch Knowe.

But first I had to pass Muckle Punder Cleugh, Cock Kaim, Ewe Brae, Yearning Flow and Havering Bog. My hopes were raised when I came upon a Forestry Commission sign saying 'HAVERING'. I was making better progress than I'd thought. Havering Bog is, according to the map, just short of Scotch Knowe.

It turned out it was the Forestry Commission who were havering*. The place where the sign was didn't match the topography on the

---

* A Scots word meaning 'talking nonsense'.

map. I could see the defiles called Nether Castle Cleugh and Upper Castle Cleugh, not to mention Black Cleugh. These are only just past Kershopehead, a bothy hidden somewhere in the dense plantations on the English side. So my hopes had been raised only to be dashed. There was still some way to the true Havering Bog, some way before I could pitch my tent and eat and sleep. I was quite pleased. It was only five o'clock and I still had some spring in my step. I would make a little more progress before nightfall.

The shadows under the trees on the opposite bank were brightened by a cushion of wood anemones, in flower a month later up here than they had been in London. The delicate white flowers lifted my spirits.

After a while, the track turned right over a wooden footbridge into England, away from the Border line, heading for Kielder. This was the last bridge between Scotland and England until Yetholm Mains, on the far side of the Cheviot. From now on, more or less, the Border follows the watershed along the top of the Cheviot Hills, until it arrives at the fertile lowlands of the Berwickshire Merse. Before I reached the watershed, however, I still had to negotiate the upper reaches of the Kershope Burn without the benefit of either track or path.

The way was obstructed by mounds of moss, tussocks of yellow winter grass, low conifer branches. I had to cross the burn into England to avoid a steep bank dropping down between the forest edge and the water. Then I met a similar obstacle on the English side. The burn continued to narrow. There were stepping stones, but it wouldn't be a place to slip out here on your own in the middle of nowhere. No one would ever know what had happened to you. Or at least not for quite some time. By then the crows would have had your eyes. Maybe your belly would have bloated and burst. Maybe your bones would have bleached.

I paid due attention to where I put my feet.

There were a few more burn and Border crossings before I reached Scotch Knowe. On my way I pondered on the old name of the place. I had in my mind it was 'Lamasisk Ford'. That name didn't appear on the OS map, though it cropped up in many historical

79

documents I'd come across. It marked the meeting of three counties: Northumberland, Cumberland and Roxburghshire. I wondered into my Dictaphone what a Lamasisk might be. It sounded like a Basilisk, that ancient creature that could turn you to stone with its stare. Maybe the Lamasisk was a beast that lived in the burn, fasting for months until some unwary traveller came by. And then, oh my, the feasting. Beware the Lamasisk, my son, it'll suck the living blood out o' ye.

Scotch Knowe appeared before me not a moment too soon. With all this talk of predatory burn-beasts and bleached bones, I was clearly suffering from exhaustion.

Scotch Knowe is a small area of flat ground beside the Kershope Burn. Three Forestry Commission signs face each other here in a triangle, marking the junction of the forests of Newcastleton, Kielder and Kershope, as well as the meeting of the three counties, and the two countries. It's a long, long way from any public road, one of the remoter spots in these islands.

There was a stone-ringed fireplace with two upright sticks holding a horizontal bar from which to hang your billy can. Three or four sawn-off logs served as seats. Most of the ground was bog, apart from a small patch of dry grass above the bank of the burn, just big enough for a single one-man tent. It was up in a moment, and soon the evening air was filled with the roar of my stove.

I had less success with the fire I attempted. The brushwood caught well, but the larger lumps of wood were sodden and would not take. After forty minutes of blowing and puffing, there was a friendly crackle and a bit of flame.

I left my fire-tending duties for a few minutes to cross the burn and inspect the place where Limy Sike entered the Kershope Burn. Then I saw a small stone inscribed with the letters 'THE LAMISIK FORD'.

So the name – Lamisik, not Lamisisk – was not entirely forgotten. It also occurred to me, belatedly, that the Lamisik was not some fabulous animal but simply a version of 'Limy Sike'. Perhaps there was some limestone further up the hill.

When I returned, the fire was looking very sad indeed. I decided to put it out of its misery. If I didn't, the chances were it would suddenly get frisky and next thing you'd know the largest man-made forest in Europe would be up in smoke.

If the fire wouldn't keep me warm, then a dram in my sleeping bag might just do the trick. I crawled into the tiny tent and nodded off before I got to the second page of my book. Overhead another skein of geese headed north into the twilight.

FIVE

UTTER DESOLATION

Scotch Knowe to Deadwater

This region cannot be called beautiful; its chief charm, if indeed it has one, is its utter desolation.

— James Logan Mack, *The Border Line* (1924)

Day Three: Sunday, 26th May 2013   It had been a cold night, punctuated by the grunts and barks of roe deer. Unzipping the tent, I blinked in the bright morning sunshine. To the sounds of birdsong and trickling water, I stripped off and washed in the burn. I knew today was going to be one of the toughest days of the walk. I was in no hurry to start.

From my camp I could see the way ahead. The Border here follows the middle of the diminishing Kershope Burn, and then runs up its principal feeder, Clark's Sike. The burn winds its way between steep banks towards the high moorland. I could make out tussocky bog and extensive areas of clear felling, littered with brushwood and stumps. There was no sign of a path.

'The Kershope Valley is peaceful enough to look at from a distance,' wrote James Logan Mack, 'but woe betide the unfortunate person who endeavours to walk alongside the Border Line up the banks of the burn.' Logan Mack was an Edinburgh academic who explored the Border in the early years of the last century. In 1924 he published *The Border Line*, a dry but scholarly account of the terrain and its history.

Up to the last bridge, I had had the benefit of a forestry track running close to the burn on its northern side. In Logan Mack's day there was no forest, and no network of forestry roads. So he had had to resort to a track on the southern side 'some little distance away' from the Border. Beyond that track, he wrote, 'lies one of the most desolate regions in Great Britain'. A 1754 map published by Emanuel Bowen, Royal Mapmaker to King George II, describes this area as 'Mountainous and desart parts, uninhabited. A large wast.'

I'd left the track behind the previous evening. Now it was just me and the large wast. Or what passes for wast in modern Britain: blanket bog and brashings – swathes of hacked-about brushwood.

84

As I followed the burn the landscape opened up. Behind and below me wedges of fir and spruce jutted across the hillsides. But up here the moorland plateau was only a hundred feet or so above me on either side. The sky was clear blue, with just the occasional puff of cloud. The day was glorious, but the going was rough. I lost count of the number of times I had to cross the burn – and the Border – to dodge steep slopes plunging into the water. Sometimes there was level ground on one side. Sometimes the level ground was on the other side. Even the level ground was barred by bollards of grass and reeds, or clumps of deep heather, or felled branches. Sometimes there was a mixture of all three. Many years before I'd tried to make my way through clear felling in a forest in Knapdale. It took me an hour to cover half a mile through waist-deep brashings. Today I was doing little better. The ground was treacherous, scratchy, ankle-snapping.

Sometimes I scrabbled across the burn by wet mossy slabs, sometimes by stepping stones, sometimes I just had to jump. At one point an overhanging cornice of turf collapsed beneath me. I jarred my knee on the hard mud below.

This was indeed a 'desart wast', but the sign of man's hand was everywhere in the landscape, from remnants of iron fence posts to expanses of felled forest. Here and there, for some reason left unfelled, stood the stripped trunk of a tree, stark against the skyline. It looked like the Western Front after a particularly heavy bombardment.

But nature was present here too, in tension with human works. At one point I found a patch of celandines, in flower two months later than they had been in London. I was several hundred miles to the north, a thousand feet higher. I might have been on a different planet.

I was more aware of my physical presence within this landscape than I would have been in a city. I constantly had to adjust my feet, my legs, my body, to negotiate its roughnesses. Wind blew soft air across my face. Unsated by the brash colours of urban signage, my eyes could feast on subtler greens, browns and yellows.

And then my nostrils caught the sharp, sweet smell of resin. The stumps I was passing were still red and raw. They could only have been cut a few days before.

In the distance were piles of logs. I knew that where there were piles of logs there would be a forestry track. That would provide an attractive alternative to the clumps of dead reeds and hidden mossy quagmires that lay in my path as the burn shrank to a trickling ditch. But I knew that forestry tracks have a habit of not going the way you want them to go. They have a different agenda, and rarely take you direct from A to B when circuits around C, D, E and even X, Y and Z might be compassed. But I was stuck with this linear project, to follow the Border line.

It wasn't always obvious where this line was. The conifer planta-tions closed in again. Sometimes I had to crawl under low branches, sometimes negotiate a fallen fir. At one point I very nearly set off in entirely the wrong direction, until put right by a very old, lichen-encrusted forestry sign. 'Bloody Bush', it said, and pointed right.

Bloody Bush, whatever it was, was marked on my map. It lay the other side of Hobbs' Flow. I checked with my compass, set myself right and so avoided the allurements of what I now realised was Queen's Sike rather than Clark's Sike. Which queen owned this sike remains a mystery, and I never followed it to its source to find out. Perhaps this queen was the Queen of the Faeries, the ruler of Elfhame, thought to lie somewhere amongst these Border hills – some say beneath the Eildons, others on a loch-topped hill near Eskdalemuir. I recalled her words in the Ballad of Thomas the Rhymer:

> 'O see not ye yon narrow road,
> So thick beset wi thorns and briers?
> That is the path of righteousness,
> Tho after it but few enquires.
> 'And see not ye that braid braid road,
> That lies across yon lillie leven?
> That is the path of wickedness,
> Tho some call it the road to heaven.

'And see not ye that bonny road,
Which winds about the fernie brae?
That is the road to fair Elfhame,
Where you and I this night maun gae.'

Her way, it was said, was neither the way of heaven nor the way of hell. But I did not take her path. I suppose something in my Presbyterian ancestry reared up and forced me down a stricter route, into the depths of Hobbs' Flow.

Hobbs' Flow, when at last I found it, turned out to be the 'braid braid' way of hell the Queen of Elfhame had warned against, a *via infernale*. Or, if not a *via infernale*, at least a *via dolorosa*, one that nearly had me weeping in frustration – had not the sheer absurdity of its awfulness made me chuckle instead. Perhaps I was away with the fairies after all.

Regarding Hobbs' Flow, Logan Mack issues this stern warning:

In a wet season its passage should not be attempted, and even in a dry one the traveller is not free from the risk of being engulfed in the morass. While I have crossed it twice in safety, I do not advise that this route be followed, and he who ventures into such solitude should keep to the west and circle round on higher ground.

The western deviation Logan Mack recommends did not look any more appealing than the direct route, so I took a bearing of thirty-five degrees, eyed up the rotten post stumps that marked the Border line across the Flow, and stumbled on.

The edge of the Flow was dotted with clumps of bog cotton, not yet in their full summer glory. The locals call these grasses moss troopers, alluding to the lawless armed bands that roamed the Border moors during the years of chaos and civil war in the seventeenth century. These freebooters acknowledged loyalty to neither king nor parliament. One of the most notorious leaders among them – perhaps the black sheep of some local landed family, or an army officer turned freelance – bore as his standard a brandy barrel stuck on top of a pike.

At first the Flow did not seem too bad. But experience made me wiser, and I found that Hobbs' Flow is very, very wet indeed. Before long the water was coming through the worn-out stitching in my boots.

Hobbs' Flow, now a nature reserve, is an example of what is known as 'blanket mire' – a large area of upland bog. It is one of several blanket mires found around and in the midst of the Kielder Forest. These mires are too waterlogged for the Forestry Commission to bother planting. The vegetation is dominated by sphagnum moss and coarse grasses, and provides a haven for moorland birds. The birds must have remained hidden in their haven, as I barely saw a single one, bar the odd white flash of a wheatear's rump.

The identity of the Hobbs of Hobbs' Flow is as obscure as the identity of the Queen of Queen's Sike. Hob was formerly a familiar name for anyone called Robert or Robin. The English soldiery gave the nickname 'King Hobbe' to their enemy Robert the Bruce and sang a rather rude song about him in Middle English (the precise meaning of which eludes the modern reader, but the general drift is clear). Hob was also a name for Robin Goodfellow, the mischievous sprite also known as Puck. Robin Goodfellow was associated with will-o'-the-wisps, the pale flares of marsh gas sometimes seen in boggy areas at night. They were thought to lead unwary travellers – who took them for friendly lanterns – into the heart of the morass, where they would drown. The Latin name for will-o'-the-wisp is *ignis fatuus* – foolish fire.

In broad daylight, there was no fire to be seen up there on the Flow. But there was, without a doubt, a fool.

I squelched on through the mosses, keeping a wary eye out for hidden traps. Once, out of the corner of my eye, I glimpsed something wriggly and reptilian scuttle under a hairy tussock. It looked too wet a place for a lizard. But if it was an amphibian, more suited to the habitat, it must have been a toad with a very long tail. Perhaps the Queen of Queen's Sike had mutated some unwanted suitor into a species unknown to our mortal taxonomies.

While pondering this question I found my foot at the bottom of a boghole. There was a dreadful sucking sound as I pulled it out. My boot and lower leg were covered in brown yuk. At least it didn't stink of slurry.

The Flow gave way at last to thick clumps of heather, but there were still mossy wet boggy bits in between. I felt the lack of what the Scots call 'heather legs' – long, strong legs fit for louping through deep heather. My legs are short, and at this point felt particularly puny.

In the distance I could see the Old Toll Pillar marked on my map. It didn't look far, but the going was so slow I knew it would take me some time to get to it. Although the ground was more or less level, I had to plunge down the defiles of the Coal Grain and the Watch Grain and up their other sides, further slowing my progress.

Eventually I reached the Pillar. It marks the intersection of the Border and the rough old track known as the Bloody Bush Road. It had taken me two and a half hours to cover the one and a half miles from my camp at Scotch Knowe. The Pillar was bigger than I'd thought, some fifteen feet high. I raised an imaginary glass to toast my arrival:

> Here's to the Bloody
> Here's to the Bloody
> Here's to the Bloody Bush Road.

Then I slumped against the pillar and brewed up some tea.

The Bloody Bush Road is now only used by mountain-bikers, but it was once an important trade route. Before the railway was built in 1862, coal was taken this way from the Lewisburn Colliery, five miles to the south, destined for the Border textile mills. The Pillar itself enumerates the charges for use of this private road, payable at the tollgate near Oakenshaw Bridge. 'Persons evading or refusing to pay at the above-mentioned toll-gate,' the Pillar intones, 'will be prosecuted for trespass.' Horses 'employed in leading coals' were charged 2d. each, other horses 3d. each. Cattle only had to pay a penny per head, while sheep, calves and swine got off with a halfpenny.

There is no bush apparent at the place by the Old Toll Pillar marked on the map as 'Bloody Bush'. But there is a story attached to the name. A band of reivers from Tynedale had been pursuing their chosen profession in Liddesdale. Returning home, they'd set up camp by a bush near here. For some reason they hadn't posted a sentry. In the night a posse of vengeful Scots fell upon them and slew them to a man. Hence the bush by the camp where they were slaughtered became bloody. No source I can find gives any more details than that, and all are very vague about the date. There is an additional story – again without any clear foundation – that no bridge ever built anywhere near Bloody Bush has survived more than a decade. Either the bridges are mysteriously destroyed in the night, or found so covered in bloodstains that the locals have demolished them. Oh, and on certain nights, it's said, you'll hear the thunder of ghostly hooves.

It sounds as if the Bloody Bush is one of the more creative achievements of the Border Heritage Industry.

I leant against the Pillar and chewed on an oatcake and cheese. As my billy came to the boil I spied a cyclist toiling up the Bloody Bush Road from Kielder. I hailed him, asked him if he'd like a cup of tea. He grinned. I told him I was going the crazy way, along the Border. He was going the sensible way, I said, sticking to the track. 'Well, I don't know about that,' he said in a Brummie accent. 'I wasn't expecting it to be so rutted.' He was hoping to get to Carlisle that night. He only had a sketch of his route. I pulled out my 1:25,000 map and hesitantly pointed out that he wasn't going in quite the right direction. 'Oh,' he said. 'Well, there was a fork a bit back.' I said it would be a lot quicker cutting down by the Kershope Burn to Liddel Water than heading northwest over the shoulder of Larriston Fells by the Bloody Bush Road to the upper valley of the Liddel. The only thing, I said, was that I'd seen a sign at Kershopebridge saying that the trail was closed till the summer due to tree-felling operations. But it had all been clear along the stretch I'd walked, I said, so it might be ok. It all depends whether the end of May counts as summer. My Brummie friend said he'd give it a go, and after swallowing his tea pedalled back down the way he'd come.

After a while another three mountain-bikers heaved into view from the English side. I had a similar conversation with them. Andy, Stewart and Rachel were from Newcastle. They realised they'd come the long way. 'Slight deviation,' they joked. 'We wanted the exercise.' One turned back, but two decided to press on over the Bloody Bush Road.

After an hour's rest, I got myself ready to go. The weather looked like it was on the turn, with the wind getting up from the southwest. There was a front forecast for the next day.

As I heaved my sack onto my back, I spotted another cyclist, head down, coming up from Kielder. Looks like the same one as last time, I said to myself. Surely not. But it was indeed my Brummie. He'd tried the trail, but it had been completely blocked by forestry operations somewhere between Willowbog and Black Cleugh. He was tired but philosophical. I suggested the Bridge Inn at Penton might be a more realistic destination for the night. He liked the sound of that.

The going was little better north of the Toll Pillar. It was still rough, tussocky ground, interrupted by more substantial obstacles, including the steep-sided cleuch of the Bloody Bush Burn. The Border along this stretch was more clearly defined, not by the topography but by a relatively new barbed-wire fence running in parallel to a broken-down wall. At one point I thought I'd found a path, at least a sheep path. I recalled the words of Logan Mack:

> In order to avoid undue fatigue, and indeed to render walking in this particular part of the country anything approaching a pleasurable experience, it is advisable to find a sheep-track and keep to it as far as possible . . . otherwise after a short time even those accustomed to hill-climbing will become exhausted . . . To those who intend to explore this stretch (which should be undertaken only by those stout of limb) the practice is to be commended of finding these tracks and keeping one's eyes usually on the ground, though now and then ahead for varying distances.

The theory was fine. However, my particular sheep path soon turned into a drainage ditch.

At last I came to the point where the Border makes a sudden and arbitrary right-angled turn and heads briefly southeastward, back into the Kielder Forest. This was my highest point that day, somewhere around 1,500 feet.

I turned round to look back at the way I'd come. Far to the southwest, beyond the moor and the forest, glinting pale gold, lay the Solway Firth. It had taken me two and a half days' hard walking to get from there to here. To the south and southeast lay a vast area of forest, and, beyond that, the rolling hills and farmland of Northumberland. There was a great sense of space, of freedom, up there on the Larriston Fells. Even with the wall and the fence by my side I felt I'd made a transition from the bounded to the unbounded. I was unrestrained by roads, or tracks, or even paths. I was far removed from the comforts and limits of civilization. It was just me and the unordered, arbitrary surface of the earth itself, a harsh landscape that offered an infinity of choices – all of them hard.

Somewhere round where the Border abruptly changes direction once stood the 'Grey Lads'. Various such lads are found across Cumbria. They are not, as you might have expected, prehistoric standing stones – like Long Meg and Her Daughters near Penrith or the Nine Ladies near Bakewell. These 'lads' are neither young men nor monoliths but piles of stones. The word derives from Anglo-Saxon *hlaed* or Old Norse *hlad*, both meaning 'heap'.

I found no heaps, only the finely crafted drystone dike that here marks the Border. Perhaps the Grey Lads had undergone a metamorphosis, dismantled and then reordered into a wall – just one more step in the story of these blocks of pale grey sandstone. They'd once been sand, deposited by ancient rivers more than 300 million years ago and then pressed and pressed by the weight of the sediments above into the hard rock we know today. The sand that had been compressed into the stone had once itself been solid rock, but over time the rock had been cracked and weathered and washed into tiny fragments. Over eons to come, the blocks that make up – for now – this Border wall will be ground down once more into tiny particles, until the whole cycle starts again. By then, humans and their walls and their boundaries will long have crumbled to dust.

The map marks a path alongside this wall. I tried both sides, but both sides were pathless, and the rough going continued. Further down the slope, though, I thought I could see what looked like a proper path. It looked recent, well maintained, shaped into pleasing curves. I presumed it had been built for mountain-bikers. I couldn't wait to get on it.

When I reached the trail I felt like a sailor who's become so used to the motion of the waves that when he steps onto dry land he can't find his feet. I soon adjusted, and strode out downhill. The trail ran parallel to the Border. I hoped it continued to do so, because the alternative was more tussocky horror. After a while the path left the open hillside and plunged under the forest canopy. It was peaceful in the dappled shade, with the wind now only a whisper in the tops of the trees. On either side there were deep ditches dripping with ruby, emerald and purple mosses, lush and treacherous.

I checked my compass. The trail was heading east, the same direction as the Border. I was encouraged, but told myself not to raise my hopes. They'd just be dashed.

A little further on the trail was intersected by a track. I looked at my map. Nothing seemed to match. In Forestry Commission land the tracks marked on the map are not always there on the ground. And often on the ground there are tracks that aren't marked on the map, and they rarely go where you want them to go.

At the intersection there was a flurry of signage. Suddenly I was back in the world of direction and advice, back into the territory of the bounded.

One sign gave emergency information, in case you and your mountain bike should inadvertently part company. The nearest public phone was '15 km' away, the sign advised, and the nearest place to get a mobile phone signal was a kilometre beyond that. And you'd have to go all the way to Hexham to find an A&E willing to put you back together. Another sign told bikers they were about to embark on the Bloody Bush Mountain Bike Trail. It is graded Red, and the sign asks, 'Is This For You?' My answer was 'No'. I was heading in the opposite direction. Another sign told me the trail I wanted was called Borderline. The significance of the name took a while to sink in. It follows the Border . . . and it's so hard that it's *borderline*. Ah yes.

Maybe my brain was slow from dehydration. I'd just finished the last of my two litres of water, and I didn't fancy the stuff in the drainage ditches beside the trail. The water was stagnant and covered with an oily sheen. Not even my chlorine dioxide tablets could cope with that.

I checked the map, looking for places where I might refill my bottles. A bit further down the Border there was Birkey Sike, and then the Duke's Well, and Bell's Burn. I'd soon be able to quench my thirst.

After a while the trail mounted a winding wooden causeway. Apparently bikers call this 'north shore'. As it was made for bikes, the slats were wide apart and I had to keep my eyes on my feet to avoid a trip. I checked my compass again. The north shore was taking me a bit more to the southeast than I would have liked. There was such thick forest on all sides that I wasn't quite sure where the Border line was any more. Then the north shore turned a bit more northward, which was more like the direction I wanted to be going in. I trudged on as the trail meandered through the densest forest I'd so far travelled through.

After a while it became clear that the net direction of the north shore was in fact southward, in diametrically the opposite direction to the Border. A sign had advised me that 'This north shore allows access across some of the deepest peats in Kielder Water and Forest Park.' So there I was, in the midst of the deepest peats and the densest forest, stuck on the wrong route. I told myself I would be mad to abandon the north shore and attempt a beeline for the Border. It would be like trying to negotiate the barbed wire and mud-filled craters of Passchendaele (although without the machine-gun fire and the gas). I just hoped that the trail wasn't going to take me too far out of my way – to Kielder Village, for example. Though there is a pub there, I comforted myself.

I also told myself that this whole area was still marked as 'Disputed Ground' in James Duncan's 1837 map, so a bit of deviationism might not be too inappropriate from a historical point of view. The Border as now marked along this section is some way from the watershed, and doesn't follow any natural boundary. Logan Mack describes it as 'an extraordinary detour'. The obvious line is further west, from Larriston Fells down past Currick, Green Craig, Rampy Sikes and Foulmire Heights. The ground under my feet now offered a damn sight better going than the horror that had been Hobbs' Flow, and the horror that would have no doubt awaited me on Foulmire Heights, if the name was any clue. In such a fashion I justified my divergence from the path of righteousness.

It was to turn into an afternoon of self-deception.

The errors of my ways became only too apparent when I came to an extensive clearing of virgin heather moor. This, I established from the map, was Purdom Pikes, a third of a mile east of the Border. And I was on the far side of the clearing, even further from where I should have been. Far beneath me in the distance I could see the blue expanse of Kielder Water, dotted with a few white sails. I imagined myself out there on the water, trimming my sail to the wind, following whichever course took my fancy. Instead, I told myself, you're stuck up here with this daft project which is all going belly-up cos you've tried to match the cartography to your convenience.

Then I heard a cuckoo calling.

Excited, I got out my Dictaphone. The previous evening, just as I was nodding off, I'd heard a cuckoo, but had been too sleepy to record it. Now the cuckoo of Kielder was coming over loud and clear.

It called again. And again.

Then an icicle of doubt slid down my back. Wasn't it just perhaps a little too loud and clear and regular, this cuckoo?

Cuckoo, it said. Cuckoo cuckoo cuckoo.

Here I was in the wilderness, with no soul seen since Bloody Bush, and some joker was pretending to be a cuckoo. Cuckoo cuckoo cuckoo. Maybe deep in the forest on the far side of Purdom Pikes a biker had a bike with a bell that went cuckoo cuckoo cuckoo?

As if in answer to my question, I heard once more the cry, cuckoo cuckoo cuckoo.

So not only had I been lured away from the Border by the duplicitous north shore. Now I was being mocked by a Mock Cuckoo.

The trail swung this way and that, very gradually making its way downhill but in no very determinate direction. There were some fine swoops and dips. They would have been especially fine if I'd been on a bike. Indeed, I made this point to the only person I met that afternoon. He was from the Reivers Mountain Bike Club, based in Morpeth, and he'd had a hand in designing these Kielder trails, he told me. The idea, he said, was to pack as much biking as possible into the limited ground available. I said I thought it would make a fantastic ride. But I had only my feet between me and the ground, and my agenda was to get from here to there as directly as I could. So it was all proving rather tiresome. We both laughed, then he jumped on his bike and sped effortlessly downhill.

And I still had found no water.

Straight ahead, across the valley in which the village of Kielder nestles, I could see Deadwater Fell with its clusters of antennae. It's an MoD radar installation controlling the local airspace, and on weekdays these hills shake with the sound of low-flying NATO jets. Beyond Deadwater Fell lay the flat top of Peel Fell. My plan for the day had been to continue over Peel Fell and make camp by the Kielder Stone, in a dip on the far side of the summit. It was only twenty past four. I was still telling myself I could make it. But it looked a long way away. Especially if the trail was going to go on zigzagging in this languorous fashion.

It did. At one point I found myself heading for something signposted as 'Purdom's Plunge'. I didn't like the sound of that at all.

Plunging was not part of my game plan for the day. So I was relieved when I encountered another sign that said 'Escape to Kielder'.

I was even more relieved when I found a trickle of water coming out of a culvert. It took five minutes to fill up a litre bottle, and another ten for the chlorine dioxide to do its work. But the water was worth the wait. As I lay back in the dappled sunlight of the late afternoon and quenched my thirst, I examined my options. I concluded that the Kielder Stone was not a realistic objective for the evening. Instead, I found on the map a little patch of deciduous woodland on Deadwater Rigg, bang on the Border and two or three hours closer than the Kielder Stone. There were springs marked nearby. It would be a good place to spend the night, I decided. And, having made that decision, I felt a further burst of relief.

Perversely, the trail – ostensibly an escape to Kielder Village – started to go uphill. My feelings of exasperation returned.

After a time I found myself approaching a strange-looking building. It stood on a rocky knoll called Cat Cairn. The structure was round and roofless, with drystone walls capped by white concrete. It reminded me of a broch, one of those ancient Iron Age towers that dot Scotland's northern seaboard. Or perhaps a Mycenaean citadel louring over the plains of the Peloponnese. But I knew exactly what it was, and hadn't expected to encounter it. It was the Kielder Skyspace. If I'd stuck to the Border, I would have missed it.

I entered through a white circular tunnel. Inside, every small sound reverberated. The centre of the floor was a circle of grey gravel, and round the walls ran a continuous white bench. Through the large circular hole in the ceiling a splash of light was projected onto the side wall in the shape of an ellipse.

Then you look up and see, through the circle of space in the roof, the sky.

It was like looking at our Earth, or perhaps another planet – Neptune, Uranus – from a high orbit. All you could see was a circle of blue, with flickers of white curling round it.

The Skyspace takes you into a different place. The world is not the same from inside it, and neither are you. It would be the place to come if you were troubled.

But I had more miles to cover before I slept, so I abandoned my meditations and took to the trail once more. As I headed down into the darkening forest I was mindful that this area had once been a sanctuary for 'wulcats'. I hoped no wildcat was going to spring onto my neck as I passed through the dense firs. I recalled with a shiver the lines of the Renaissance makar Gilbert Hay:

> Thare wyld cattis ar grete as wolffis ar
> With ougly ene and tuskis fer scherpare . . .

The forest floor was lightened here and there with the delicate white flowers of wood sorrel. But the only animals I spotted were scores of black slugs making their sluglike way along the trail. Who knows what business they were intent on. Perhaps they were after a chomp on the sorrel's tangy trefoils.

I came at last to tarmac road, and the whiff of burnt petrol. The road took me in a few minutes to Kielder. The village is still a remote place, but not as utterly out of the way as it was in the middle of the eighteenth century when the then Duke of Northumberland described the inhabitants as 'all quite wild'. His Grace continued:

> The women had no other dress than a bedgown and petticoat. The men were savage and could hardly be brought to rise from the heath, either from sullenness or fear. They sung a wild tune the burden of which was 'Ourina, Ourina, Ourina'. The females sang, the men danced round and at a certain part of the tune they drew their dirks which they always wore.

Today Kielder is more hospitable. I contemplated the many temptations the village has to offer: the hostel at Butteryhaugh, the campsite at Catcleugh, the Anglers Arms with its 'traditional freshly cooked British fayre'.

But what I needed above all was water. I tried the petrol station.

There was a man filling his four-by-four. I asked him whether there was a tap. He said there wasn't. We fell to chatting. Although he was originally from Derbyshire, he'd discovered this place while living in Newcastle and decided to settle here, a few miles north of the village, just short of the Scottish Border. 'That is the beauty of it,' he said. 'People get to Kielder then turn round, don't explore further.' He told me his name was Jonathan.

I asked Jonathan if he could give me a lift up the road to Deadwater. He said of course. As I'd put in a lot of extra unintended miles during the course of the day, I didn't feel I was cheating. I was merely being restored by four-by-four to my proper place on the Border.

I told Jonathan I was thinking about camping on Deadwater Rigg. 'I had a chap calling by,' he told me, 'wanting to wild camp, but wasn't sure if he could. I said you can walk and camp anywhere you like on the Scottish side. But he wasn't sure on it. Don't know what he ended up doing.'

Jonathan dropped me off at Deadwater Farm. 'If you go to the farmhouse, Tony the farmer's up there, and he'll sort you out with some water. Ask him where the source of the Tyne is as well. Tell him Jonathan says.'

It turned out that there'd been some experts from Newcastle University had recently decided that the true source of the North Tyne lay somewhere on the flanks of Peel Fell above Deadwater Farm. There was some talk of erecting a monolith to mark the spot. They'd need a helicopter to put it in place.

Sheila, the farmer's wife, was taken aback to find a vagabond on her doorstep. But when I explained I was just after some water and would be on my way, she smiled, and took my bottles to fill them. The family were eating round the table, so I didn't want to linger. Their Jack Russell ran round my ankles, barking. Sheila laughed, said the dog was confused by my big blue rucksack. Apparently I wasn't quite human, and therefore needed a good barking at. I let myself be seen off. I never did get to discuss the source of the Tyne. But I'd got my water.

I walked a few hundred yards back down the road towards Kielder, looking for the right-of-way marked on the map. It should have taken me straight up to Deadwater Rigg. But where the path should have been, it wasn't. I followed its theoretical line up the edge of the Deadwater Plantation, squelching through bog, squeezing under low branches, ducking my head down to avoid putting an eye out. It was hopeless. So I made a break for the open hillside to the west, because whatever path there may once have been was now completely overgrown. The only sign of human passing was an old camping chair lying on its side, covered in mildew. It didn't explain what it was doing there.

Straddling two barbed-wire fences, I escaped from the forest, and then crossed the ditch of the Deadwater Burn.

I don't quite know why 'Deadwater'. In *The Romance of Northumberland* (1908), A.G. Bradley tells us that in a 'wild hollow' under the English slope of Peel Fell 'the North Tyne springs from peat mosses, and on its way down lingers silently for a time in a rushy flat known to the borderers as Deadwater, a name now embalmed in the timetables of the North British Railway'. The implication here is that 'Deadwater' refers to the marshy floor of the valley (called 'Ye Red Mosse' in a survey of 1604), where the various streams that come down from the fells merge and mingle and lose their identity in the general wetness, before dribbling out the southeastern end of the moss as the River North Tyne. It's not long before it too becomes lost in Kielder Water, the largest artificial lake in Britain. The marshes of Deadwater, and in particular the burns called Rashy Sike and Dead Sike, also form the source of the Liddel. The latter flows west towards the Solway, while the Tyne goes east to the North Sea. So at Deadwater I was at the middle of the Border, at least in watershed terms.

Bradley's reference to the 'North British Railway' alludes to the fact that 'There is here a Lilliputian station displaying with laconic pathos on its narrow platform a name embalmed in Border song and story . . . Who uses it, I cannot imagine.' Deadwater Station was a lonely spot on the forty-two-mile Border Counties Railway that ran from Hexham via Bellingham to Riccarton Junction, where it met the Waverley Line. One might ask why such a desolate place should ever have been deemed worthy of a station, but in fact Deadwater was in the eighteenth and nineteenth centuries something of a mecca for people suffering from 'cutaneous and scrofulous complaints', who would flock here to take the waters. Deadwater Well lies just north of the old station, and there was once a 'Bathing House', still in use in the later nineteenth century. But by the 1920s Deadwater was once more becoming a backwater, and the station mistress was only authorised to issue tickets for six stations down the line, and no further. Later, the station became unstaffed, and passengers wishing to join the 6.55 a.m. southbound train were requested to notify the station master at Riccarton Junction before 5.00 p.m. the previous evening. The station was closed to passengers in 1956, and completely closed in 1958. Now Deadwater has rediscovered that remoteness that my friend Jonathan relished so much that he came to live here.

As I walked up the side of the Deadwater Burn, a wagtail danced above the water, its yellow breast catching the evening light. Above me a lark sang. I plodded due north up the hillside through a pathless tract of rough, reed-studded pasture, rich enough to support a handful of cattle. I could see them ahead of me. One of them was giving me a look. I hoped she had no malevolent intent. More likely she thought I was wrong in the head. This place was hardly fit for cows, let alone an unsturdy, hairless biped.

As I approached my little copse at the top of the rig, leaving the cows far below me, I could see the trees were barely in leaf. There was just a slight downy dusting of green, no more than a hint of spring. The trees – mostly birch, some alder – were stunted, exposed as they were on their knoll to the prevailing westerlies. But this evening there was no wind. And I would be able to watch the sun as it set.

It was now nearly eight o'clock, ten hours after I'd left Scotch Knowe. I wandered into the wood, looking for a spot on the greensward to pitch my tent and sleep. Branches and trunks twisted in all directions, draped in lichens, lit by a rosy light from the west. I felt I'd entered some old legend, probably involving gnomes and a pot of gold – or one of the Border equivalents of gnomes, such as fatlips, redcaps, or the brown man of the moors.

I dined on pumpernickel and Portuguese sardines in a piquant tomato sauce, followed by rice and sweet-pepper sludge. For dessert there was a Snickers bar, accompanied by a glug or two from my very own pot of gold.

Birds sang as the sun set. The sky dimmed through a lattice of winter-bare branches. With the sun gone, the wind rose a notch, bringing a chill. I'd put on all my clothes and a gnome-like woollen hat from Peru.

Although tent and sleeping bag beckoned, I was reluctant to leave the boundless for the bounded. Out here the birds tossed fragments of phrases to and fro, daring each other to pick up the theme and play.

In the distance, sheep conversed in the timeless way of sheep.

I'm here, one said.

I'm here too, said another.

Where's my mum, said a third.

Over here, dear, the mother said.

I'm here, one said.

I'm here too, said another.

Where's my mum, said a . . .

Ba. Baa. Baaaa.

The rest of the world was inside, bordered by their four walls, watching the telly.

I was in a magic wood that time had forgot, a thousand feet above the sea.

SIX

AMONGST THESE ENGLISH ALPS

Peel Fell to Carter Bar

... the North [Tyne] is out of Wheel Fell sprung
Amongst these English Alps which as they run along
England and Scotland here impartially divide.

– Michael Drayton, *Poly-Olbion* (1612, 1622)

Day Four: Monday, 27th May 2013   Today we call it Peel Fell. Michael Drayton called it 'Wheel Fell', while on an 1837 map of the Deadwater District it is marked as 'Pearl Fell'. I was to find that Peel Fell was no pearl – more like the swine one should not cast pearls before. And I suspect that Michael Drayton had neither visited the Cheviot Hills nor the Alps, as the former are as rounded as the latter are spiky. But they do have this is common: uncompromising wildness.

> On Kielder-side the wind blaws wide;
> There sounds nae hunting horn
> That rings sae sweet as the winds that beat
> Round banks where Tyne is born.

So wrote Swinburne in 'A Jacobite's Exile'. The wind was fair blawing wide when I poked my head out of the tent in the morning, and the clouds were shutting down the sky. The promised front had come. The wind was from the southwest, but it was distinctly chilly. I was in shelter on my greensward in the wood, but there was commotion in the tops of the trees. I ate my breakfast huddled in sleeping bag and hat.

I was hoping I might race the rain eastward. But I knew there wasn't going to be much racing today.

I'd run out of water again, so stumbled down below the wood where the map marks four thin blue fingers. The ground was covered in reeds, and the patches in between had been trodden by cows. Out of the shelter of the wood I could feel the bite of the wind and wished I hadn't left my gloves in the tent. Even the celandines had closed up against the cold. It was 27th May, Bank Holiday Monday.

I couldn't find any sign of running water, just a patch or two of oily-looking drip and drool. I looked further down, where the little fingers were supposed to join to form a head of water. I found the confluence, but it was no more than a bog that cows had shat in.

At least it wasn't a hot day. I would have to make it waterless over to the far side of Peel Fell, to Kielderstone Cleugh, down which I hoped a stream would run.

By the time I'd broken camp the rain had arrived, though not much more than a drizzle. I'd put on all my waterproofs, hat, hood, gloves and over-gloves. At least the wind was behind me. 'From here to the top of Peel Fell,' writes Logan Mack, 'is a long tramp over very rough ground . . . There is no pleasure to be had from it until the heavy tus-socks are left behind and the higher reaches of the Fell attained.'

The Border here follows a somewhat irregular line up the hill, in a northeasterly direction. On the English side were mature conifers, while on the Scottish side was a plantation of young birches. I crossed over a barbed-wire fence and followed the Border along the mossy top of a broken-down dyke. Here and there I had to divert into the bog or clear-felling either side to avoid a young self-sown spruce or a fallen fir. Some of the fallen trees had hauled up their roots as they fell. These roots were draped with mosses, giving them the look of giant, hairy spiders.

When at last I emerged onto the open hillside, I was surprised to find a path. There was a sign. 'Kielderstane Walk' it said. It was going my way. It was a good honest hill path and it gave me a good honest uphill slog.

And so I came to Jenny Storie's Stone, a cuneiform buttress of Northumberland sandstone jutting out of the rim of the Peel Fell plateau. If I hadn't been alone, if it hadn't been raining, and if I'd had my rock boots with me, I would have tried a few of the tempt-ing lines up the front face, using water-worn pockets and shapely horizontal breaks. Northumbrian sandstone is a delight to climb. But I was alone, it was raining, and I didn't have my rock boots, so I let Jenny Storie's Stone well alone.

I never did find out who Jenny Storie was. She still keeps her secret. But on a night of full moon I can imagine you might hear her here, wailing for her demon lover . . .

Peel Fell, at just under 2,000 feet, is the highest point in the western Cheviots. Just where its summit is wouldn't be easy to tell if there wasn't a cairn to mark the spot in the middle of a flat expanse of peat hags. The tops of the hags are festooned with moss and heather, and here and there you find the stumps of an old Border fence. The going's not as easy as Logan Mack would have you believe, but it's not in the Hobbs' Flow league of awfulness.

Nestled amongst the hags I came across a little lochan, its surface whipped by cat's paws in the strengthening wind. It was now blowing from the southeast, but it felt like it had whistled in from Siberia. I had heard that after the first front passed another front, a cold one, was going to be moving down the country. It had arrived.

I found my burn sooner than expected, on the near side of the Kielder Stone. There were no sheep up here amongst the heather, so I didn't bother with sterilising tablets. A bit of grouse dropping never did anybody any harm, I told myself as I swallowed mouthful after mouthful. Go back go back go back, said the grouse.

If you're approaching via Peel Fell, you come to the Kielder Stone from above. From this viewpoint it looks like a huge table, part covered with a cloth of moss and heather. It is in fact a gigantic block of Northumbrian sandstone, 26 feet high, 133 feet in circumference and weighing perhaps 1,400 tons (Logan Mack measured it). The sides are generally sheer or overhanging, though they are replete with all the wonderful features you find in Northumbrian sandstone – little pockets, vertical cracks, nubbled walls, flakes of finely layered horizontal strata, jutting noses, water-worn grooves. Again, if the sun had been shining, and I'd had my rock boots, and didn't have ground to cover, I'd have had a happy time bouldering here. There's a soft landing in mossy bog if you fall.

'The eastern face of the rock is certainly unclimbable,' Logan Mack opines, 'and to the ordinary individual so are the other three, but to the skilled mountaineer the north-west corner presents no great difficulty.' As if to prove his point, he includes a photograph of himself and his friends posed halfway up the Stone.

He also recounts the story of 'some foolhardy lads and lasses' who managed to make their way to the summit, but then found they could not descend. One of the more timorous members of the party, who had remained earthbound, walked several miles to raise the alarm, and returned with a group of rescuers carrying a ladder. Perhaps the stranded youngsters had tempted fate by walking round the Stone three times widdershins (contrary to the direction of the sun), which is said to bring ill fortune.

Apart from this tale, the Kielder Stone remains silent about its history, although it bears the inscribed initials of some of its more self-promoting visitors. If 'PS' and 'AC' are reading this, you should be ashamed of yourselves.

Such an obvious feature would have provided an important signpost in these featureless wastes, and a rallying point for countless raiding parties. As such, it will no doubt have seen its fair share of bloodshed. It certainly inspired the imagination of Dr John Leyden, whose poem 'The Cout of Keeldar', is included in Scott's *Minstrelsy of the Scottish Border*. The eponymous Cout rashly ventures on a hunting expedition into Liddesdale, incurring the wrath of William, Lord Soulis, the vicious warlock of Hermitage Castle (who could only be killed, Leyden tells us in another poem, if he was wrapped in lead sheeting and boiled alive):

> And onward, onward, hound and horse
> Young Keeldar's band have gone;
> And soon they wheel, in rapid course,
> Around the Keeldar Stone.
> Green vervain round its base did creep,
> A powerful seed that bore;
> And oft, of yore its channels deep
> Were stain'd with human gore.
> And still, when blood-drops, clotted thin,
> Hang the grey moss upon,
> The spirit murmurs from within,
> And shakes the rocking-stone.

The only murmuring I could hear was the wind, while the rain had washed all trace of blood and gore from the rock (which, contra Leyden, does not in fact rock).

The Kielder Stone is perhaps the most prominent landmark anywhere along the Border, which now runs straight through it. It wasn't always thus; these wastes were long disputed between the Earls (later Dukes) of Northumberland and the Earls of Douglas. It seems that whichever bits of land each of them decided belonged to their own private estate determined the territorial claims of their respective nations. It wasn't until 11th May 1778 that the lawyers put the matter to arbitration and fixed the line of the Border between Peel Fell and Carter Fell. I was to find that this line was anything but logical. In fact it was to prove exasperating, exhausting, soul-sapping. Definitely the result of horse-trading on the part of a bunch of well-feed and unscrupulous lawyers.

I'd had my first slip of the day walking down to the Kielder Stone. After ending up on my backside I'd turned round to examine the spot, expecting to find skidmarks in a patch of peat. But there was nothing to be seen but steep grass, slippery as ice in the wet. After that I made a special effort to dig my heels in on the downhills, and the edges of my boots horizontally into the slope on the ups. But it was far from the last slip of the day.

It was just after noon when I left the Kielder Stone. According to my original schedule I should have been at Carter Bar by now. I thought it might take me another couple of hours to reach the A68. As it turned out, I was not to reach the road till five o'clock, averaging something like one mile an hour. These Border miles are triple-strength.

After the Kielder Stone the Border jerks crazily about through a nightmare of cleuchs* and sikes. The heather on these fells is so dense and deep you could call it scrub. These were not the manicured

---

* On the Scottish side of the Border it is a *cleuch*, while on the English side it is a *cleugh*.

heather moors of the grouse shoots. The Border line is marked by the rotten stubs of fence posts. First they take you across Wylie's Sike, then over Haggie Knowe, down again to the junction of the Green Needle and the Black Needle. Neither of these two feeders of the Scaup Burn reflected their names; both were peat brown, readying themselves for the spate to come.

Stumbling up the east bank of the Black Needle I had to contour the flank of the heather-black hill called the Trouting. Despite the wind and the rain I sweated with the effort. I'd take a step up, then my foot, hidden somewhere deep in the heather, would slip sideways. Or my ankle would get caught in an unseen hole. In places it was two steps forward, one step back. Or even two steps back. It was harder than breaking trail through deep snow in the winter hills. I thought of the line in *King Lear*:

> The worst is not
> So long as we can say 'This is the worst.'

But I'd pretty much plumbed my own personal depths. Even a bank of primroses above the Black Needle failed to rouse my spirits.

I was not the first – nor, I suspect, the last – to curse these almost impassable fells. 'If I were further from the tempestuousness of the Cheviot Hills,' wrote Peregrine Bertie, Thirteenth Baron Willoughby de Eresby, 'and were once retired from this accursed country, whence the sun is so removed, I would not change my homeliest hermitage for the highest palace there.' Bertie was Warden of the English East March, clearly not a job he enjoyed. He died of a cold in 1601.

On a sunny day, with nowhere particular to go and no deadline, I would have loved to laze by these burns among the hills. As it was, I slumped briefly for a drink and a snack, conscious of the chill and the wet down my back, then plodded on.

I tried to raise my spirits by moaning into my Dictaphone: *Down Green Needle, up Black Needle, plunging down, gasping up another steep-sided cleuch. Deep heather, deep deep heather. No path. This is*

mad, totally illogical, this Border line marked by these rotting old posts.
One I've just taken a photograph of has just been shat on by a moorland
bird. Well done it.

Who on earth designed this Border? There's a far better route up there,
you know, along the watershed, without all this dropping down, clamber-
ing up, only to drop down again.

The Border kinked north, then southeast. Any fool could see that
this was an entirely unnecessary deviation from the general northeasterly drift of the Border line. I was exasperated, so angry with the
Border-makers that, to spite them, I cut the corner and slogged up
deep heather onto Knox Knowe. So I missed out the source of the
Black Needle and the stretch of featureless nothing called Duntae
Edge, which Logan Mack describes as 'the most evil piece of ground
which I encountered on the Border from sea to sea'. I saved myself
maybe 400 yards and, in the process, by walking this new bound,
annexed an insignificant triangle of worthless land for Scotland.

On Knox Knowe there were cloudberries in flower, a rare treat. At
one point a snipe burst out of the ground beneath my feet, zigzagging
away from any merlin that might be on its tail.

Despite the wind and the rain, the cloud was still above the tops.
Behind me dark grey ridges gave way to paler and paler grey shoul-
ders, fading into the distance towards Deadwater Fell. To the north,
peaking over the horizon, I could just make out the tops of the highest band of conifers in Wauchope Forest. Ahead of me I spotted the
mobile mast on the side of Carter Fell. It still looked like a long, long
way away. But I got a signal, phoned my sister, told her how very,
very late I was going to be. I was apologetic. She was sympathetic.
'Poor you,' she said. Poor fool, more like. 'No, no,' I said. 'Don't
worry, I'm fine.' Well, I was. Just cold and wet and late. But still able
to put one foot in front of the other.

Which is what I did, one foot in Scotland, the other in England,
one foot among blaeberries, the other treading on bilberries – the
same plant, with the same delicate pink bell-like flowers, but with
different names on either side of the Border. If it had been August, I

would have hunkered down and stuffed my face with the tart purple fruit.

I was ridiculously happy to find, at last, one of the Border Stones that had been marked on the map as 'BSs' for some miles, but which had remained hidden in the heather. Here was a fine specimen of grey sandstone, part covered in white lichen. It had N on the English side, for Northumberland (the Duke, that is), and D on the other, for Douglas. Except that the D was reversed. Either the mason who'd carved it was illiterate, or he'd had an inbuilt anti-Caledonian bias, and thus saw fit to upend the dignity of the Scottish Earl by boule-versing his D.

And so I made my way across Carter Fell. The going was certainly better than it had been down in the cleuchs, but there were still plenty of traps for the unwary – not only shake holes and old mineshafts, but also mosses, morasses, quagmires, all ready to suck you in and swallow you. If you'd put a foot wrong by one of these wobbling green horrors, you'd sink and sink and never be seen again.

I shuddered. The bogs juddered, quaking with silent boggy laughter.

I came at last to the trig point on Carter Fell, the first trig point on the walk so far. After that it was downhill, and the going got considerably better. In fact there was a grassy path, and as I strode down it towards Carter Bar and the A68 I could make out two Blue Saltires fluttering vigorously in the strong southerly wind. Beyond them, far away in the distance through the rain, at the other end of a long snaking line of hills, I could just make out the Cheviot itself. It still wore a big patch of snow on its southwestern flank.

The car park when I got there was virtually empty. No one with any sense was going to stop here today to admire the view. But as I passed one solitary vehicle a man stepped out into the wind and the rain. He was Chinese, and his car had diplomatic plates. Inside I could make out a woman and a baby. I asked him if this was his first time in Scotland.

'Ya,' he said.

'What do you think of it?' I asked inanely.

'Really lovely. Fantastic.' Clearly a diplomat. 'You?' he asked.

I told him I came from Scotland, that I was walking the Border from the west coast to the east coast.

'Alone?' he said, with some concern in his voice – for both my safety and my sanity, perhaps.

'Yes,' I said.

'Very good,' he said encouragingly. He probably thought it best not to upset this maniac. Then he returned to the warm interior of his car.

Then I saw my sister's car. Inside were not only my sister Tricia but my brother-in-law Jem, and also my daughter Claire and son Archie, with whom I was to continue my walk over the Cheviots.

That had been the plan. But I was half a day late, and the forecast for the two to three days it would take us to traverse the high Cheviot was not good. There was going to have to be some kind of rethink. That night we should have been camped at the Roman fort at Chew Green, several miles east along the main Cheviot ridge. We examined our options. There were some possible places to pitch a tent on the edges of the woodland on the Scottish side of the Border pass. I mulled over the prospect. I was wet and cold, it was still wet and cold and windy outside, and the following days were also supposed to be wet and cold and windy, at least up high where we would be.

And then I remembered the words of Jean-Luc Godard. 'A film should have a beginning, a middle and an end,' he said. 'But not necessarily in that order.'

If that was true of a film, I thought, it could also be true of a walk.

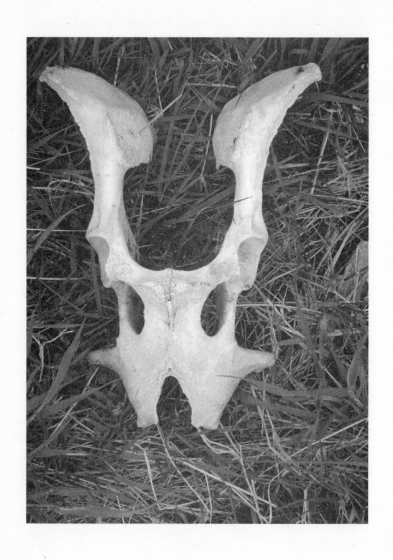

SEVEN

A TRUE PERAMBULATION BETWEEN THE KINGDOMS

Kirk Yetholm to the Tweed

The business on which they had met being opened, they elected six knights for England and six for Scotland, as jurors, to make a true perambulation between the kingdoms.

— Hugh de Bolebec, letter to King Henry III of England,
13th October 1222

Day Five: Tuesday, 28th May 2013 'There's honesty. And white nettle in flower.' I was pointing out the treasures of the hedgerow to my children. 'Wild roses too – oh, and a little white cranesbill.'

'Yah, white nettle in flower. Ooooh, and wild roses!' Claire was on my case. 'And oh oh oooooh an itsy little white cranesbill!'

It is better, I thought to myself, to travel alone.

'My weary eyes cross the fields of lemon-yellow rape!' Claire was on one. 'And I *behold – BEHO-O-OLD* – the *li-mi-nality* of my *Aye*-den-titty.'

You can tell she's been studying anthropology.

'Am I Scottish?' she continued. 'Am I English? Am I *YA-HA-HA-HA*...'

BANG. There was a loud bang. We all jumped in the air.

'Fuckzat?' Archie enquired.

We were, bizarrely, approaching England from the south. This is what happens when you walk north along the road from Kirk Yetholm.

Perhaps the Border guards were jittery.

BANG. Again.

'Shit,' I said. It was my turn to swear. Then I realised what it was. 'It's a bird scarer.'

'A people scarer more like,' Claire said.

'Let's assume it's a bird scarer,' I said.

'I've broken out in a sweat,' Claire said.

'Well, I wasn't expecting that,' I said.

'Neither were the birds,' Claire said.

'Were there any birds?' Archie asked.

'They're dead or flown, Archie,' I said. 'Dead or flown.'

Pebble-studded mudflat where Solway meets Sark, and the Border is sucked inland.

Gravestone in Gretna.

DLO Longtown, an MoD munitions dump that was once part of a vast First World War cordite factory that spread for miles either side of the Border.

Dead moles strung on a barbed-wire fence by the River Sark.

Sign by the old Waverley Line on the English side of the Liddell Water. No right to roam here.

The ditch called Clark's Sike forms the Border beneath Hobbs' Flow.

The toll pillar on the Bloody Bush Road.

Border wall on the eastern flank of Larriston Fells.

Border stone between Peel Fell and Carter Fell. The 'N' stands for the Duke of Northumberland, who fixed the Border here with his neighbouring landowner the Earl of Douglas in the 18th century. There's a mirror-image 'D' on the other side of the stone.

The Border stones at Carter Bar.

Ascending back up Clennell Street to the Border by Windy Gyle, having found water down in the forest.

The Border fence between Randy's Gap and King's Seat, on the west side of the Cheviot.

Skull on the Border fence on Bowmont Hill, north of Kirk Yetholm.

Riders relax after their gallop up Branxton Hill during the Flodden Ride-Out.
(Photo: Joyce Nicholls)

Approaching Flodden Cross for the laying of the thistles. (Photo: Joyce Nicholls)

'Yella, yella yella. Any colour you like. Very cheap.' Coldstream High Street on the last night of Civic Week. (Photo: Joyce Nicholls)

The climax of Coldstream's Civic Week. 'It was as if all the devils of hell were after the souls of the slaughtered.' (Photo: Joyce Nicholls)

Masonry at Norham Castle

Sticker on the back of a road sign, Cornhill on Tweed.

Road sign on the English side of the Tweed.

Graffito in Berwick

By the mouth of the River Sark: 'It might once have been an ash, but now it was more like some prehistoric monster lurching from its lair, a knot hole for an eye, a root for a snout, the body scaly and green with algae.'

The M6 crosses the River Sark and halfway across becomes the M74.

Looking down on the Sark from the Scottish side.

Nature reclaims her own on the old Waverley Line, south of Liddel Water.

Following the Kershope Burn towards Scotch Knowe.

The crook-maker at Dalston Fair. (Photo: Joyce Nicholls)

In Kielder Forest: 'On either side there were deep ditches dripping with ruby, emerald and purple mosses, lush and treacherous.'

My campsite on Deadwater Rig.

Jenny Storie's Stone, on the flank of Peel Fell.

The view south from Carter Fell into Northumberland.

Dere Street by Coquet Head, from the Roman camp at Chew Green.

The Carham Burn leading the Border into the Tweed.

The proprietor of Coldstream Crafts and her cat. 'It's a place that the nastiness of the world has passed by,' she says. (Photo: Joyce Nicholls)

View from the wild camp on Ba Green, the tiny Scottish exclave on the south side of the Tweed.

Children watch the horses pass on Coldstream High Street, en route to Flodden Field. (Photo: Joyce Nicholls)

Four generations of Peebles Cornets take a break on Branxton Hill. (Photo: Joyce Nicholls)

The Coldstreamer lowers the Earl of Home's standard over the sod of earth cut from Flodden Field. (Photo: Joyce Nicholls)

Inside Rajdhani Spice, Coldstream. The town also has a Chinese takeaway, and Anthony's, an Italian chippy.
(Photo: Joyce Nicholls)

Mr Forman, butcher of Norham and custodian of its castle. Although born in Edinburgh, he has always lived in England. He thinks of himself as neither Scottish nor English, but as a Berwicker, as that was his mother's town.
(Photo: Joyce Nicholls)

The torchlit procession on the last night of Coldstream's Civic Week.
(Photo: Joyce Nicholls)

From the south bank of the Tweed towards either Dreeper Island or Kippie Island. The former is entirely in England, the latter entirely in Scotland, but both form parts of the same island.

Window shutter on a fisherman's hut near Paxton House, on the Tweed.

The wall that keeps a thousand free-range pigs out of Scotland, near Halidon Hill.

A full moon rises over the North Sea at the end of my journey.

'Dead or flown, Archie,' Claire repeated.

Merciless they are, merciless.

'I had to do an experiment to scare birds, how to quantify it,' Archie told us. He's studying ecology. 'My plan was to put some birds in a cage and put a thousand cups of seed on the ground, so you could then work out how close they would dare to go near a model, a human or a predator.' He paused. 'I didn't do as well as I should've.' His tone was becoming indignant. 'I was like – *There's no flaws in this!*' He laughed. He takes his studies very seriously.

The previous evening, as we'd huddled on Carter Bar with the wind rocking the car and rain spattering the windscreen, we'd come to a decision. We'd leapfrog the eastern Cheviots, save them for more clement weather, and instead take Tricia's offer of a lift to Kirk Yetholm, the village that nestles at the northeastern end of the Border hills. There was a hostel there, and a pub, both well-known and welcome to those finishing the Pennine Way. From here we would walk the low-level section of the Border to Coldstream, rather than committing ourselves to a multi-day high-level traverse in worsening weather.

So there we were, under dry grey skies, walking along the wide strath of the Bowmont Water between low, nubbly hills. The hills were covered in grass and gorse and patches of woodland. The hedges either side of the little road were mostly hawthorn, the hedgerows dominated by cow parsley.

We were, as I said, doing an unusual thing to be doing in Scotland. We were walking north towards England.

ScreeeeeeeROOOOOOOAAAaaaaaaarrr. A fighter jet flew low overhead, at one moment in Scottish airspace, the next over England. The jet, a Tornado or a Typhoon, was followed by another, swooping up the valley towards the Cheviots. With such metallic angels looking over us, how could we come to harm?

A John Lewis van drove past. Civilisation was being kept safe for shopping.

This is the posh end of the Borders. The fertile alluvial soils of the

Merse – the lowlands either side of the lower Tweed – have made its farmers rich. And the area is close enough to Edinburgh and maybe Newcastle to provide rural havens for those who've made their fortunes in property or finance or law.

We got our first taste of this wealth at Venchen Old Toll, just short of the Border. Behind the old toll cottage, away from the road, the owner has attached a substantial new house, designed in the local vernacular. The two windows and door of the old toll cottage itself, facing directly onto the B6352, have been bricked up – not with bricks, but with matching undressed stone. The place had turned its back on its original function. No pennies to be made these days on the B6352.

A pair of SUVs were parked up on the driveway in front of the house, while in the paddock beyond two girls were jumping their ponies. We felt like vagabonds, stravaigers, sturdy beggars.

The north end of the paddock where the girls jumped their ponies was the Border. It crosses the B6352 and cuts up the hillside alongside a drystone dike to a saddle between Bowmont Hill and Castle Hill, the one with an ancient settlement on its top, the other with an Iron Age fort.

As if to remind us of the long-dead builders of these places and of our own mortality, the hillside by the Border wall was littered with the ruins of animals: the skull, spine and pelvis of a sheep; a still fresh stoat curled up in death, the black tip of its tail touching its gaping snout. The fur on its belly was a warm yellow.

A sign on the electricity pole said DANGER OF DEATH. Against a yellow background, within a black triangle, a prone man was suffering what looked like a lightning strike.

Crossing the saddle between Bowmont Hill and Castle Hill, we descended towards Wideopen Moor. A herd of cows – heifers or bullocks, I don't remember, but they were young and daft and saw us as predators – locked into formation and, heads down, crowded in on us.

I raised my arms, Archie raised his, Claire hers, we strode towards them waving our arms and shouting 'Go on! Go on! Go on!' in as masterly a manner as we could manage. They flicked their long-lashed eyes, seemed to calculate, panic. Then backed off. Oh – them, they maybe said. Those humans. Best back off.

When I was young we never worried about cows, only bulls. But now you hear about walkers butted over and knelt on till their ribs crack and their hearts burst.

The herd dispersed. We let go our held-in breath, strode down by the old hawthorn hedge between a field of fodder on one side and rough plough on the other.

The Border fence was black with flies hanging along every wire, twitching. They were in pairs, each one clasped onto the back of another. They were fornicating. Not only the wires but the air was thick with them, paired up on the wing, their long legs trailing. In the midst of death we were in life.

But death still stalked us: the fused vertebrae of a bird; another sheep skull; and then, close by, an amorphous blob of sinew, tendon and tight white curls. We couldn't classify it beyond: Animal, Part of, Dead.

Oblivious to the transitoriness of existence, or perhaps only too well aware of it, the flies swarmed on in a fervour of copulation.

The countryside we were walking through could have been many places in Britain: a gently rolling landscape of fields dotted with coppices of broadleaves and conifers, some marked on the map as fox coverts. There were nettle-filled ditches, unnamed burns, stone walls, electric fences. There was silage, rape, barley, pasture, soft brown plough. Blue speedwell and yellow and purple heartsease dotted the field edges, and in the hedgerows wild cherry and blackthorn were in flower. A heady scent of coconut came off the golden gorse as the day grew warm and humid. The sun glowed hazily behind burnished cloud.

We followed the Border along walls, dodged it when it plunged along an overgrown ditch or through a particularly dense covert. Past Hoselaw Mains, between Pressen Hill and Hazelcleugh, the Border briefly follows the B6396, before turning right down a minor road and then wandering off again through the fields towards Duke's Strip and Nottylees.

This whole stretch of the Border, from White Law to the Tweed, was for many centuries ill-defined. Unlike the 'natural' barriers provided by the Sark, the Liddel, the Kershope Burn, the Cheviot Hills and the Tweed, there were no clear frontier lines. These were the eastern Debateable Lands. And, as this was fertile ground and thus more desirable than the mires of the Debatable Lands of the west, much blood was shed over them.

Through the Middle Ages the line wandered to and fro. One year the local Scots would cross what the English regarded as their frontier and plough the fields and sow their seed, and when the English saw this they would come and burn down the crops. And the next year there'd be English incursions into what the Scots regarded as Scotland, and the English would plough the fields and sow their seed, and the Scots would come and destroy the English crops.

An early attempt to define the Border here was made in 1222, when Henry III ordered the Sheriff of Northumberland and the Bishop of Durham, together with Hugh de Bolebec, Richard de Umframville, Roger de Morlay and 'such other discreet and loyal knights of the shire' to meet the representatives of Scotland at Carham, and there agree how the march should be defined hereabouts. Appearing on behalf of the Scottish king were David de Lindesay, Justiciar of Lothian, and Patrick, Earl of Dunbar, together with many other knights. When the parties met, de Bolebec reported, they agreed to elect six knights on each side 'as jurors, to make a true perambulation between the kingdoms'.

De Bolebec recounted how the six English knights 'with one assent proceeded by the right and ancient marches between the kingdoms', while the Scottish knights 'totally dissented and contradicted them'. So both sides then agreed to elect another twelve knights, six from each side, to join the first twelve in walking the marches. To no avail: the two sides differed as before.

De Bolebec then took it upon himself to swear in another two dozen English, who on oath duly declared that the 'true and ancient marches between the kingdoms' were as follows: 'from Tweed by the rivulet of Revedeneburne [Redden Burn], ascending towards the south as far as Tres Karras [unidentified], and from thence in a straight line ascending as far as Hoperichelawe [unidentified], and from thence in a straight line to Witelawe [White Law]'. But when the English party then determined to set off to 'make the perambulation', the Scottish representatives, 'resisting with violence, hindered them by threats from so doing'. And so the debate over the Debatable Lands continued . . .

As we meandered along stone walls and ditches and field boundaries, there was nothing bar the map to tell us that sometimes we were in Scotland, sometimes in England. Barley grew on either side, a lapwing danced its crazy aerial dance – dipping, curling, jerking one way then the other – oblivious of any line of demarcation.

And so we came to the Carham Burn, the last leg of the Border before the Tweed. It may be just a change in nomenclature, but the minor stream called the Redden Burn mentioned by de Bolebec no longer forms part of the march between the two countries. The Redden Burn now dribbles into Hadden Stank, which in turn feeds into the Carham Burn just before the latter enters the Tweed.

The banks of the Carham Burn – which is itself little more than a burbling brook – were lush with butterbur, red campion and apple blossom. At one point the burn enters a duck pond formed by a concrete dam. There weren't any ducks. Then we saw hunters' hides on the far side. Any duck daring to land on this small pond would be blasted out of the water.

Although the Carham Burn is a delightful stream, worthy of an Augustan pastoral idyll, its confluence with the Tweed is an undignified affair. The flow stagnates to a standstill and the surface of the burn is sheeted in froth and scum and the debris of twigs, bottles and polystyrene food trays.

But the Tweed itself is a mighty and fast-flowing river, with complex eddies and currents, its surface busy and troubled as it swept past us, like the White Rabbit in a panic, late for its rendezvous with the North Sea. The river has certainly evoked its share of poetical effusions:

> Delightful stream! tho' now along thy shore,
> When spring returns in all her wonted pride,
> The shepherd's distant pipe is heard no more,
> Yet here with pensive peace could I abide,
> Far from the stormy world's tumultuous roar,
> To muse upon thy banks at eventide.

Thus William Lisle Bowles, sonneteering in 1789. We too found ourselves musing upon the river's banks at eventide, and brewed a cup of tea the better to aid our musings. The shepherd's distant pipe remained unheard, but the world's tumultuous roar was apparent in the form of a Fed-Ex van on the B6350.

As it was indeed eventide, and there was still some way to walk to Coldstream, we eschewed the pathless banks of the Tweed for the tarmac joys of the Cornhill–Kelso road, running east in parallel to the river. It was a weary plod, past Carham, past Wark, both places redolent with history but now small, sleepy backwaters without even the benefit of a pub. On our right rose Gallows Knoll and Gallows Hill, the names attesting to the means by which power and ownership were once maintained in these parts.

It's been over a thousand years since Carham hit the headlines. In 1018 (or perhaps 1016) Malcolm II, king of Scots, allied with Owen the Bald, the last king of Strathclyde, defeated the Northumbrians under Earl Uhtred – 'a young man of great energy most suited to war' – at the Battle of Carham. Some said the Scots thereby gained Lothian, fixing the Border along the Tweed, although others believe Lothian was already de facto Scottish territory. The chronicler Simeon of Durham, in his *Historia Ecclesiae Dunelmensis*, gives a somewhat histrionic account:

In the year of our Lord's incarnation ten hundred and eighteen, while Cnut ruled the kingdom of the Angles, a comet appeared for thirty nights to the people of Northumbria, a terrible presage of the calamity by which that province was about to be desolated. For, shortly afterwards (that is, after thirty days) nearly the whole population, from the River Tees to the Tweed, and their borders, were cut down in a conflict in which they were engaged with a countless multitude of Scots at Carrun [Carham].

Just across the Tweed, the village of Birgham is remembered as the place where the Treaty of Birgham was signed in 1290. Guaranteed (or imposed) by Edward I of England, the treaty sought to defuse the rival claims on the Scottish throne of the Bruces and the Balliols, and to support the claim of the late Alexander III's granddaughter Margaret, the Maid of Norway. Edward conceded the independence of Scotland on condition that Margaret married his son, the Prince of Wales. This plan unravelled when Margaret died on her voyage to Scotland. There followed decades of warfare, only ending when Scottish independence was won by force of arms at Bannockburn in 1314. Although quite in what sense Scotland became 'independent' from England is muddied by the fact that the victorious Robert the Bruce (aka Robert de Brus), like John Balliol (aka Johan de Bailliol) and the French-speaking Edward I himself and his son Edward II, were all of Norman lineage. Indeed, Bruce claimed descent from Henry I of England, son of William the Conqueror, and had extensive estates in England as well as Scotland. So the 'Scottish Wars of Independence' can be interpreted as little more than a dynastic squabble among different families of Anglo-Norman adventurers.

A mile or two to the east of Birgham, on the English side of the Tweed, a stark mound butts up against the road. This is all that remains of a once powerful Border fortress, Wark Castle. It was built as a motte and bailey in the early twelfth century, and subsequently occupied by both Scots and English. It was demolished and rebuilt several times, the last time as an artillery platform in the reign of Henry VIII. There is a story that Edward III founded the Order of the Garter here, when he gallantly swept up the fallen garter of the Countess of Salisbury at a ball. Other accounts have this wardrobe malfunction happening at Calais.

Beyond Wark the road, pressed between high hedges, crosses an extensive flat haugh (floodplain or water meadow) on the south side of the Tweed. Tired and footsore, we stuck out our thumbs in the hope of a lift the last few miles to Coldstream, but the SUVs and Jags and Audis (this is rich farming land) sped by, blinkers firmly in place. It was as well they did, otherwise we would have missed a magical evening.

If you look closely enough at the OS map, you'll see between Wark and Coldstream that the Border does something odd. For a few hundred yards it abandons the middle of the Tweed and comes ashore on the south side of the river, forming a little triangular enclave, the only piece of Scottish territory south of the Tweed between Carham and the sea. No name is given to this field on the OS 1:25000 map, but in old documents it's called 'Scotch Haugh'. It also has another name, 'Ba Green'. There is a story that every year on this field the youths of Coldstream would play the youths of Wark at handba (a form of free-for-all football, with teams of unlimited size and little in the way of rules). If the Scots lads won, the field would be Scottish for the following year; if the English lads won, it would be English. But as Coldstream grew in size, and Wark remained no more than a hamlet, it became clear that the Coldstreamers, vastly outnumbering the Warkers, were winning every time. And so it was amicably agreed that the field should remain a part of Scotland in perpetuity.

The fact that the Ba Green is north of the Border was an advantage to us weary walkers. It meant that Scottish access law applied, and this meant we could wild camp there, as long as we kept off the enclosed land. So we slipped into the field and walked its margin down towards the river. At the foot of the field there was a steep bank, overgrown with nettles and butterbur, and at the foot of the bank there was a hidden sandy flat, dotted with willows and with enough room for two small tents between the bank and the river. It would be a fine secluded place to camp, as long as it didn't rain heavily overnight over all the hills that feed the streams that feed the Tweed, from the Manor and the Lyne to the Ettrick and the Yarrow and the Teviot. I hoped the forecast – that it would stay dry till morning – would still hold.

Claire gathered pieces of driftwood for a fire while Archie and I pitched the tents. Archie began to sing 'Old Man River' as the Tweed rushed by, only a few feet away. It turned out he'd been under the impression that it was the River *Twee*. 'I *did* wonder,' he said. 'It doesn't look at all *twee*.' Claire asked what it would be like to swim in. I thought it would be fine as long as you were prepared to be swept downstream at a rate of knots and not make landfall for a mile or two.

As the fire crackled and the sun set behind silhouetted willow branches, we ate an improvised supper of whatever we had in our packs. We'd intended to dine in Coldstream, either at the Bangla sit-in or the Italian chip shop, but happily made do with oatcakes, fish paste and some gritty powdered soup. The highlight was the pepper roasting on an open fire. Thinking of the chestnuts in 'White Christmas', I felt another song coming on, and launched into my best Bing Crosby impersonation. But even my best was not good enough for Claire. 'Mmm,' she said. 'You sound like you're *actually* mental.'

She could have been right.

Day Six (part – the first): Wednesday, 29th May 2013   I couldn't hear any rain on the tent when I woke the next morning. But when I put my hand out I could feel the fine drizzle the Scots call smirr. At the other end of the Border this is called a Liddesdale drow, a meteorological phenomenon that is said to 'drench an Englishman to the skin'.

We broke camp and packed before the forecast downpours should arrive. Breakfast could wait till Coldstream.

It turned out to be a long, hungry tramp along the B6350 as

Range Rovers and timber lorries roared past. By the time we came to Cornhill, the village across the Tweed from Coldstream, the rain had begun in earnest.

I paused by the war memorial. It listed thirteen men from this small parish who had perished in the 'Great European War' – Johnsons, Elliots, Dalgleishes, Aflecks, Jeffreys, Lauries, Reids, Humes. Four more names from the 'Great World War, 1939 to 1945' were inscribed on the side. I was to note that even the smallest villages along the Border had their own memorials, their own long lists of the dead.

The sight of Coldstream Bridge was a welcome one – as it no doubt had been to its first users on its opening in 1766. Before that the only way to cross here was to ford the 'cold stream' of the Tweed. As it was the lowest point on the river where this was possible, the crossing was used by many armies, from that of Edward I in 1295 to General Monck in 1660.

The crossing maintained its strategic importance. At the outbreak of the Second World War Coldstream Council dismantled the plaque previously placed at the Border line in the middle of the bridge. This plaque, to welcome returning Scots, was inscribed with a line from Sir Walter Scott: 'Oh Scotia, my dear, my native land!' It was removed in case it should provide vital geographical information to any German parachutist landing nearby.

But Coldstream has no shortage of signage. First, on the Scottish end of the bridge the old toll house has a slab indicating that the place was once a rival destination to Gretna for runaway couples from England:

MARRIAGE HOUSE
WEDDINGS CONDUCTED
HERE UNTIL 1856

Then there's the big brown 'Scotland Welcomes You' sign. Then there's a rowing boat on the side of the road planted with pansies above which there's a sign on the wall:

Coldstream Gateway Association
welcomes you to
COLDSTREAM
IN BLOOM

The welcoming is far from over:

Welcome to
Scottish Borders

is followed by

Welcome to
Coldstream
Home of the Regiment
The First True Border Toon.

When you reach the Robert Burns Lay-by, all welcomed-out, there's an exhaustive interpretation board that supplies you with a detailed account of Burns's visit to Coldstream on Monday, 7th May 1787. Here he made his first foray into England and, according to his companion Robert Ainslie, on reaching the further shore he doffed his hat, knelt down on the road and recited the last two verses of 'The Cottar's Saturday Night'. Apparently this little piece of theatre was intended as a homage to Scotia, his dear, his native land. Rather like a court circular, the interpretation board tells us that the poet then returned to Coldstream, where he had lunch with a farmer called Mr Foreman. They discussed Voltaire. He then took tea with the local gentry in the persons of Mr and Mrs Patrick Bryden at Lennel House, and was 'extremely flattered' by his reception.

Beyond the lay-by there's a fine viewpoint looking down on the Tweed. This is the head of Nun's Walk, and there is a new wooden shelter for those, like me, anxious to get in out of the rain while admiring the view. A couple of elderly gentlemen were in residence. We fell to talking. I told them about my Border project, and my book.

'Do you know why it's called Coldstream?' one asked me. He spoke with a precise and careful Border accent, just Scottish, but sometimes with a Geordie inflection. 'It was General Monck brought the troops over, and they said it was a *cold stream*. That's the story. They crossed from over there. You're writing your book. You'd better put *that* in.'

I said I would.

'Have you been to Flodden?' he asked me. 'This is the 500th anniversary of the battle. In August there's going to be 500 horses riding out there from the town. And the Guards'll be there too. They'll get the freedom of the *Toon*.' He stressed the word for comic effect. 'They get it every year.'

He was a font of local knowledge. 'If you stand here,' he says, 'you'll get two chapters of your book.'

'That's why I'm lingering,' I tell him.

'You'd better not linger, your sister's looking for you.' He was right. He'd heard me talk to her on my mobile. We had a rendezvous.

'Come back in August,' he said. 'There'll be a lot of people here.'

I walked on through the rain along the high street. I stopped to buy a local paper, and asked the newsagent where she was from. 'Northumbria,' she said. I asked whether she felt English. Or was she more Scottish now she lived and worked in Coldstream?

'We're all reivers,' she said.

I asked her if she thought the bridge was significant.

'I find it a bit odd, all this "Let's have Scottish independence",' she said. 'I've a feeling that the Borders are going to say you can do what you want but we're just going to be the Borders.'

It turned out she'd looked into her family history. 'Many generations ago it was Armstrongs, they were all over, they were quite a nasty lot. Then there were Scotts, Inneses from further up the east coast of Scotland, Bowlums and Ingrams from Northumberland.'

'You know what it was like,' she continued. 'They used to fight with each other. It didn't matter which side of the Border they came from. I don't think there was much to choose between any of them. They were all reivers. Like we are today. We've just given up on the fighting.'

EIGHT

GREY WAVING HILLS

Carter Bar to Chew Green

I beheld a mere succession of grey waving hills, line beyond line, as far as my eye could reach . . .

> – Washington Irving, quoted in John Gibson Lockhart,
> *Memoirs of the Life of Sir Walter Scott* (1837–8), vol. 2

Day Six (part the second): Friday, 19th July 2013   In 1817 Washington Irving, the first notable author produced by the pubescent United States, visited Sir Walter Scott on his home turf. The great man took him on a ramble over the hills to admire the view. 'I have brought you,' Scott told his guest, 'like the pilgrim in the Pilgrim's Progress, to the top of the Delectable Mountains, that I may show you all the goodly regions hereabouts.' Scott went on to point out the glories of his native land, from Lammermuir to Teviot, Ettrick, Yarrow and the Tweed, 'names celebrated in Scottish song ... most of which had recently received a romantic interest from his own pen'.

Irving was singularly underwhelmed. 'I gazed about me for a time with mute surprise,' he wrote, 'I may almost say, with disappointment.' He elaborated:

> I beheld a mere succession of grey waving hills, line beyond line, as far as my eye could reach, monotonous in their aspect, and so destitute of trees, that one could almost see a stout fly walking along their profile; and the far-famed Tweed appeared a naked stream, flowing between bare hills, without a tree or thicket on its banks; and yet such had been the magic web of poetry and romance thrown over the whole, that it had a greater charm for me than the richest scenery I had beheld in England.

Irving confesses that 'I could not but help giving utterance to my thoughts.' He goes on to record the great man's response:

> Scott hummed for a moment to himself, and looked grave; he had no idea of having his muse complimented at the expense of his native hills. 'It may be pertinacity,' said he at length; 'but to my eye, these grey hills, and all this wild border country, have beauties peculiar to themselves. I like the very nakedness of the land; it has something

bold, and stern, and solitary about it. When I have been for some time in the rich scenery about Edinburgh, which is like ornamented garden land, I begin to wish myself back again among my own honest grey hills; and if I did not see the heather, at least once a-year, I think I should die!' The last words were said with an honest warmth, accompanied by a thump of the ground with his staff, by way of emphasis, that showed his heart was in his speech.

Anyone who has stood at the top of Carter Bar on a clear day and gazed on the distant Eildon Hills in the north and then panned their eyes a quarter of the compass clockwise cannot fail to endorse Scott's admiration for these 'honest grey hills'. Looking east the sinuous crest of the Cheviot Hills unfolds before you, rounded ridge winding behind rounded ridge as the Border snakes towards the distant sea. The bright clear shades of the nearby hills give way to fainter and fainter hues, until land and sky are indistinguishable. Here it is possible, perhaps more than in any other spot in these islands, to count the seven receding horizons that in Norse myth foretell the end of the world.

The litany of names suggests the long and lofty meandering the walker faces who sets off to follow the Border along this ridge: Wooplaw Edge, Arks Edge, Leap Hill, Fairwood Fell, Catcleuch Hill, Hungry Law, Hawkwillow Fell, Greyhound Law, Brownhart Law, Black Halls, Scraesburgh Fell, Broad Flow, Raeshaw Fell, Lamb Hill, Beefstand Hill, Mozie Law, Windy Gyle, King's Seat, Auchope Cairn, the Schil, the Curr, Black Hag, White Law, Burnt Humbleton, Coldsmouth Hill.

No road crosses the range after the A68 at Carter Bar. I would be entirely reliant on the contents of my rucksack. I estimated it would take me two and a half to three days to complete this leg, with two or three wild camps along the crest.

My spirits were high as I cadged a lift south from Edinburgh. It was now late July, in the best summer in Britain for seven years. The Leader Water and the Jed could have been the Aveyron or the Dordogne in southern France. Mirages flickered above the hot black tarmac, the roadside grass was burnt yellow, the sky clear blue, the sun blazing.

The Carter Bar where I was dropped off in the early afternoon was very different from the Carter Bar I'd last visited in cold wind and rain a few weeks before. Tourists spilt out of coaches, milled about in the sunshine, posed for their photographs beside the piper – a man canny enough to realise the punters preferred pop songs to pibrochs. The ice-cream vendor was doing a roaring trade.

A quiet breeze combed the grasses of Wooplaw Edge, my first, gentle hill. I was grateful for the cooling it brought, as down in Jedburgh it had been uncomfortably hot – or what passes for uncomfortably hot in Scotland.

There were thistles in flower both sides of the Border, alongside sedges, reeds and grasses – red, green, yellow, intermixed with white tufts of bog cotton. There was an intermittent path, broken up by tussocks, but the going was smoother than over the thick heather to the west of Carter Bar.

Far to the northeast, nearly twenty miles away as the crow flies, I could make out the hazy whaleback of the Cheviot itself. The large snow patch I'd seen at the end of May had gone. The Cheviot didn't look as far away as it was. In other ways it looked almost impossibly distant.

To the north there was a lower line of shapely hills, patterned with fields in different shades of green. The fields alternated with strips of conifers, patches of yellow and orange mountain grasses, rich green bracken. Farm tracks wound between the hills, like roads in a children's picture book.

Redesdale to the south was more sombre, its moors clad in forestry. There was less sign of agriculture, no hint of habitation. Four centuries ago William Camden described this remote valley as 'a dale too voide of inhabitants by reason of depredations'.

In 1575, shortly before Camden embarked on *Britannia*, his massive topographical and historical survey of this island, the head of Redesdale witnessed one of these bloody 'depredations'. This was the notorious Redeswire Fray*, celebrated in a famous Border ballad, 'The Raid of the Reidswire':

---

* Named after the source of the River Rede in a *swire*, Old English for a hollow on top of a ridge.

> The seventh of July, the suith to say,
> At the Reidswire the tryst was set;
> Our wardens they affixed the day,
> And, as they promised, so they met . . .

It was meant to be a Truce Day on the Middle March. The Scottish Warden, Sir William Kerr of Cessford, sent his deputy, Sir John Carmichael, Keeper of Liddesdale, to Carter Bar to discuss matters of mutual interest with the English Warden, 'Old' Sir John Forster. Forster was accompanied by his deputy, Sir George Heron of Ford.

All went amicably enough until they came to an item on the agenda concerning one 'Farnstein' (thought to be Harry Robson of Falstone). This man had been accused of some misdemeanour by the Scots and at a previous meeting the English had agreed to hand him over. But on this Truce Day there was no sign of 'Farnstein'. Despite the fact that Forster promised to produce the accused at the next Truce Day, Carmichael stood on his dignity and, in so standing, lost his temper. As the ballad has it:

> To deal with proud men is but pain;
> For either must ye fight or flee,
> Or else no answer make again,
> But play the beast, and let them be.

Mutual recriminations turned to hard words, and hard words turned to sharp deeds as a band of Fenwicks from the English party loosed off their arrows. The Scots – many of whom were drinking, playing dice or otherwise amusing themselves as their superiors saw to matters of state – were put on the back foot, and fled back over the pass into Scotland. Here they met a troop of Jeddart callants (men of Jedburgh), who were coming late to the meeting. The Jeddart callants put heart into the fleeing Scots, and retreat turned into advance:

The swallow taill frae tackles flew,
Five hundredth flain into a flight,
But we had pestelets enew,
And shot among them as we might.

With help of God the game gaed right,
Fra time the foremost of them fell;
Then ower the knowe, without goodnight,
They ran with mony a shout and yell.

Heron was killed in the fray, and a number of English worthies captured. The Scots poured down into Redesdale, taking the opportunity to inflict another depredation. They returned home with several hundred head of English cattle.

Like the freeing of Kinmont Willie two decades later, the Redeswire Fray threatened diplomatic relations between the two countries. On this occasion Regent Morton of Scotland and Queen Elizabeth of England were eager to smooth things over. Morton sent the English prisoners back with gifts of hawks, prompting some wag to observe that this was an exchange of 'live hawks for dead Herons'. For their part, the English were aware that 'Old' Sir John was not entirely blameless, nor entirely trustworthy, having made alliances with various Scottish Border families who as a consequence were able to raid on the English side with impunity. Nevertheless, Sir John kept his job as Warden for another twenty years, by which time he was ninety-four and far gone in 'imbecility and weakness'.

Leaving behind Wooplaw Edge and the scene of the affray, I strode out towards Leap Hill and Fairwood Fell. On the Scottish side, stands of young Scots pine had been allowed enough space to spread into their natural shapes. Long grasses grew on the English side, grazed by sheep. In the distance I could see a herd of hardy cows. They must have been a tough breed to thrive on these uplands where the pasture is so poor one of the hills has earned the name of

Hungry Law. So I came to Catcleuch Hill and its cairn marked on the map as Phillip's Cross. But it is not a cross, and no one seems to know who Phillip was.

By the time I reached Greyhound Law the grasses were growing on the Scottish side, and the conifer plantations to the south. When googling Greyhound Law to find out what, if any, connection it had with greyhounds, I found instead a scientific paper by H.F. Barron published in the *Scottish Journal of Geology* in 1989. Reading this I found that Greyhound Law has inspired its own poetry, albeit lacking any mention of hunting dogs or the chase:

> Six samples from the SE margin of the Greyhound Law Inlier on the southern slopes of the Cheviot Hills yielded diverse, moderately well preserved middle Silurian palynomorph assemblages. The taxa present suggest a mid- to late Sheinwoodian or earliest Homerian age ... Thick-walled *Leiosphaeridia*, suggestive of deposition in a hemipelagic environment, are common in the assemblages and are associated with diverse non-sphaeromorph acritarchs ...

Such stuff is dense and incomprehensible and mesmerising – as dense and incomprehensible and mesmerising as the 400 or more million years that separate us from the making of these Border hills, built when the separate continental plates containing Scotland and England collided, squeezing the sediments of the disappearing ocean floor upward between them like a couple of bulldozers. I thought of the lines from Hugh MacDiarmid's meditation 'On a Raised Beach':

> What happens to us
> Is irrelevant to the world's geology
> But what happens to the world's geology
> Is not irrelevant to us.

As dense and incomprehensible and mesmerising is the 400 or more million years of evolution that separates us from the tiny organisms whose remnants made up the rocks beneath the turf on which I walked.

Past Greyhound Law I came to the Heart's Toe, a piece of flattish ridge between Crooked Hope and Hoggerel Cleugh. Here I disturbed a big bushy-tailed dog fox. He bounded away, leaping over the tussocks, looking back to make sure I wasn't following. Then he darted into the trees on the English side. Maybe the hens are sweeter on that side of the Border.

Past Ogre Hill and Grindstone Law I left the last of the forest behind and found myself surrounded in all directions by open moorland. At a junction of paths between Yard Shank and Coquet Head I joined the Pennine Way. This last section of Britain's longest long-distance path, from Byrness across the Cheviots to Kirk Yetholm, is said to be one of the tougher sections of the route. For me, with its well-marked and often-paved path, its stiles and its signposts, it was to provide some of the easiest walking of the whole Border line.

At the same time, I was entering a militarised landscape. I was now on the northern edge of the MoD's Otterburn Ranges. On the map the edges of the Ranges are delineated by red triangles. On the ground there are frequent signs.

Military Firing Range.
Keep out when
red flags or lights
are displayed
or barriers closed.

Danger
Do not touch
any military debris.
It may explode
and kill you.

The strange thing is, this has been a militarised landscape for millennia. Ahead of me lay Dere Street (Anglo-Saxon for 'Roman road of the stags'), on which the legions marched north into Caledonia. It was built in the first century AD by Julius Agricola, the first Roman governor of Britain, and so predates Hadrian's Wall.

Just before Dere Street crosses the Cheviot watershed there is the site of a Roman fort, together with several overlapping camps and fortlets. Even a mile or so away I could make out the lines of ramparts, throwing shadows in the early evening light. It is a vast area, on sloping ground nearly 1,500 feet above the sea. The largest camp was intended to accommodate two legions plus auxiliaries, totalling 16,800 foot and 1,800 horse.

Today the place is known as Chew Green, though it is more sheep-cropped moor than manicured lawn. In medieval times there was a settlement here called Kemelpethe – Dere Street in this section being known in former times as Gemelspath or Gamel's Path. There is a tradition (possibly mistaken) that the Romans called Chew Green *Ad Fines* – 'to the ends' – indicating what a remote place they thought it was, and also suggesting that it marked the boundary of their imperium.

This stretch of Dere Street is littered with Roman camps. Such defences were constructed even if the legion was stopping only for a single night. The men would dig a ditch and pile the earth up into a rampart, upon which they erected a palisade. To the north of Chew Green the next camp is at Pennymuir, and the most important fort beyond that is above the Tweed on top of the triple-peaked Eildon Hills, known as Trimontium to the Romans. To the south, across the high treeless moors that now form part of the MoD artillery ranges, there are several more camps before you reach Rochester, the hamlet on the A68 that has the remains of the Roman fort called Bremenium. From the scant records that remain, we know that at various times soldiers from all over the Empire were stationed here – Lingones from Burgundy in central Gaul, Dalmatians from what is now Croatia, Vardulians from the Basque country. This was 'free movement of labour', Roman style. Two thousand years ago the EU was the PR – the Pax Romana.

For the antiquarian William Camden the whereabouts of Bremenium – mentioned in the first century AD by the Alexandrian geographer Ptolemy – was uncertain, although he had a shrewd idea:

> May we not hence guesse that Bremenium, for which there hath beene made so long and great search, was here? Whereof Ptolomee hath made mention in this very site and position of the country, and from which Antonine the Emperour beginneth the first journey of Britaine, as from the utmost limit of the Romane Province in Britaine at that time. And the limites or Bounds of a Dominion were seas, great rivers, Mountaines, Desert lands and unpassable, such as be in this tract. Trenches also with their rampiers, walles, mounds of trees cut downe or plashed [stripped], and Castles especially built in places more suspected and daungerous than others, to all which there are to be seene remaines heere every where about. Certes, when the Barbarous nations, after they had broken through the wall of Antoninus Pius in Scotland, harried all over the country and laid all wast before them, and the wall of Hadrian lay neglected unto the time of Severus, we may well thinke that even heere was set downe the limit of the Roman Empire, and that from hence the old Itinerarie which goes about under the name of Antoninus beganne thus, *A limite*, that is, *From the Bound*.

This was where I was to pitch my tent in the midst of the Roman camp at the one-time limit and bound of the Roman Empire, among 'Mountaines, Desert lands and unpassable'.

Then something strange happened. As I approached Chew Green a bright yellow light appeared in the eastern sky. It sank slowly to earth somewhere near the Roman camp. I couldn't quite believe what I was seeing. The light had a faint trail of smoke after it. I assumed it must have been a flare, but why you'd need to fire a flare in the bright seven o'clock sunshine of a July evening I have no idea. I hoped I wasn't going to find myself in the midst of some military exercise. And if I was, was I about to be surrounded by a bunch of squaddies with blacked-up faces aiming their SA80s at me? Or would I find myself at the sharp end of a Roman *pilum*?

There was neither squaddie nor legionary when I arrived at Chew Green. Only sheep. Scores of them. What Camden fails to mention, never having had to pitch a tent in the midst of Chew Green Roman Camp, is that the whole place has now become a vast sheep's lavatory.

There was poo everywhere. I plodded about, looking for a level spot, kicking great piles of the stuff off the close-cropped turf.

Satisfied that I'd established a turd-free zone, I began to pitch the tent. Then, as I knelt down to peg it out, I felt a squelch beneath my knee. Not entirely turd-free, I noted, as I wiped something fresh, sloppy and green off my trousers with a handful of grass.

After a while two Pennine Wayers passed by, heading for the mountain refuge between Raeshaw Fell and Lamb Hill. They still had some miles to go, but had a heads-down steely look about them, so I don't doubt they made it. About an hour and a half later another walker turned up. He was slower, older, bigger-bellied. He stopped for a smoke. I offered him a dram. He said he would probably camp a mile or two up. Both parties were hoping to get to Kirk Yetholm the following day. That would be a hard, long walk. I preferred to take a bit more time.

As the sun sank towards the western horizon I tried to make out the course of Dere Street on the hillside to the south. The low light picked out no single clear line. Instead, a whole network of small paths became apparent, meandering down over ridges and bumps towards the infant River Coquet and up to the old Roman camp where I sat.

It was as if – in apparent contradiction to Roman military discipline and the rigid straightness of the Roman military road – each soldier, or each line of soldiers, had taken their own path, following the natural contours of the hill. There must have been thousands of them to make so many different paths.

I tried to imagine them pouring down over the ridge some evening 1,800 years ago. Each man would be weary after a hard day's march, weighed down with his helmet, body armour, shield, javelins, sword, dagger, food enough for a fortnight, wineskin, cooking pot and a pair of stakes for the palisade. Their spirits would have lifted at the sight of where they'd sleep, but their work for the day was not yet over. They'd still have to dig ditches, build ramparts, hammer in stakes.

The military had not yet done with this landscape. Just to the east of Dere Street I could see a strip of fresh-laid tarmac cutting steeply up the hillside into the heart of the Otterburn Ranges. It links to the minor public road that ends at the head of Coquetdale. It's not marked on the map.

Every now and again I'd hear the distant swish of tyres. Then I'd see a landcruiser coming down the hill, this way and that. The first one was black. Then, some minutes later, a white one drove uphill in the opposite direction. For some hours these two vehicles patrolled up and down the road at irregular intervals. They might have been farmers. But would their sheep have needed such constant attention through a balmy July evening?

As the light faded I heard a low distant growling. Two heavier vehicles, headlights blazing, came over the southern horizon. Then they drove slowly, very slowly down the road. I could hear every gear change, but couldn't make out what they were until they came closer. Two large military trucks in convoy. I watched as their white headlights slowly approached, watched as their red tail-lights receded slowly, very slowly, down Coquetdale.

In the east a martin darted under a yellow moon. Later, perhaps after the same fly, a bat flicked across the corner of my eye then disappeared into the dark.

So there I was in the midsummer night with the ghosts of Basques, Burgundians and Slavs . . . Forsters, Fenwicks, Herons and Hawks . . . palynomorph assemblages, thick-walled *Leiosphaeridia*, non-sphaeromorph acritarchs . . .

Lulled into sleep by the distant mournful bleating of sheep and the trickle of the Coquet burn, I dreamt my midsummer dream, as True Thomas once had done by the Eildon Tree . . .

I was trying to follow the Border. I was among the Cheviots, but they were not the hills of daylight, but like all the hills in dreams there were unveilings of places and things and thoughts I thought I once knew but had forgotten, remembered, forgotten again. The Border, in my dream, was around here somewhere, intermittent, indeterminate, marked here and there on the map, going nowhere in particular.

In a place that might be but isn't there was a building on a shelf of the hill above a slope of pine trees, overlooking the Merse. This side of sleep I know this place is just grass and sedge. On the outside the building was a half-ruined concrete outhouse. I entered through a hole in the wall. The dark interior was lit by slits of light shining down from gaps in the roof. There were bright Eastern carpets on the floor, shelves lined with books, portraits of someone's loved ones on the wall.

I unhooked a picture, took some books from the shelves. Then I was aware of a voice. I'd be very grateful, the voice said, if you could return the things you've taken. Yes, I said, I'll put them back. When I'd done, the voice said, You haven't put everything back yet. I'm sorry, I said. There's this and this. And when I'd put those things back I thought I felt the spirit of a thank you.

There was someone there in the house with me. She was not a ghost but a flesh-and-blood young woman with pink punk hair. Or she might have been the ancient sorceress Circe on her island, in which case I wasn't sure if I was to play Ulysses or one of his men transformed into a pig. Then it became clear that this ageless woman with the laughing eyes was none other than the Queen of Elfhame, come here from under the Eildon Hills. And, to borrow the words of an old Scots ballad, with her laughing eyes 'she coost her glamourie ower me'.

Later – it may have been seven seconds, seven days or seven years – the time came to leave. So I wandered in my loss through the summer hills along a track, oak and ash on one side, yellow grass and blackthorn on the other.

I heard a noise, turned round. Three black Cadillacs with darkened windscreens sped towards me down the track.

I waited for the impact. I was not to return to the world of mortals. At least, not without my memory banks wiped clean.

NINE

THE BONNY ROAD

Coquet Head to Clennell Street

And see not ye that bonny road,
Which winds about the fernie brae?
That is the road to fair Elfhame,
Where you and I this night maun gae.

— Anon., 'The Ballad of Thomas the Rhymer'

Day Seven: Saturday, 20th July 2013   I woke up to the bleating of sheep and low cloud covering the slopes above the tent. There was a desperate rattling between the flysheet and the inner. It was a pair of craneflies waving their legs about, clamped tail to tail in a frenzy of coition.

I was still half in my dream, in that strange world between sleep and waking where boundaries dissolve. Up here alone in the wilds the past was here and now. The Queen I'd visited in my dream had been all ages at once: girl-child full of laughter, young woman full of love, old woman full of wisdom. I too contained all my past and my future in this moment: infant, schoolboy, lover, father; bones, ashes, dust.

Mixing with the denizens of Elfhame can be a risky business. In 1576 a woman called Bessie Dunlop was accused of witchcraft on this count. She had told her interrogators that she had met a group of gentlefolk, eight women and four men, who greeted her and asked her if she would go with them, but she declined. They were, it turned out, 'the gude wights that winnit in the court of Elfame'. When she met them again, passing Restilrig Loch on the edge of Edinburgh, they were on horseback and 'with mony a hideous rumble' they rode hell-for-leather into the loch. They were, she said, 'the gude wights that were riding in middle-eard'. These tales were enough to commit her to the flames. Her executioners could not accept that there was a third road, neither the narrow path of righteousness nor the braid braid path of wickedness. This third road was the 'bonny road / Which winds about the fernie brae':

> That is the road to fair Elfhame,
> Where you and I this night maun gae.

Needing to clear my head, I stumbled down through thick reeds and bracken to the headwaters of the Coquet. It's only a small burn here, but there was a peaty pool. I stripped off and ducked in. It did the trick.

I might have done better washing the sleep from my eyes over the hill to the south. There's a burn there that goes by the name of Fool Sike.

After such a night, the day's walking felt flat and grey. 'This section,' writes Logan Mack, 'may lay claim to be the most desolate of the whole Border Line.' The going is easier these days. Much of the path over the boggier stretches of the Pennine Way is now paved with flagstones that became surplus to requirements when hundreds of mills and factories across the north of England closed down during the 1980s.

North of Chew Green I followed Dere Street/Gemelspeth into Scotland for a hundred yards or so, then back into England for a few hundred yards. At this re-entry into England there was a sign reminding me that access laws in England are different from those in Scotland. I was told to keep to the marked paths. Still walking north, I followed Dere Street/Gemelspeth back into Scotland, where it parts from the Pennine Way. In the Middle Ages, Gemelspath was one of those places agreed by the Wardens of the Middle March for Borderers to settle their differences by single combat.

I left Dere Street at Blackhall Hill and followed the Border over Scraesburgh Fell and Broad Flow. After Hobbs' Flow I was suspicious of any ground with 'Flow' in its name. Broad Flow turned out to be rough and tussocky, full of bog cotton waving in the breeze, but the yellow mosses in between the tussocks had been dried up by weeks of hot weather. As I crunched through the Flow meadow pipits flew ahead of me, calling in alarm. They must have had nests nearby, perhaps with the year's second brood.

It was worth making the tougher diversion from the Pennine Way along the Border over Raeshaw Fell. On this hill, also known as Rushy Fell, there is a spectacular earthwork in the form of a long rampart. I thought initially it must be Iron Age. But rather than forming a circle round a hillfort, the rampart is linear, extending in a more or less straight line for some two-thirds of a mile. Logan Mack avers that it was constructed in the thirteenth or fourteenth centuries to mark the Border. If so, like Scots' Dike, its function was more symbolic than military.

Perhaps unsurprisingly, I was to meet more people on the Pennine Way section than on any other part of my Border walk. It was probably as well, otherwise I might have stayed away with the fairies.

The first mortals I'd met on waking were a couple from Australia, walking in the opposite direction. They were in their sixties, he unfit but willing, she fit as a whippet and with short-cropped hair and a diamond stud in her nose. 'She's the walker,' he told me. 'She's doing the whole Pennine Way. I'm just doing this bit cos it's downhill.' I wondered why they'd come all the way from Australia to walk these desolate moors. 'Someone sent me a magazine article,' she told me. 'I was captivated. There's nothing like this in Oz.' Ironically, it had been so hot the last few days they'd been setting off at four-thirty in the morning and finishing at two in the afternoon, spending the remainder of the way resting in the shade.

It was still chill and misty when I stopped for lunch at the mountain refuge hut on Yearning Saddle, beneath Lamb Hill. Through the afternoon, as I made my way over Beefstand Hill, Mozie Law, Plea Knowe and Foul Step, the sky cleared and the sun came out over Scotland. But on the other side Northumberland was still swathed in a bank of cloud. A couple I met from Consett told me it had been raining that morning when they'd left. They said on the other side of Windy Gyle the ridge and the tops were all in mist.

I was lucky, though. I took the sun with me. The mists parted, and by the time I reached Windy Gyle – the highest point on the Border before the broad shoulder of the Cheviot itself is reached – all the hills roundabout were bathed in sunshine. Windy Gyle belied both parts of its name: Gyle comes from Old Norse *gil*, a ravine, but the hill itself is a rounded lump; and today it was not so much windy as gently caressed by a balmy breeze.

Windy Gyle has one of the largest summit cairns I've ever seen. It isn't just the result of generations of walkers each adding their own individual stone to the pile. It goes back long before people walked for pleasure, probably to the Bronze Age. It must have been a mighty chieftain who could command such a burial mound for his mortal remains. We do not know who he, or she, was. But the cairn today is known as Russell's Cairn.

Unlike the Phillip of Phillip's Cross, we know all about the Russell of Russell's Cairn. He was Lord Francis Russell, a local magnate who on 27th July 1585 accompanied his father-in-law, Sir John Forster of Bamborough, to a Truce Day at the pass on the Border called Hexpethgate, about half a mile northeast of Windy Gyle. Forster was the English Warden of the Middle March, while on this Truce Day his Scottish counterpart was Sir Thomas Kerr of Ferniehurst. It was only ten years since the Redeswire Fray, at which Russell had been present, and both parties arrived mob-handed and armed to the teeth. The English account of the day, written by Forster himself, describes the Scots as 'standinge ranged in order of battell with ensigne pensell fyfe and drumes'. No doubt the English would have put on a similar martial display, for there were always unsettled scores in the backs of the minds of all those present on such days.

Nevertheless, according to their duties, the two Wardens sat down to their task, working their way through the agenda. Then, somewhere off to the side, there was a kerfuffle. An English youth had been accused of stealing a pair of spurs, and voices were raised. Sounds of the disturbance reached the negotiators, and Russell marched off to investigate. The next thing anybody knew he had been 'cruelly slaine with a shot'. All hell broke loose and, according to Forster's report,

... divers gentlemen of Scotland, with their footmen and horsemen and their whole force followed, and maintained the chardge fower miles unto the realme of England, and toke sundry prisoners and horses, and carried them into Scotland, which they deny to redeliver againe.

Today there is nothing to remind you of this violent past apart from the name. The yells have long faded into silence, the blood seeped deep into the ground.

Other names nearby also tell of lawless times. On the Scottish side of Hexpethgate there's the burn called Thief's Slack, while on the English side there's not just one but two Murder Cleughs, one by Trows Plantation, the other by Davidson's Burn. At the first of these there is a stone stating simply that 'Here in 1610 Robert Lumsden killed Isabella Sudden'. The victim and perpetrator involved in the second Murder Cleugh are unrecorded. All I found on the Border path itself was a dead shrew.

By now glorious afternoon was turning into glorious evening. There was no water to be had on the ridge, though I spotted a flat spot to pitch the tent at Hexpethgate. I hoped I might find water a little further on, at the head of Buttroads Sike.

The search for water in Buttroads Sike turned out to be a wild goose chase. The course of the sike was plain – a wide grassy hollow flowing down the hillside in between banks of heather into the forestry below. I plunged into the long lush grasses, hoping for a squelch. All I got was a crunch. The sike was dry. I strode on down the hill, full of thirst, ears alert for a trickle. No trickle came. Sometimes I staggered down the bed of the sike, struggling with tussocks of sedges and reeds. Sometimes I took to the heather-thick flanks, ducking under the low branches of sitka spruce.

A track cut across the sike, but the culvert underneath it was dry. I had a choice. I could either descend further, to Davidson's Burn – on the assumption that a burn might be a bigger, wetter beast than a sike – or cut back along the track to the southwest, parallel to the Border, in the opposite direction to my journey, and hope that one of the four further sikes that cut across the track might be running.

The first sike was unnamed. And dry. The second sike was Tod Sike – the fox's stream – but there was neither fox nor stream. The third sike ran down Outer Hare Cleugh.

I heard a tinkling, peered over the edge of the track and spotted a length of yellow corrugated piping. Out of the pipe's mouth dribbled a trickle of water. The fourth sike could wait. I scrambled down the steep bank, thinking this is no place to turn an ankle, crouched under the spout and let the water splash on my face, my neck, my mouth, then filled my bottles.

Although Outer Hare Cleugh is marked on the 1:25000 map, Inner Hare Cleugh – presumably the next sike on – gets no mention. Perhaps the locals were anxious to keep its whereabouts secret. Long ago, Inner Hare Cleugh was the site of Rory's Still, just one of many illicit stills making mountain dew in these hills. The name gives us a clue as to where the expertise came from. The eponymous Rory was probably originally Ruaridh, one of many Highlanders who slipped away from the retreating Jacobite army in 1746 to pursue their traditional skills in the Southern Uplands.

I could have camped down there in the forest. But, in shade and shelter, it would have been midge hell – or rather heaven for midges, hell for humans. The alternative was to continue southwest along the track until I met a path leading back up to the ridge. I'd noted a good spot to pitch the tent up there at Hexpethgate, in the sun and the breeze. If I took this course I would have walked an extra couple of miles to get to the place I'd been a couple of hours back. But at least I'd be watered and midge-free.

It was a good path back up to Hexpethgate, along the line of the medieval road called Clennell Street. Clennell Street starts at Alwinton in Northumberland and continues over the hills into Scotland, down to the farm at Cocklawfoot. Although today the only public road over the Cheviots is the A68 at Carter Bar, Clennell Street is just one of the many old trade routes that once crossed the watershed. A document dating from 1543 lists a total of seventeen 'ingates and passages forth of Scotland upon the Middle Marches'. In the space of just a few miles there's five. Gemelspeth follows the Roman Dere Street. The road simply known as the Street (and on a 1775 map as 'the Clattering Path') crosses at Black Braes between Mozie Law and Windy Gyle. Clennell Street, up which I was toiling, crosses at

Hexpethgate. Then, a little further east, there's Salter's Road (which joins Clennell Street just short of the Border) and Butt Roads. Salter's Road was sometimes known as Thieves' Road, while in 1829 Butt Roads was described as a 'miserable track impassable in winter . . . frequented by smugglers and vagabonds of every description'. The smugglers would no doubt have done a roaring trade in the 'innocent' whisky distilled in these hills. They delivered their contraband to their customers in remote farmhouses in large stoneware bottles known as 'grey hens'. Today the only traffic on these abandoned trade routes consists of honest walkers and mountain-bikers – and not many of those.

As I plodded up Clennell Street out of the dense conifers to the watershed, the reeds on either side were spattered with white gobs of cuckoo spit, outshining even the bog cotton. It had been an unexpected diversion, but on a walk such as this the unexpected is always welcome. Within reason.

Hexpethgate would not be the place to camp when Windy Gyle is windy. But on a calm July evening this exposed shoulder was perfect. All the hills were clear, bar the Cheviot itself, which was capped with a rosy beret of mist. The cloud bank still loomed over Northumberland, but to the north the sun set gloriously over Scotland. After supper I dug out my very own grey hen and raised a mug to Scotia, my dear, my native land.

TEN

MOSS-HAGS AND OOZY PEAT-FLATS

Skirting the Cheviot

. . . a desolate looking tract of treacherous moss-hags and oozy peat-flats, traversed by deep sykes and interspersed with black stagnant pools.

> — William Weaver Tomlinson,
> *Comprehensive Guide to Northumberland*
> (1888)

Day Eight: Sunday, 21st July 2013   I was jerked out of sleep by the clang of metal on metal. Gates banged, gears clicked. Fit men panted, wheezed.

'Hoch, a great hill climb!' yelled one.

'Fair got yer lungs pumpin'!' bellowed another.

'Hey Davy, whit's fer breakfast?'

'Who's fer sausage and beans, eh?'

'Whaur's Wull?'

'Ah'm here,' puffed Wull. 'Jeez-o!'

I prised my eyes open, peered at my watch. Seven-thirty on a Sunday morning and these guys had already peaked. I pulled my sleeping bag over my head, hid in my tent. The last thing I want to do at seven-thirty on any morning is engage in happy banter. I barely dared breathe. I didn't want to be discovered, drawn into conversation. I'd be mocked as a sluggard and a sleepyhead.

'Ok, wha's leadin'?'

'Dave, eh?'

'It's doonhill frae here.'

'Nae fallin, mind yer speed.'

'Oh kaaaaaaay!'

And with a clanking and a clattering, some grunting and some shouting, they hurtled off down Clennell Street into England. In a moment the noise was gone. But still my nerves jangled, my lungs pumped in sympathy.

I put on the tea and made my porridge.

The mist had crept in overnight, slinking northward over the Border from Redesdale, fingers reaching over the ridge. It had been a cold night, dreamless as far as I remember. The mist was already beginning to clear by the time I began to pack up. There was a fresh breeze. The flysheet flapped anxiously.

A couple of young women strode past in bandanas, shorts and leggings. They gave me a cheery greeting as I squatted in the door of my tent. I felt like a bleary-eyed dwarfie. They were Geordies, fit, glad and kind. They'd spent the night in the mountain refuge hut, been walking the Pennine Way for the past five years. Today they'd be completing it. I wished them well, said I doubted I'd catch them up. I'd be stopping to take lots of photos, I said, an old man's excuse. I'd be burbling into my Dictaphone, I said, for this book I was writing. What's more, I was, I confessed, a sluggard and a sleepyhead.

By a quarter past ten I'd sorted myself enough to set off. The fresh breeze kept it cool. The Cheviot was still in cloud.

July in the Highlands is the peak time for mountain flowers, but there was no great variety here on these more southerly hills. I found thyme, speedwell, little patches of cross-leaved heath, tormentil, a fruiting cloudberry, a few bog asphodels – but not the swathes you'd find in a Highland bog.

But the bog cotton spread in wild profusion across the moors, like snow in summer. It seems the Cheviot may be white in any season:

> A snowstorm drifting down the Bowmont vale
> A little hour ago made Cheviot white,
> And left him glistening in his silver mail,
> The day's last champion in the lists with night.*

Happily, I was blessed with midsummer Cheviot white, of the fluffy variety.

This section of the Pennine Way is well paved. The flagstones make for rapid progress, but the hard surface jars the shins. Here and there across the bogs are signs of the old duckboards that the paving has replaced.

---

* Will H. Ogilvie, 'Sunset', from *The Land We Love* (1910).

On top of a post of the Border fence – somewhere up by Randy's Gap and King's Seat – someone had planted an upside-down weather-beaten boot with a busted toe. It reminded me of me.

And so I made my slow way up the broad western shoulder of the Cheviot to the highest point on the Border, marked on the map as 743 metres (2,437 feet). You wouldn't know it. All the ground hereabouts seems much the same height.

The only point of interest round here is a feature called the Hanging Stone. Somehow I failed to find it. I didn't even find the False Hanging Stone. Given the violent nature of life along the Border, the origin of the name of this small outcrop is a surprising one. It was never the site of a gallows. Rather the name is said to commemorate a passing peddler who slipped here. His pack fell over the edge of the rock, but the strap caught round his neck and he was strangled to death by the weight of his own goods. In medieval times, the Hanging Stone was bang on the Border, and marked the divide between the Middle and Eastern Marches. Today it is unequivocally in England.

I was only thankful the Border doesn't (and never did) divert northeast to the indistinct, mist-shrouded, peat-hagged summit plateau of the Cheviot itself, which, at 815 metres (2,673 feet), would require even more effort.

When Daniel Defoe made his ascent of the Cheviot in the 1720s, he was full of foreboding: 'the height began to look really frightful, for, I must own, I wished myself down again'. At one point he refused to urge his horse further, fearing the summit would be a pinnacle, 'and we should only have room enough to stand, with a precipice every way round us'. He was persuaded by his guide to continue: 'he assured us there was room enough on the top of the hill to run a race, if we thought fit, and we need not fear anything of being blown off the precipice, as we had suggested'. His fears thus allayed, Defoe continued the ascent:

I must acknowledge I was agreeably surprised, when coming to the top of the hill I saw before me a smooth and with respect to what we expected a most pleasant plain, of at least half a mile in diameter, and in the middle of it a large pond . . .

In fact, something like a third of a square mile on the top of the Cheviot is much the same height. 'Any spot within this area,' writes Logan Mack, 'may claim distinction to be the actual summit.' Be that as it may, the Ordnance Survey have marked the place they believe is the very top with a trig point. This stands on top of a vast stone-built pile, itself resting on some kind of platform to prevent the whole thing sinking deep into the mire (apparently the fate of two previous pillars).

Other travellers have loathed the Cheviot, not for its horrid cragginess, but for its bogs. 'The summit is a desolate looking tract of treacherous moss-hags and oozy peat-flats, traversed by deep sykes and interspersed with black stagnant pools,' wrote William Weaver Tomlinson in 1888 in his *Comprehensive Guide to Northumberland*. Ten years later, the aptly named Edmund Bogg wrote of 'a long bog trot over the proverbial swamps' until he attained 'the highest point of the cold bleak back of the mountain'*. More recently, I have met hardened mountaineers who have spoken of the peat hags of the Cheviot with nothing less than dread. Only the recent provision of a paved path has made the ascent of this hill something less than purgatory.

Happily leaving the Cheviot to the English, I strode northwest down the slope to a more pronounced summit, that of Auchope Cairn. This fine viewpoint is marked, as the name might suggest, with a fine cairn – in fact, two fine cairns. These are not just higgledy-piggledy heaps, but carefully crafted drystone structures with vertical sides, much like chimney stacks. By the summit cairn I met the two young women who'd passed my tent earlier. They'd diverted to the Cheviot summit, otherwise I'd have never caught up with them. We sat down and ate our lunch, chatting and joking, with the long Border ridge extending before us towards Kirk Yetholm.

---

* Edmund Bogg, *Two Thousand Miles of Wandering in the Border Country, Lakeland and Ribblesdale* (1898).

Auchope Cairn turned out to be a busy place this particular sunny Sunday. There were mountain-bikers, walkers, birdwatchers. One man in a baseball cap and football shirt asked me whether I'd seen any aircraft wreckage. He clutched a map, a GPS, a booklet, a camera. He had a way of speaking to someone over your left shoulder, someone who wasn't there. I said I hadn't seen anything like that, only some pallets of flagstones waiting to be laid, and a JCB abandoned for the weekend.

It turned out that the Cheviot has had its share of air crashes – seven during the Second World War alone – attracting a certain kind of enthusiast to search out the wreckage.

On 15th January 1942 a Wellington bomber, returning from a raid on Hamburg, overshot its base in Yorkshire. The radio was out, the navigation equipment not working, and in the blizzard conditions the pilot had no idea he was approaching high ground. Then he hit West Hill, the western shoulder of the Cheviot.

The fate of the Wellington might have remained a mystery had not three local shepherds noticed a smell of burning coming down from the plateau. They made their way up to the crash site, where they found three of the crew had been killed outright. Two more were fatally injured, and died the next day. Only one man survived.

Nearly three years later, on 16th December 1944, West Hill was again the site of a fatal accident. Lieutenant Kyle of the USAAF was piloting his nine-man B-17 Flying Fortress back from a raid on Ulm. The raid had been aborted due to the worsening weather, and as he tried to find his way back to his base in Cambridgeshire across the North Sea, Kyle was deceived by false navigation signals transmitted by the Luftwaffe. Although he didn't know it, he was far to the north of where he should have been. In an attempt to get a visual fix on his whereabouts he took the B-17 under the cloud, only to find the snow-covered shoulder of the Cheviot dead ahead. Kyle managed a crash landing of sorts. The B-17 skidded across the bog, eventually coming to rest on West Hill. Two of his crew were killed in the crash. The rest of the crew – some of them badly injured – managed to scramble out of the wreckage. Kyle and two others who had escaped with minor injuries struggled down the hill to raise the alarm, while the remaining men took shelter in the lea of a peat hag.

Two local shepherds, John Dagg and Frank Moscrop, set out to look for survivors, together with Dagg's dog Sheila. Sheila quartered the ground around the Cheviot's featureless wastes, moving much more quickly than the men could. Then Dagg heard barking. Following the sound, Dagg found Sheila licking the face of Sergeant George P. Smith. The two shepherds helped the four airmen down the slopes to the safety of lower ground. Just as they reached shelter there was a series of thunderous explosions. The B-17's entire bomb load had gone off.

Pilot George Kyle died, aged eighty-two, on 20th September 2005. He left a last wish that his ashes be scattered by Braydon Crag on West Hill, the site of the crash that had almost claimed his life six decades before.

The aircrew who survived these crashes were lucky not to perish in the bitter winter conditions of the high Cheviots. A number of walkers have not been so fortunate. The Stuart Lancaster Memorial Hut – a wooden shelter on the saddle below Auchope Cairn – is named after a man who perished in a snowstorm nearby.

More dramatic – if less well attested – deaths and disappearances are associated with the great chasm that divides West Hill from Auchope Cairn, just on the English side of the Border. This is the Hen Hole – also known as the Hell Hole – between whose crags the College Burn descends in a series of dramatic waterfalls. In this secluded, shady spot, a 'snow egg' sometimes persists into the summer.

The Hen Hole provides the setting for the climax of the ballad of 'Black Adam of Cheviot'. Black Adam, also known as the Rider of Cheviot, was an infamous outlaw who lived in a cave among the crags of the Hen Hole. One day he burst in on a wedding at Wooperton intent on villainy. He seized the jewels of the women, raped the bride-to-be, and then stabbed her to death. The would-be groom, Wight Fletcher, had been away to fetch the priest, and returned only in time to hear Adam's callous laugh as he made good his escape. Picking up his beloved's blood-stained handkerchief, Fletcher set off through storm and darkness in pursuit, all the way up to the wilds of the Hen Hole. Here Black Adam leapt the chasm to reach his cave. But Fletcher leapt across too, and the two locked in combat so fierce that they lost their footing and fell together to their deaths:

> Slowly right owre then they fell,
> For Fletcher his hold did keep;
> A minute and their twa bodies
> Went crashing doun the steep.
>
> Loud and lang Black Adam shrieked,
> But naething Fletcher said;
> And there was neither twig nor branch
> Upon their rocky bed.

Another local legend about the Hen Hole tells of a party of hunters who, in pursuit of a roe deer, 'heard issuing from this chasm, the sweetest music they had ever heard, and forgetting the roe which scoured away unheeded, they were impelled to enter, and could never again find their way out'*.

Another source identifies the leader of the lost hunters as a member of the Percy family, who for centuries have been Earls, then Dukes, of Northumberland:

There is a small cavern in the face of the highest cliff on the right bank of the ravine, still accessible, we believe, to the venturesome, though dangerously so; and into this it is said that one of the early hunting

---

* Moses Aaron Richardson, *The Local Historian's Table Book, of remarkable occurrences, historical facts, traditions, legendary and descriptive ballads connected with the counties of Newcastle-upon-Tyne, Northumberland and Durham* (1846).

Percys, along with some of his hounds, went and never returned. He and the hounds, if we may credit the legend, still lie in the cavern, bound by a magic spell – not dead, but fast asleep, and only to be released by a blast of a hunting horn, blown by someone as brave as ever Hotspur was, and more fortunate.*

It was, of course, a dispute over hunting rights between the Percys and the Douglases that led to the Battle of Otterburn. That at least was the explanation put forward by the anonymous author of 'The Ballad of Chevy Chase', who recounts that Henry Percy ('Hotspur') crossed the Border to hunt on Douglas land, thus outraging James, Earl of Douglas:

> Show me, said he, whose men you be
> That hunt so boldly here
> That, without my consent do chase
> And kill my fallow deer?

In historical fact it was Douglas who had encroached on English soil, not on a hunting expedition but at the head of a Scottish army, intent on taking advantage of the turmoil in England, as the great magnates moved to knock Richard II off the throne.

Having (supposedly) captured Hotspur's lance pennon at Newcastle, Douglas rode back north in triumph, stopping only to lay siege to Otterburn Castle in Redesdale, on the south edge of what are now the MoD ranges. Here, on 15th August 1388, Hotspur caught up with his quarry, his men falling on the Scots with cries of *Percy, Percy!* 'The night was far on,' according to the French chronicler Jean Froissart, 'but the moon shone so bright as an it had been in a manner day.' Douglas was, Froissart tells us, 'young and strong and of great desire to get praise and grace, and was willing to deserve to have it and cared for no pain nor travail'. There followed a 'sore fight',

---

* *Monthly Chronicles of North-Country Lore and Legend* (1887).

For Englishmen on the one party and Scots on the other party, when they meet there is a hard fight without sparing. There is no 'Ho!' between them as long as spears, swords, axes or daggers will endure, but lay on each other.

At first the English, who outnumbered the Scots, had the advantage.

Then the Earl of Douglas, who was of great heart and high of enterprise, seeing his men recoil back, then to recover the place and show knightly valour he took his axe in both his hands and entered so into the press that he made himself way in such wise that none durst approach near him, and he was so well armed that he bare well of such strokes as he received. Thus he ever went forward like a hardy Hector, willing alone to conquer the field and to discomfit his enemies. But at last he was encountered with three spears all at once: the one struck him on the shoulder, the other on the breast, and the stroke glinted down to his belly, and the third struck him in the thigh, and sore hurt with these strokes, so that he was borne perforce to the ground, and after that he could not be again relieved.

In the dark the English did not realise whom they had felled, thinking Douglas was just another man at arms. Tradition has it that Douglas ordered that he be hidden in a stand of bracken, so that his imminent death would not give cheer to the enemy. Asked by Sir John Sinclair how he fared, Froissart tells us Douglas replied,

Right evil, cousin, but thanked be God there hath been but a few of mine ancestors that hath died in their beds. But, cousin, I require you to think to revenge me, for I reckon myself but dead, for my heart fainteth oftentimes.

The Scots were in the end victorious, and – again according to tradition – it was to the stand of bracken where the dead Douglas lay that Hotspur conceded the victory.

In another ballad, 'The Battle of Otterbourne', Douglas foresees his own death thus:

> But I hae dream'd a dreary dream,
> Beyond the Isle of Skye;
> I saw a dead man win a fight,
> And I think that man was I.

Froissart and the ballads depict a battle in which gallantry and chivalry rather than gore and fear and sheer bloody aggression dominate the field. I suspect the reality would have been very different.

It's a steep knee-jarring stomp down Auchope Rig from Auchope Cairn to the mountain refuge hut, but then you stride along a long, level shoulder towards the Schil. An afternoon breeze stirred the grasses, fluttered a scrap of black bin bag caught in the barbed wire of the Border fence. In Logan Mack's day the Border here was marked by tall pine posts to let guests of the sporting estates on either side know where the limit of their shooting lay. They presumably didn't want a repeat of the Percy–Douglas Spat.

At the top of the Schil there is an outcrop of rock that might to the timorous eye of Daniel Defoe have seemed a pinnacle, but which is only a few feet high. Shored against it are great heaps of stones, which, according to Logan Mack, 'must have been piled together by prehistoric hands for such purpose as seemed fit to their owners'. It may be another Bronze Age burial cairn, but as far as I know it is yet to be excavated. When I passed by, three words were spelt out in stones on the flat grass next to the summit:

I LOVE YOU

I stuck to the Border up to Corbie Craig and Black Hag (circumvented by the Pennine Way), along Steer Rig to White Law and past Whitelaw Nick. Here the Pennine Way leaves the Border for good and heads downhill to Kirk Yetholm. I had thought that by the time I reached this point it would be evening, and I'd have to make camp. But it was only four o'clock in the afternoon, so, even if I followed the Border northward for a couple of miles past Coldmouth Hill and Burnt Humbleton to the Shotton Burn and Yetholm Mains, and then walked the mile or so south down the road to Kirk Yetholm, I'd still be in time for dinner at the pub and bed at the hostel. That was an altogether more tempting prospect than pitching the tent on Tuppie's Grave – however beautiful these upland grasslands, golden ripe in the summer sun. A third night on rice and ready-made sauce was not so appealing as what was on offer at the Border Hotel: pan-roasted rump of Border lamb on spiced puy lentils, with dauphiniose potato and a red wine and rosemary jus. Besides, the old grey hen was nearly empty.

I didn't regret my decision. Leaving the Pennine Way behind, I recovered a sense of adventure, of striding into the unknown. At one point the no-man's-land between the Border wall and the parallel Border fence was filled with meadowsweet, foaming like cream at the top of a pail.

Eventually I came to the saddle between Humbleton Swyre and Coldsmouth Hill. Although the general direction from Auchope Cairn had been downward, there had been quite a few ups on the way. But from here it was entirely downhill. As I turned a corner a roe deer panicked just in front of me, burst into the thick bracken and hid somewhere up by the Border wall. Beyond and above it there was a thick conifer plantation. A buzzard mewed, another answered. To this mournful soundtrack I stumbled down what might have once been a path, but had since been hijacked by cows. The ruts and hollows they'd made in the mud with their hooves had hardened in the sun, making for an awkward, ankle-twisting descent.

The going continued like this along Countrup Sike and the Shotton Burn. At one point I crossed the burn, its banks dotted with yellow mimulus, to take advantage of the right of way marked on the map on the English side. The way was barred by a large bull. I had no intention of embarking on a legal debate with a bull, so I cautiously backtracked and continued down the Scottish bank.

I left the Border at Yetholm Mains, where there's a road bridge over the Shotton Burn. This was the first road I'd met since leaving Carter Bar. Perversely, on the north side of the bridge lies England, on the south side Scotland. There's not much at Yetholm Mains apart from a large farm and a few pebble-dashed council houses.

A man was digging his garden. Aware of the geopolitical peculiarities of the place, I asked him, 'Are you Scottish on this side and English on that side?'

'Scottish,' he said.

'You feel Scottish?'

'I don't know whether there's such a feeling as feeling Scottish,' he said. Obviously I'd asked another stupid question.

I told him I was heading for the pub to eat.

'You've got about twenty minutes to go,' he said.

'Really?' I said in alarm. Maybe Sunday was early closing.

'Or twenty-five minutes. Along the road.'

'Oh, I see,' I said. 'I thought you meant until they closed.'

It was a weary, footsore twenty-five minutes along the tarmac, but there was an open pub at the end of it. I was sweaty, long unwashed.

I told myself I'd just have a quick pint, then have a shower and change of clothes in the hostel before returning to the pub to eat. But then the two young women I'd last seen on Auchope Cairn came in. They'd been to the hostel, washed and changed. I just sat there on my barstool in my T-shirt and stank. But being honest Northern lasses they didn't turn their noses up. They even bought me a pint.

Photo: Joyce Nicholls

ELEVEN

UNTIL THE NIGHT CAME UPON THEM

Flodden Interlude

. . . the fight continued sharp and hot on both parts until the night came upon them . . .

> – William Camden, *Britannia* (1586–1607),
> on the Battle of Flodden

> All the lords of this land were left them behind.
> Beside Branxton in a brook breathless they lie.
> Gaping against the moon their ghost went away.

> – Anonymous song from Cheshire,
> celebrating the defeat of the Scots at Flodden

Interlude: Wednesday, 7th August 2013   Down at Tweed Green, the meadow between the town of Coldstream and the river, a plump southerner in shades and waders stood waist deep in the water.

'It's chuffin cold in here,' he told the world at large.

It's a notoriously chilly river, the Tweed. Hence the name Coldstream. Before the bridge was opened in 1766 this was the lowest place along the course of the Tweed where the river could be forded. Edward I's army waded across in 1296 on their way to seize Berwick. What happened next is described by the fifteenth-century *Scotichronicon* of Walter Bower:

> When the town had been taken in this way and its citizens had submitted, Edward spared no one, whatever the age or sex, and for two days streams of blood flowed from the bodies of the slain, for in his tyrannous rage he ordered seven thousand souls of both sexes to be massacred . . . So that mills could be turned round by the flow of their blood.

In 1513 James IV took his army across the Tweed in the other direction, on the way to annihilation at Flodden.

It was a quiet sunny evening when we arrived on Tweed Green. I was with my photographer friend Joyce Nicholls. Among the lush vegetation on the bank a young red-haired officer of the Coldstream Guards cast his line into the river. The Guards turn up every year during Coldstream's Civic Week. Many ex-Guards turn up too, and I spoke to some of them. Despite their name, they told me, the Guards don't recruit on the Scottish side of the Border. They draw on the youth of Northeast England and, oddly enough, Cornwall.

'We always wind them up that they're a Scottish regiment,' a non-Guard told me. 'Well they are, Coldstream is in Scotland.' But, he said, they were actually founded in Northumberland, in Fenwick and Hazelridge. This was during the English Civil War. In 1650 Colonel George Monck drew on these Parliamentary militias to form Monck's Regiment of Foot.

Under Monck's command the regiment marched north against the Scots, who by then had come out in support of the future Charles II. Having defeated the Scots at Dunbar, the regiment stayed in Scotland until 1st January 1660, when Monck and his men forded the Tweed at Coldstream and marched south to support the restoration of that very same Charles II to the thrones of both countries. Subsequently, Monck's regiment became known as the Coldstream Guards.

But the main event of Coldstream's Civic Week, the event that was going to fill the next day, was the mass ride-out south across the Border to Flodden Field. There, 500 years previously, the largest army that Scotland had ever mustered met with utter disaster.

One young man every year takes the role of the Coldstreamer, the principal rider, and this 500th anniversary year they hoped he would head up a ride-out of 500 horses.

To cater for the inundation of visitors, Tweed Green had become a temporary campsite, with a hosepipe and a row of portable loos. The visitors weren't tourists. They were participants. There was one marquee for ex-Guards, another for former members of the King's Own Scottish Borderers. And there were tents and caravans and mobile homes, many flying flags, all full of drinkers and revellers and riders. Most of them were from other Border towns: Kelso, Hawick, Selkirk, Jedburgh, Duns, Peebles, Galashiels, Langholm. All these towns have their own weeks in which troops of horsemen and horsewomen ride the marches of the burgh. This was traditionally done to mark the territory in which the citizens maintained their privileges against the feudal claims of the local landowners.

The principals have different names in different towns. In Coldstream he is the Coldstreamer, in Jedburgh the Jeddart Callant, in Kelso the Laddie, in Peebles the Cornet, and so on. In most cases there is also a female principal. On Tweed Green we found ourselves camping next to three ex-principals from Duns, tough women whose ages spanned the generations. They were hard riders, generous with their drink, kind with their advice. They'd wanted to join in the ride-out to Flodden the next day, but there was not a single horse left for hire, they said, anywhere along the Border.

As we wandered up into the town in the golden evening I said hello to a cat, enjoying the last of the sun. Then the cat's owner appeared in her doorway, and we talked in a leisurely way of this and that. She was semi-retired, but ran a little shop with her husband.

I said it felt like Coldstream was a town out of time. 'Yes,' she said, 'it's like Brigadoon. It's a place that the nastiness of the world has passed by.' She paused, then added, 'No one lies here dead three days unnoticed.'

Interlude: Thursday, 8th August 2013

'Voddy voddy voddy!'
  'Oi oi oi!'
  'Voddy voddy voddy!'
  'Oi oi oi!'
  'C'mon, darling! Sing! FUCKIN' SING!!'
  'I've got all my love to give . . .'
  'More! Louder! FUCKIN' SING!!!'
  'I will survive!'
  'More! Louder! FUCKIN' SING!!!'
  'I will survive!!'
  'I will survive!!!!'

I was blasted out of sleep. One o'clock in the morning and the campsite had exploded into life. These Borderers certainly know how to party. It didn't stop. At least not for another couple of hours. I pulled a T-shirt over my head, but the decibels broke through.

At one point I stumbled out in the dark to the portaloos for a pee. Three young men in jeans and T-shirts carrying cans stumbled past. 'Oh, look at him!' one jeered. 'He's all cosy-wosy in his jimmy-jammies!' If only I was, I thought, tucked up and fast asleep all cosy-wosy in my jimmy-jammies. I might have said I was too old for all this. But half the revellers still up and about were even older than me.

'FUCKIN' DANCE, GIRLS!!!'

'*I . . . SHALL . . . SURVIVE!!!!*'

Eventually someone pulled the plug, and silence fell.

Later that morning, as the town clock struck ten, I stood dazed and confused in the breeze and sunshine in Coldstream's Market Square. A crowd had gathered round a cluster of worthies on a ribbon-decked podium. Among them was the Fifteenth Earl of Home, a tall, gaunt man with a smoker's pallor slouching in a baggy suit with aristocratic ease. Beside him the Lord Lieutenant of Berwickshire stood straight as a ramrod in his full dress uniform, sash, sword, medals and all. The Master of Ceremonies at their side was a shorter, plumper man, bespectacled, ruddy, stiff with civic dignity. I presumed he represented the citizenry of the burgh.

'Lord Lieutenant, Lord and Countess of Home, Ladies and Gentlemen,' the MC intoned. He reminded us that if we'd been standing in the same place on 22nd August 1513, dominating the landscape would have been Coldstream's abbey, and passing through would have been the vanguard of King James's mighty army, led by Alexander, Second Lord Home, distant ancestor of the present Earl. According to Sir Walter Scott in *Marmion*, Lord Home was to follow King James's orders

> And strike three strokes with Scottish brand,
> And march three miles on Southron land,
> And bid the banners of his band
> In English breezes dance.

'Today,' the MC continued, 'we go the same three miles on southern land, and our banners will dance to an English breeze. Ladies and Gentlemen, please welcome the colour standard, the Coldstreamer and his Right- and Left-Hand Men.'

There was a skirl of pipes, and to the tune of 'Blue Bonnets Over the Border' the Coldstreamer and his Right-Hand Man and his Left-Hand Man marched into the square. Dressed in dark blue bonnets and dark blue jackets, white riding breeches and black boots, they sported blue-and-white sashes, the colours of the town. They had the awkward bow-legged gait of men more used to the saddle than the pavement.

As the pipes fell silent, the Earl of Home cleared his throat.

'Coldstreamer,' he said in the tones of the effortlessly upper class, 'I, David the Fifteenth Earl of Home, charge you to lead the cavalcade assembled here in Coldstream today to Flodden Field, as my ancestor did in 1513, there to lay a wreath in homage to the slain of that fateful day. I also charge you to return with a sod of earth cut from the field.'

This part of the ritual commemorates the role that Isabella of Pringle, Abbess of Coldstream, played in the aftermath of the battle. Hearing of the carnage she ordered her nuns to bear the bodies of the Scottish nobility back from the battlefield to Coldstream Abbey to be given a Christian burial. The sod of earth that the Coldstreamer brings back every year is laid on a stone capital on Tweed Green, one of the few relics of the Abbey that survive.

'Sir,' the Coldstreamer declared in a broad Border accent as he received the Earl of Home's standard, 'I solemnly promise to carry out your charges to the best of my ability.'

The Countess of Home then pinned a rosette to his lapel.

The Coldstreamer turned to the crowd and shouted, 'Hip hip!'

'Hooray!' the crowd roared back.

'Hip hip!'

'Hooray!'

'Hip hip!'

'Hooray!'

With that the pipes struck up again and the Coldstreamer and his Right-Hand Man and his Left-Hand Man marched from the square.

We made our way up the High Street. People were lining up on the pavements, peering towards the west to look out for the approach of the great parade. I asked a shop assistant sitting on her step whether this was Coldstream's big day. 'It is, yes,' she said. 'This year especially, because of the Battle of Flodden.' She'd been born in Gateshead and still had a Geordie accent, but had lived in Coldstream for thirty-two years. She said a lot of Geordies ended up there. 'You get a right mixture in the Borders,' she said. 'Which is nice.'

I asked another woman standing in the entrance of her shop whether everything closed down for half an hour until the horses passed. 'Not really,' she said. She was a somewhat taciturn Scouser. But she was as anxious as any to watch the riders go by.

Outside the Besom pub a young man with shaved ginger hair was clutching a pint. Beside him was a woman in a tracksuit and a child with a dummy in its mouth. 'Are you locals?' I asked. 'Aye,' said the young man. Then he saw my Dictaphone. 'No, Ah'm no wanting recorded,' he told me firmly. 'Ok,' I said, 'I'll turn it off.' This vox pop business wasn't going so well.

A retired couple proved more forthcoming. They were originally from Yorkshire, but had moved here to be equidistant from one daughter in Leeds and another in Edinburgh. They'd lived in Coldstream for five years.

'The town's not changed since 1951,' he said. 'A strange and mysterious place. How we ended up here I will never know.'

I mentioned the comment by the woman the previous evening that no one lies here dead three days unnoticed.

'When I drive in over the Tweed Bridge,' he said, 'my wife knows I'm home before I do.'

I asked about the demographic make-up of the town. He told me there was a split. 'Those who are all related, and the rest of us.' He thought that almost half the population were now incomers.

As the pipe band at the head of the procession came into view, I began to offer a commentary to my Dictaphone. 'A big police four-wheel drive has stopped in the middle of Coldstream high street, and now – ' The woman in front of me jumped with fright then burst into laughter. She hadn't expected some idiot to be chuntering into a microphone.

'And now here come a couple of police bikes with flashing lights, and the band and a whole lot of riders following on.' It was difficult to keep a straight face, but I persisted. 'The Coldstreamer and his Right-Hand Man and his Left-Hand Man, and then the whole cavalcade coming through. Some in bright waistcoats, some in tweed jackets, some in riding jackets, all in white riding breeches and boots. Some with sashes, some with rosettes. All ages – kids, teens, right up to sixty-somethings, all with a sense of occasion. The women chat companionably. The men keep a stony silence. Here's four young girls, aged maybe ten, proud and pleased, riding side by side.'

The town rung with the sound of hooves on tarmac. Rider after rider shouted 'Hip hip', and the crowd roared back 'Hooray!' There were hundreds and hundreds of riders. It must have taken the best part of half an hour for all of them to pass. Children in the crowd held their noses and pointed and shrieked as horse after horse lifted its tail and shat on the road. The August air filled with the smell of dung.

If it took five hundred riders half an hour to pass through Coldstream in 2013, how long, 500 years before, would it have taken James IV's great army of thirty to forty thousand knights, men at arms, pikemen and camp followers to ford the Tweed on 22nd August 1513?

King James IV, Scotland's great Renaissance prince, had done all he could to avoid war with England. After all, his queen, Margaret Tudor, was elder sister to Henry VIII of England. But her brother was determined to strut upon the European stage, and to this end joined with Spain and the Holy Roman Empire in war against France, Scotland's traditional ally. For Henry this was the game of kings. He dismissed James's attempts at diplomacy, blithely stating, 'I am the very owner of Scotland.' Such claims had not been heard from an English monarch for 200 years.

Perhaps unwisely, James felt he had no option other than to launch a diversionary raid across the Border to distract Henry from his French campaign. And so, in the words of William Camden, James 'marched forward in great courage and greater hope with banner displayed against England'.

Unusually for a Scottish king, James had the support of virtually all the great magnates of the realm, together with considerable aid, in money and arms, from the French. 'The Scots lacked nothing necessary for the wars,' wrote Thomas Ruthal, Bishop of Durham, 'but only the grace of God.'

Having forced the surrender of the great English Border fortress at Norham, a few miles down the Tweed from Coldstream, James and his army of perhaps 20,000 fighting men took up a strong position on Branxton Hill, a mile or two northwest of Flodden.

Thomas Howard, Earl of Surrey, had led an English army of roughly the same size north to meet the Scottish threat. Surrey, at seventy years old, may have been, as the Scots said, 'ane cruikit cairll', but he was a wily commander. Initially Surrey invited James to fight him on level ground to the south, near Milfield. But James sensibly refused to surrender his strong position. So Surrey marched round to the north of the Scottish army, cutting off their line of retreat, and took up position on Stock Law, a lower height beneath Branxton Hill.

It was 9th September, and the rain fell incessantly. Visibility was poor, made worse by smoke from the campfires. The two armies were only a quarter of a mile apart when they came into view of each other. It was not until late in the afternoon that battle was joined, beginning with an artillery exchange. The Spanish diplomat Pedro de Ayala had observed that James 'does not think it right to begin any warlike undertaking without being himself the first in danger'. Accordingly, when the guns fell silent, James led his men down the hill through the rain and smoke to fall upon the English army, intent on neutralising the English longbowmen while their bowstrings were still wet.

In other circumstances the Scottish formations of pikemen – a tactic evolved by Swiss mercenaries – had proved an effective shock weapon. But in this terrain the Scots found their fifteen-foot pikes lacked sufficient versatility. Advancing down a steep slippery slope it was difficult to maintain the right angle and momentum, and when the pike squares reached the lower ground they found themselves bogged down in thick mud, making them vulnerable to the more manoeuvrable billhooks and halberds of the English foot soldiers. With the axes of their weapons the English could chop off the tips of the Scottish spears, while the stabbing blades of the bills outreached the Scottish swords.

Even so, the Scots fought on determinedly. 'They were so mighty, large, strong and great men,' Bishop Ruthal reported, 'that they would not fall when four or five bills struck on one of them at once.'

> Howbeit, our bills quit them very well, and did more good that day than bows, for they shortly disappointed the Scots of their long spears wherein was their greatest trust: and when they came to hand-strokes, though the Scots fought sore and valiantly with their swords, yet they could not resist the bills, that lighted so thick and sore upon them.

William Camden picks up the story:

> . . . the fight continued sharp and hot on both parts until the night came upon them, uncertain as then whether [which] side had the victory. But the day ensuing manifested both the conqueror and conquered, and the King of Scots himself, with many a mortal wound, was found among the heaps of dead bodies.

It turned out to have been a close thing. At the start of the battle Lord Home and the Earl of Huntly had overwhelmed the English right, and James himself had fallen within a spear's length of where the elderly Earl of Surrey had taken up position to command his forces. But in the end the English victory was absolute.

No prisoners were taken, no quarter given. Dawn revealed a dreadful sight: Flodden Field was littered with the corpses of ten thousand Scotsmen, and perhaps fifteen hundred English dead. It was said that there was not a family in Scotland that did not lose a son, a husband or a father. As for James himself, according to the English antiquary John Stow, he had suffered 'divers deadly wounds',

> . . . his throat cut half asunder, his left hand in two places almost cut off, and many other wounds, as well with arrows as otherwise . . .

Although the nuns of Coldstream brought back the bodies of the Scottish nobility for burial, there is no record as to what happened to the mass of the dead and wounded. They were no doubt stripped of their arms and armour, and then left naked on the field for the fox and the crow to grow fat on.

On Stock Law today, near where Surrey oversaw the slaughter and King James fell, there is a monument, in the form of a sturdy cross. On it there is a plaque, which simply states:

FLODDEN

1513

TO THE BRAVE OF BOTH NATIONS

It was here that we awaited the 500 riders. Most of the cars and four-by-fours and the horseboxes and the spectators were up above us, on the top of Branxton Hill. This was a quieter, more poignant spot.

It was a warm August day, but the sky was busy with clouds manoeuvring to match the drama of the occasion. It was a day of long views, long memories. In this fine summer the corn had already been cut in Flodden Field, leaving a clear run of stubble for the 500 horses.

There was a quiet expectation among the two score spectators around the cross, their words whipped away by the breeze. After a few minutes someone made out a movement along the hedge-lined lane below. We saw the horses before we heard them. Five hundred horses clattered on tarmac, huffing and blowing, then the cries of marshals brought the procession to a standstill. A marshal dismounted, opened the double gate into the field of stubble, into Flodden Field.

There was a dip in the hill below us, a steepening, so the riders were hidden for a while after they came through the gate. Then suddenly they reappeared, charging up the hill over the near horizon towards us. At their head was the Coldstreamer, banner flying. Close behind came his Right-Hand Man and his Left-Hand Man.

Hundreds more followed, some on their own, some in small troops, some walking, some trotting, some of the friskier ones taking a quick canter. Then they mustered beyond the cross, at the foot of Branxton Hill, in the level ground where most of the Scots had been slaughtered. Five hundred riders seemed to fill the field. It was impossible to imagine what that same field would have looked like five hundred years before, littered with the bodies of ten or twelve thousand dead or dying men.

I followed after the riders, puffing up a path through a steep field of barley to watch the climax of the day. The five hundred massed in the lane by the ruins of Branxton Stead. Then the Coldstreamer and his Right-Hand Man and his Left-Hand Man set off at a gallop diagonally up the final grassy slope of Branxton Hill, while the crowd above roared with approval. More and more gallopers followed, the crowds cheering wildly. The horses waiting their turn grew restless, turning this way and that, snorting. Their riders, under orders from the mounted marshals, worked hard to hold them back until their turn came. The ground shook, the air was beaten with the blows of hooves. The biggest cheers of all were reserved for the last rider – a young lad of only six or seven, on a small white pony. I don't suppose he'll ever forget the roars of the crowd that day.

On my way up the hill after the gallopers I met a man on horseback leading a riderless horse.

'Where's the rider?' I asked.

'In hospital,' the man said.

At the top of the hill the riders mixed with the crowd. I passed a young girl holding the horse of a man in a red waistcoat. When he came back from the refreshment tent, he slipped her a tenner. The wealthier riders had their grooms and horseboxes lined up waiting for them. Two adolescent riders, a boy and a girl, smartly accoutred in waistcoats, jodhpurs and stocks, dismounted by their picnicking parents. As they rested, their ponies were groomed and watered by another boy and girl of much the same age, dressed in jeans and sweatshirts. The slogan on the girl's back said 'FABULOUSLY BRITISH'. I couldn't make out whether they were family or paid retainers. They all had strong Border accents.

Walking around on foot among horsemen, one is only too aware of one's own lowly station. There's something about being on top of a horse that gives the rider an assumption of superiority over lesser mortals. It is not necessarily expressed. It's just there.

I overheard snatches of conversation. 'Ah canna believe the view,' one rider said. 'I've been here once before but I was so pissed I canna remember.' Another rider, about sixty-five or seventy, gave a loud yawn. 'Aye, it's a hard life,' said his friend as they rode off, beginning the long hack back to Coldstream. I came across a frantic man in a pink jumper, part of the ITV team filming celebrity Geordie Robson Green gallop up the hill for a series about Northumberland life. 'I can't find him, basically,' he whined into his Bluetooth. 'I don't know *where* I am.'

A woman rider passed by with a head-cam attached to her helmet. A young lad wore a pompom on his. A small company of army cadets, both boys and girls, strutted around. I was unclear what their function was today, but they certainly seemed to feel important. Uniform, whether military or equestrian, can have that effect. All around me there were proud men and women on horses, straight-backed, waving to the onlookers. I caught a glimpse of the Coldstreamer himself. He seemed to have lost his standard, but I've never seen a happier face. 'Hip hip,' he shouted, and the crowd yelled back, 'Hooray!'

As the riders went off in one direction and the onlookers returned to their cars, we made our way back down the north slope of Branxton Hill in the footsteps of King James and his commanders, Lord Home and the Earls of Huntly, Errol, Crawford, Montrose, Bothwell, Lennox and Argyle. Five hundred years before they'd been at the heads of four or five great pike squares, each some four thousand men strong, sixty files broad and sixty ranks deep. Of the commanders, only Huntly and Home survived the battle, while fully half the Scottish army were slain, together with a great swathe of the nobility, including the Lord Chancellor of Scotland. It was the largest battle ever fought between the two kingdoms.

With the crowds left behind, Flodden Field fell silent. All I could hear was the gentle breath of the wind through the ruins of Branxton Stead.

Ahead of me, on the skyline leading up to the monument, I spotted two men silhouetted against the northern sky. The two men turned out to be a priest and a piper.

Then a procession of some twenty men in dark suits appeared and made their way in single file towards the monument. The piper played a march, bringing up the rear. I thought of the scene in *The Seventh Seal* where the Reaper leads the peasants and the gentlemen, the priest and the knight in a dance of death against a brooding sky.

The twenty men in dark suits lined up before the cross. Then the priest or minister began to speak, his words sometimes blown away in the wind.

We come as representatives of families, local communities, and of our country, to remember our forebears and predecessors, and also to reflect on the thousands of men who lost their lives in that dreadful battle . . . So that we may, in our own time, plant rather than uproot, build up rather than break down, heal rather than kill, make peace rather than war. Amen.

Then the MC who had spoken after the Earl of Home in the Market Square that morning recited Jean Elliot's 'The Flowers of the Forest', a lament for the dead of Flodden written two and a half centuries after the event.

> I've heard the lilting, at the yowe-milking,
> Lassies a-lilting before dawn o' day;
> Now they are moaning on ilka green loaning,
> The flowers of the Forest are a' wede away.

The Forest in question was the Ettrick Forest, then covering most of Selkirkshire. The flowers were its menfolk, cut down by English bill hooks.

One by one the men in dark suits walked forward to place a single thistle at the foot of the cross. The MC intoned their names as the August breezes whipped around the hill. Some of his words were flung away by the wind, unheard, like the names of all the unnamed dead who fell here.

The People of Berwick . . . Sir David Home and his son George of Wedderburn . . . Sir John Home and his eldest son Cuthbert of Fastcastle . . . Sir John Stuart of Minto . . . John Murray of Bowhill . . . William Hague of Bemersyde . . . David Pringle and his three uncles, John, William and Alexander . . . Patrick Gillies, Borough Treasurer of Peebles . . . The Free Men of Penicuik . . . Sir Andrew Kerr of Cessford . . . Sir William Cockburn and his eldest son Alexander . . . James Stuart of Traquhair . . . The Lord Provost of Edinburgh . . . For all souls buried at Yetholm who fell here . . . For all the Border men who fell . . . For all the Northumbrian men who fell . . . For all the Scots who fell.

When all the thistles had been laid at the foot of the cross, the minister raised his arm and gave his blessing. Then the piper struck up a lively march and the dignitaries processed away, leaving the cross to the silence of the summer day.

Early that evening a sombre crowd gathered on Tweed Green for the Abbey Ceremony. A row of dignitaries faced the crowd, their backs to the river. I recognised several faces from the thistle-laying ceremony at the Flodden Memorial. On one side the Earl of Home was having a smoke and chatting with the minister.

At the far end of the Green the Coldstream Pipe Band was assembling, alongside a small unit of Coldstream Guards in full dress uniform. The band struck up 'A Scottish Soldier' and began to march. Then a solo piper played a lament. A speaker read a translation of the Abbey's charter, then the MC told us just one of the sad tales from Flodden. Among Lord Home's vanguard was his kinsman, Sir David Home.

Sir David Home from Wedderburn Castle near Duns was accompanied by all of his seven sons, George, David, Alexander, John, Robert, Andrew and Patrick. They were known as the Seven Spears of Wedderburn. It was custom in those days that in time of war the heir would remain at home to continue the family line in case the rest of the family were killed. George was sent from the Scottish camp when the English were first spotted within the vicinity of Flodden Hill. On his way back George stopped at Coldstream Priory, where his mother, Isabella of Pringle, persuaded George to return to his father, safe in the knowledge that the king's mighty army would never be defeated. Home's men were the first to engage the English on that fateful day, and during the battle Sir David Home and George were slain. The six remaining brothers wrapped the bodies in the Home banner, which was a green saltire, and carried them back to Wedderburn.

The minister then offered a prayer. He said we were all children in the eyes of God, so sounding that old Scottish egalitarian theme, summed up in the saying, 'We're a' Jock Tamson's bairns.' It was a tonic against all the talk of kings and earls, baronets and abbesses, hierarchy and division, a reminder that, to cite another old Scots expression, 'We're a' ae oo' – we are all woven out of the same wool. I was glad to see an Afro-Caribbean face amongst the Coldstream Guards on the Green.

A soprano sang 'The Flowers of the Forest', unaccompanied. Then a solo piper picked up the lament.

In single file and slow march the Coldstreamer and his Right-Hand Man and his Left-Hand Man advanced towards the stone capital of the abbey, positioned on the turf of the Green. The Right-Hand Man in front held a folded Blue Saltire, the Left-Hand Man behind held the Earl of Home's standard, while the Coldstreamer himself bore the sod of earth cut that day from Flodden Field.

The Right-Hand Man draped the Blue Saltire over the capital. Then the Coldstreamer bent forward to place the sod of earth upon the Saltire. The Left-Hand Man passed the Home standard to the Coldstreamer, who lowered it over the Blue Saltire in homage to the fallen.

'By the right . . .' barked the drum major, 'quick march.' And the band broke into 'Scotland the Brave'. *Exeunt omnes*, leaving the sod on the Saltire, a poignant relic of Scotland the Foolhardy.

It's been said that the Scots like to dwell on disaster. That may or may not be true – though I doubt few people south of Newcastle have ever even heard of Flodden. But maybe staring disaster in the face is a way of putting things in perspective, owning up to one's own fallibility, keeping hubris in check.

There's a relatively new ritual in Coldstream that upholds this spirit. It kicks off shortly after the Abbey Ceremony, and turns tragedy into farce. It's been going for perhaps four or five years, according to the young man I found myself standing next to in a little square off the High Street. The place is known as the Stump.

'Aye,' he says, 'this is the ceremony where all the principals from all the Border towns who've fallen frae their horses during a ride-out have tae explain themselves in verse. And spray champagne at the same time.' Apparently about thirty past principals were lined up for humiliation. The first, standing on the eponymous stump, began to sing.

Three men from Carntyne and a bottle of wine went to join the party . . .

'Do they come clean?' I asked. 'Or does everybody just know?'

Three men from Carntyne and a bottle of wine and five woodbine went to join the party . . .

'As soon as somebody falls off,' he told me, '*every* rider knows. Everybody finds out. You won't get away with it.'

Three men from Carntyne and a bottle of wine and five woodbine and a big black greyhound dug ca'd Boab went to join the party . . .

I remembered a snatch of conversation I'd heard on Branxton Hill. 'This guy was denying it,' a rider had chortled to his friend, 'but I've got a photograph of him. *On the ground!*'

Three men from Carntyne and a bottle of wine and five woodbine and a big black greyhound dug ca'd Boab went to join the party . . . AND somebody fell aff and got a sore knee . . .

I asked my friend where he was from. 'Frae Innerleithen,' he said. He told me each principal wore a sash with his or her town's colours. The principals didn't just come from the Border towns, some came from Lanarkshire or the Lothians, from towns such as Biggar, Penicuik, Musselburgh – even Edinburgh. It turned out that the exception was Innerleithen. 'We're bad enough at trying to walk,' he said, 'never mind ride.' So they don't have a ride-out. 'Ride-outs are about protecting your boundaries,' he said. 'This is ours, this is the town's, not the laird's.'

'Do the principals who've fallen have to bring their own champagne?' I asked.

'Aye. And if you fall off in your own week's festival, you need to bring two bottles of champagne. There's somebody from

Musselburgh who fell off in their own week, twice. Cost him four bottles of champagne.'

I'd thought the champagne might be a perk. But it turns out it's a penance.

The young woman now standing in smiling shame on the stump and spraying the crowd was belting out a pastiche of an old Monkees song. Like those of all the other fallen principals, her rendition was joyful, shouty and tuneless.

Hey hey wur the Dunsies! she might have sung. Or maybe it was *Hey hey wur the Kelsies!* I never did quite grasp what her excuse was.

Little children scuttled about, squealing and giggling with delight when the spray hit them.

It was the start of a long night, after a long day. All the riders and many of the spectators would be dressing up later for the Grand Ball, commencing at nine. I was told that the Ball rarely came to an end before four o'clock in the morning. I decided to give it a miss. I do not have the stamina of a true Borderer.

Interlude: Friday, 9th August 2013   Things were still going strong in Coldstream the following evening. Everybody was gearing up for the torchlight procession that brings the town's Civic Week to a close. Down on Tweed Green campers were milling about, getting some cans down them before hitting the pubs. I got caught up in an ever-shifting conversation with some ex-Coldstreamers, some former KOSBs, a couple of teachers from Dumfriesshire and the founders of the 1513 Club. Some belonged to more than one of these subsets, but I never quite worked out who was what.

I asked my usual question about accents along the Border.

'You go to Annan,' one man said, 'and you get yow and my and the backdoor kye.'

'And if you go to Hawick,' said another, 'you'll get yow and me and I'll have a cup o' tea.'

A woman who farms at Old Graitney, where the Lochmaben Stone is, said, 'You can go just ten miles from Gretna – to Annan,

Kilpatrick, Langholm, Longtown – and you have about thirty different accents within that ten miles.' She herself had a Cumbrian accent, though she insisted she was Scottish born and bred.

The conversation moved on to identity politics in Dumfries and Galloway. 'An inspector came to the college in Dumfries,' one of the teachers told me. 'He asked, "How do your students cope with having other students of a different ethnic background in the class?" "They don't have to," I said. "What do you mean they don't have to?" "Well," I said, "it's very, very seldom that they have to. But what they *have* got to cope with is someone coming from Gretna, or Stranraer, or from Castle Douglas. *That's* more of a confrontational situation."'

'They're clans,' his female colleague told me. 'Annan, Kirkcudbright, Dumfries, Castle Douglas, Dalbeattie – they're all just a wee bit insular.'

And so we drifted onto the subject of the Border.

'I've got mates on both sides,' one man said.

'I'm actually two hundred yards from the Border,' another said, 'but I'm in Englandshire. Born and bred here, though.'

'And I live in Scotland, though I come from over there,' an Englishwoman said. 'It doesn't make me a bad person.'

The Scotsman who lives just over the Border in Englandshire told me he'd named the place where his house is the Scottish Principality of Howburn – 'Cos there's three people live there and they're a' Scots. Ma dug's the queen, ma ither dug's the prime minister, an' ma bidie-in's the royal housekeeper.' (A *bidie-in* is a live-in partner.)

I asked what the line-up of activities was for the evening.

'Drink.'

'Well obviously that, but any cultural activities of a higher order?'

'No.'

'But look here,' said another man pointing to a third, 'this man wrote the book about the battle.'

'More than just the battle,' the author said. 'More than just knocking shite out of each other.'

'Was it the fault of the French?' I asked.

'Everything's the fault of the French.'

'Was James IV not a bit stupid to invade just cos the French asked him to?'

'Well, he was in between a rock and a hard place. But how he managed to lose that battle with the tactical position that he had . . . Having said that, had the pubs not been open all bloody day we wouldnae have lost.'

'Was it not,' I offered, 'a lot to do with long pikes and unsuitable ground? Pikes against halberds?'

'Light cannon against heavy cannon,' the author said.

'And he got outflanked,' said another man.

'Done over,' said a third.

'He wiz nae good.'

'Na, he wiz nae good at a'.'

'It's a bit like Scotland every time it goes into the World Cup. Gets to the first round and then . . .'

'Another glorious defeat.'

'Against the odds we manage to lose.'

'Aye, another glorious defeat.'

We wandered up to the High Street. If anything, the streets were busier than the day before. As it grew dark, the pavements outside every pub in town grew thick with drinkers. There were a lot of police in evidence, keeping a beady eye out. I asked one young policeman if this was the busiest night of the year. 'No,' he said, 'but it's the funnest. We had a bit of trouble here last year, but this year we're going to come down heavy.' Then he looked at me. 'I can see you're not going to cause trouble. You're a gentleman.' One has to question the officer's judgement.

We looked into a Chinese takeaway. There were no customers, only a lad behind the counter. 'Bit of a quiet night for you guys?' I asked. 'Is Civic Week not a good time for you?'

'Ok I suppose,' he said.

'Not too fond of it?'

'Everybody seems to enjoy it, apart from us. We have to work, don't we? You enjoying it?'

I reassured him that I was, but said he looked very sad.

'I'm not really enjoying it. I have to work. It's a family business.'

He'd been brought up in Scotland, attending primary school in Coldstream and secondary school in Duns. He was now studying sports science at Napier University in Edinburgh. I asked how it felt living in a place that was very Scottish and very English at the same time.

'I prefer the English,' he said.

Joyce asked whether she could take his picture.

'I'm not really a fan of photographs,' he said.

'That's ok,' I said. 'Don't worry.'

If we hadn't already eaten, we would have ordered a Special Feast for Four just to cheer him up.

There was a very different mood at Rajdhani Spice, Coldstream's only curry house. I'd seen a poster by the bridge saying 'Happy Civic Week From Rajdhani Spice Indian Restaurant & Take Away'.

'We are in Coldstream just one and half years, so we are not very well known about this place,' the patron explained. 'Very nice place, calm and quiet, people are very friendly. You want to take some pictures with us? You take some picture? You take some picture?'

Another young man appeared. 'Is this a family business?' I asked. 'Your brother?'

'This is my nephew,' he replied. 'Family business. Originally we're from Bangladesh. You been Bangladesh? We're from Newcastle. I learn cooking from South London.' Then he produced a photograph of a baby. 'This is the kaffir, the boss. Any drinks for you?'

I politely declined. It was clearly going to be a night for pacing oneself.

Among the 'English Dishes' on offer at Rajdhani Spice were Tikka roll, Mixed roll, Skeek roll, and Fish and chips. A Tikka roll sounded more Brick Lane than Burton upon Trent. A Mixed roll obviously had some kind of identity crisis. And I've no idea what a Skeek roll is – the only skeek turned up by Google is an entry from www.urban-dictionary.com. I leave it to the reader to pursue the definitions there.

But the place to go for fish and chips in Coldstream is Anthony's. Anthony himself has got a strong Mediterranean face, as mobile as his gestures, quick and deliberate like the way he shovels chips into a poke. On his pale blue T-shirt it says 'ITALIA'. He's been in Coldstream for fourteen or fifteen years. Before that he'd lived in Edinburgh. His family came from the coast between Rome and Naples.

I observed that it seemed to be the Chinese, Bangladeshis and Italians who fed Coldstream. 'They'd all starve without you guys,' I said.

'Not many people appreciate us,' Anthony replied. He had a big smile on his face.

I asked him why the Italians were so good at fish and chips.

'I don't know,' he said. 'Must be a natural thing. All the good things're Italian.'

'Haggis and chips, please,' said a customer. The place was hoaching.

There was also a young man serving. I took him to be Anthony's son until I heard him speak. His accent was southern English. I asked him how he'd ended up here. He laughed. 'I'm from Edinburgh,' he said. I think he was joking.

'We're all the same,' said Anthony.

I asked if he'd still got family in Italy. 'Yes,' he said. 'I go summer, winter, whenever I can. Whenever I get the chance.'

Outside on the High Street it was buzzing. Police officers in high-viz jackets paced up and down. The citizenry milled about in the balmy evening. The sounds of karaoke leaked out of the Newcastle Arms, drinkers spilled out onto the pavements. Further along three young people with guitar, moothie and bongo sat on a step belting out 'Whiskey in the Jar'.

> *As I was goin' over*
> *The far-famed Kerry mountains*
> *I met with Captain Farrell*
> *And his money he was counting.*

Two men in party hats were waving light sticks about, blowing huge bubbles out of some bubble-blowing thing.

Yella yella yella!

Any colour you like!

Very cheap!

'Are you travellers?' I asked.

'He asks a lot of questions, this man,' said the older man. He had a Geordie accent.

> *I first produced my pistol*
> *And I then produced my rapier,*
> *I said stand or deliver*
> *Or the Devil he may take ya —*

Yella yella yella!

Any colour you like!

Very cheap!

'Asks a lot of questions,' said the younger man. He had a Geordie accent too.

'Show people,' the older man said. 'We've got the fair up at the top there. 'We've got hookah-dooks.'

I wasn't sure what they were. 'Cool hats,' I said.

'Flashing hats,' the older man said.

Yella yella yella! shouted the younger man.

> *Musha-ring dum-a-do dum-a-da.*
> *Whack for my daddy-o,*
> *Whack for my daddy-o*
> *There's whiskey in the jar!*

'You're going to exhaust yourself twirling that around,' I said.

'They've got batteries in them.'

'But your arm hasn't.'

'Look at the camera, Jack,' said the older man. *Woohoo, free bubbles!*

'Can I have a light?' said a passerby.

'What kind of light d'ye want?' said the younger man. *Yella yella yella!*

> *I took all of his money*
> *And it was a pretty penny.*
> *I took all of his money*
> *And I brought it home to Molly –*

'Are you related? I asked.

'I'm his father,' said the older man. *Woohoo, free bubbles!*

'That's me dad over there.'

'You ask too many questions,' said the older man.

'He's the taxman, I swear,' said the younger man.

Yella yella yella!

I denied this, told them I was writing a book about the Border. I asked them where they worked the shows.

'We do all over the country,' said the older man. 'Bournemouth to top end of the Hebrides.'

Woohoo, free bubbles!

'What's the season?' I asked.

'March, May, June, like this is the peak.' In the winter he did painting and decorating work in the northeast of England. Three years before he'd won a big plastering contract in Fort William.

'So you were there through the winter? I asked.

'Ooh, fuckin aye,' he said. 'I felt it as well. Then you've got the helicopters landing, these crazy people who want to go and climb Ben Nevis. You know when they die in the middle of Ben Nevis, you know how they find them? In the spring when the birds are flyin' aroond. We were there when the helicopters were landing, at daft o'clock in the morning. Do you get paid for this?'

'Barely,' I said.

'It's the dream,' he said, then burst into song. '*Life is but a dream . . .*'
Yella yella yella!

'I'm down Hartlepool tomorrer,' he continued. 'There's a big parade there. I'm going down with all this first thing, then I'm down Whitby. Whitby's nice, beautiful place.'

'And here's the police,' I said. 'Out in force. Just making sure.'

'Aw hell,' a woman said as she walked past.

'Aw hell,' said her friend.

> *She swore that she loved me*
> *Never would she leave me*
> *But the Devil take that woman*
> *For you know she tricked me easy –*

I could hear a faint drumbeat in the distance. All around there was drunken laughter, shouting in the street.

'You like bubbles, eh?' the older man asked Joyce. 'When I'm moving away like that?'

'You've done this before,' I said.

'All over the country, mate,' he said. 'For photographers.'
Woohoo, free bubbles!
Yella yella yella!

> *Musha-ring dum-a-do dum-a-da.*
> *Whack for my daddy-o,*
> *Whack for my daddy-o*
> *There's whiskey in the jar!*

Yella yella yella!

I looked at my watch. There was just time to grab a drink in the Besom before the parade arrived, if the place wasn't stowed out.

The cheerful young woman behind the bar pulled me a pint of Old Golden Hen. I asked where it was brewed.

'I've no idea,' she said. Her accent was from this side of the Border. 'Dunno.'

'Way down south,' a man said.

'After a hard night's pulling pints, you're standing up to it very well,' I said. She laughed. 'I thought it'd be more crowded in here.'

'They're all waiting for the parade,' she said.

A big motherly woman at the other end of the bar was in full flow. 'The girls'll get your money,' she told a customer. 'I'm pulling pints on this side.'

'Two pints of cider and a red wine,' said someone.

'That'll be five thirty-five,' said the younger woman.

'It was me you were serving,' someone else said.

'Oh it's been a long day,' she said.

'And it's not over yet,' I said.

Outside people were rushing past. There was a feeling of growing excitement. Someone peered out the door. 'Aye, they're comin',' she said, and everybody piled out onto the pavement.

You could hear the drums, then the pipes. They were playing 'Scotland the Brave' – no lamenting now, just sheer bravura. A police four-by-four cruised into view, blue light flashing. Then the Coldstream Pipe Band, the drum major at its head, marching out proudly. They'd abandoned their kilts and dress jackets for jeans and hoodies. Then came troops of kids with their parents. Some shook buckets at the crowd, raising funds for who knows what.

Oggy oggy oggy! someone shouted.

Oi oi oi! came the reply.

Danny!

Penny!

Hip hip!

Hooray!

Scores, hundreds of people – mothers, fathers, kids – processed past, many holding small torches. There was nothing as outrageously dangerous as the flames of Lerwick's Up-Helly-A or the whirling fireballs of Stonehaven or the burning tar barrels of Burghead.

Yella yella yella!

Hurrah! Hurrah! Hurrah!

This was not the dark-defying of the midwinter fire festivals further north, not a demonstration of pagan machismo. Nor was it the proud show of yesterday's horsemen and horsewomen, riding high above the crowds. This was a family occasion. The faces all bore big smiles, flickering in the torchlight. It was more of a harvest festival, a night to celebrate family, food, contentment, community. For the children, it was the last late night of the summer holidays, before school started. I remembered the words of the minister, praying at the Abbey Ceremony: 'Remind us that home is not gourmet meals or fancy furniture, but commotion mixed with contentment, problems mixed with prayer, gentleness, kindness, laughter and love.' There, before me, walking happily down Coldstream's High Street, were just some of Jock Tamson's bairns.

Then it was a rush down to Tweed Green again, to welcome the pipers and the marchers after their tour through the town. In the old days, the marchers would hurl their fiery brands into the river, but now they more decorously dunk them in a bucket.

The spectators lined up in rows on the steep banks on the town side of the Green. Dress was informal compared to the smart riding costumes of the day before. Only the female teens were done up to the nines, many in long dresses, tricked out in jewellery and slabs of make-up. They wandered about, arm in arm, making eyes and giggling. It was the place to be seen, perhaps the one night in the year when the town had its very own *passeggiata*. The teenage boys seemed largely indifferent. Or perhaps they were too drunk or too shy to make a move.

Everybody was looking at their watches, waiting for 10.30. There were still some streaks of light in the west. Then, at the appointed hour, the sky across the Tweed was filled with multi-coloured explosions. The crowd roared with approval.

There were crackles, pops, bangs, wheeees. *Ooooh*, went the crowd. *Aaaaah*.

As the fireworks grew to a climax, the air filled with a crescendo of furious screaming. The crowd screamed back. It was as if all the devils of hell were after the souls of the slaughtered.

It had been my intention to go to bed straight after the fireworks. Tonight I was prepared for a better night's sleep. I'd bought earplugs.

But I had not reckoned on the hospitality of the drum major. I was just returning from brushing my teeth at the hosepipe when I found myself lured into his capacious campaign tent with the promise of beers unlimited. He and his friends from the Coldstream Pipe Band turned out to be a fount of stories.

When I asked the drum major about the big police presence in the town, he said that in the old days the police would intercept English revellers heading for Coldstream during Civic Week and turn them back. Otherwise there was always trouble. The police effectively acted as border guards.

He used to go the other way, south across the river, to get into trouble. 'When I was young,' he said as he pulled the ring on a can – 'I *was* young once, believe it or not – the pubs closed at ten o'clock and we used to go to Cornhill for the last half-hour. Same on the Saturday, pubs used to close at two o'clock, half two here, three o'clock in England, so we used to go across the Border for the last half-hour.'

He was rightly proud of the Coldstream Pipe Band. 'There's three guys who started in our band who went on to be drum majors in the KOSB. It's an amazing achievement for a little band.'

I said it was good to see a lot of young faces playing the pipes and drums.

'We've always had kids, always have,' he said. 'But the problem with the kids is you get them in the band, you teach them, they get to the age of sixteen, seventeen, eighteen – and other things take over. But they always come back. I was away for a good ten years, came back. It was because I got an ultimatum, my marriage or the band. And in the end I got divorced so I wish I'd kept with the band. That's rock and roll for you.'

He remembered that when he was young the band used to play Thursday night in Berwick, and when they stopped playing they'd close the bar. 'So we'd go to the nightclub and get absolutely hammered. And some of the lads had to get up for school the next day. I don't think I was a bad influence. All part of growin' up. I think they had a good upbringing. They werenae roamin' the streets, they were in the band.'

I told him I'd seen English home rule posters on the back of the sign welcoming visitors to Cornhill, on the other side of the Tweed.

'Ah, I wouldnae pay any attention to that,' he said.

'The English Defence League?' I asked.

'I dunno. It's no goin' to happen anyway. My sense is that the Borderers are dead against it. Cos if they get it – I live in England, just, and I get a lot of work in Scotland. So where do I pay my taxes? Do I pay them to Scotland, do I pay them to England? Do I have to show my passport every time I cross the bridge?'

'The vodka's finished,' said a woman with an English accent. 'And the flat coke's half empty.'

'The vodka's finished?' he asked.

'There was only a little bit in it,' she said.

'Bloody English, drinkin' all ma drink.' He laughed. 'Have you ever got off the train at Berwick? Well, if you were going down onto the platform, there's a big sign saying that this station is on the site of the Great Hall of Berwick Castle. And that's where Edward I held court, where he summoned the contenders to be king of Scotland, and he decided on John Balliol. That's where that happened. And during the Wars of Independence the English captured Robert the Bruce's wife and they hung her in a cage frae the walls of Berwick Castle for weeks . . .'

He looked wistfully into the middle distance, as if the past lay there, then took a sip from his can. 'In 1296 Edward crossed the

Tweed here. The English ransacked the abbey and the prior of the time wrote to them and asked for compensation, and he got it. Got money in compensation.'

He laughed. 'And then fae here Edward went to Berwick and he slaughtered seven thousand people. They reckon he only stopped because he saw one of his soldiers with his sword in a pregnant woman. And he said that's enough. Seven thousand.' He paused. 'He was a vicious man.'

There was a silence. Then in a quiet voice he said, 'History's a funny thing, in't it?'

TWELVE

A PLEASANT PASTORAL STREAM

Coldstream to Horncliffe

... the Tweed ... is a pleasant pastoral stream ...

– Tobias Smollett, *The Expedition of Humphry Clinker* (1771)

It wasn't until November that I travelled back north to complete the journey begun six months before. At the top edge of Berwick a Cross of St George flew in the garden of a pebble-dashed semi backing onto the East Coast Line. It must have been the most northerly Cross of St George in England.

Over the Border, as the sun lowered across the Merse, the ploughed fields turned deep red, then purple in the dusk. Other fields were green and purple with beets, neeps, cabbages, sprouts. Beyond lay unseen cliffs dropping into the steel-grey sweep of the North Sea.

It was dark by the time the train drew into the caverns of Waverley. Walking up the steep ramp out of the bowels of the station I'd expected to be greeted by the chill, damp gloom of a November evening. Instead there was light, colour and music. Above me the stern Victorian façade of Jenner's department store had been transformed by pink floodlighting into something French and frothy. And on the corner of Waverley Bridge and Princes Street, where for years an old lag had belted out 'Scotland the Brave', 'Speed Bonny Boat' and a couple of other standards, there was a fresh-faced young piper – it might have been a boy or it might have been a girl – in a beanie hat playing passionate pibroch, weaving dazzling variations out of reeds and wood and air. The notes spiralled like a buzzard in an updraft.

Day Nine: Friday, 15th November 2013　And so I found myself on a chilly morning back at Coldstream, this time on the English side of the bridge. Below me the Tweed rushed through the narrow passage between the bank and the wide weir called the Cauld. My old friend and climbing partner Bob Reid had given me a lift south from Edinburgh, and he was going to accompany me for the last two days of the walk.

As it happens, the site engineer responsible for the construction of Coldstream Bridge some two and a half centuries ago was also called Robert Reid. Eyebrows were raised when he used some of the funds for the bridge to build a house for himself (this is the house that later became the Toll House and the Marriage House*). John Smeaton, the designer of the bridge, argued that the house actually helped to support the bridge. He apparently felt that Reid, a fellow engineer, was entitled to some perks, given the miserliness of his pay.

Late autumn, when the colours on the trees are burning at their brightest, is a fine time to walk the lower Tweed. On the Scottish side of the bridge a cherry tree blazed like a bonfire. On the English side we stood beneath a row of old beeches, their leaves golden in the grey light.

The River Tweed is above all else a salmon river, and for the first few miles we'd be walking the Tillmouth Beat. In a few hundred yards we came to a well-appointed fisherman's hut. A rather grand-looking man emerged, dressed in a casual jumper. He reminded me of Max Hastings. He was talking to a younger man in jacket and tie who carried a clipboard and laptop.

We gave them a merry hello, got into conversation. The older man was a member of the syndicate that owned the Tillmouth Beat. He was from down south. The younger man was the factor. They'd been holding a meeting to discuss the next season.

I told them about my walk, about the book.

'You know about the law, do you?' the older man said.

Uh-oh, I thought. Are we trespassing? Surely this was a public right of way. Maybe walkers here were prohibited from wearing anything brighter than brown for fear of frightening the fish. Bob – a fisherman as well as a climber – had suggested a green Barber rather than a bright red mountain jacket might make it easier to blend in with the natives.

---

* See chapter seven.

'You mean the law on this side and that side, or the river?' I answered cautiously. 'What do you have in mind?'

'Well, *normally* the law on rivers is that if you own one bank you can go out to the middle line and fish the other side.' The older man warmed to his theme. I think he shared my fascination for the vagaries of Border law. 'And if the river moves – and the river does move with erosion – under those circumstances the median line moves as well. *But* . . . this is the national boundary between England and Scotland, and it doesn't move, it's a fixed line. So there are places where if you want to fish the other bank you have to come to an arrangement with the opposite neighbour to trespass. If there's an island in the middle, for example – we have a pool down there where there's an island in the middle – we have to trespass onto their land to be able to fish where the fish are.'

I said I didn't think there was such a thing as trespass in Scotland. But Bob gently reminded me that we were talking about fishing rights, not the right to roam.

Logan Mack relates another story concerning the vagaries of Border law hereabouts. He says that fifty years before his time – so that must have been around 1870 – a man had been arrested for throwing stones from Coldstream Bridge at a boy bathing in the river below. One of the stones had hit the boy, although the injury was not serious. However, 'pains were taken to ascertain exactly where he stood on the bridge when he threw the stone – as it was a question of bringing him before a Sheriff in Scotland, or before a Justice of the Peace in England'. Logan Mack goes on to ponder the following question:

> If one person stands in Scotland and assaults another admittedly at the moment on English soil, in which country was the offence committed? If the *intention* proves the crime, it was committed in Scotland, but the *assault*, that is to say the actual spot where the missile impacted on the head of the victim, took place in England.

No doubt arguing on such matters could keep chambers of lawyers in port and brandy for a dozen years. As far as I know, the question has not yet been brought before the House of Lords.

Shortly after leaving the fishermen's hut the path climbed up above a line of steep bluffs plunging into the Tweed. At the top of the bluffs the map marks Cornhill Castle, but today there's nothing more than a shapeless earthern mound in amongst the tangled trees.

With ground to cover, we cut a corner of the Tweed over Brownridge Bank to Oxendean Burn. The path followed the edge of a field of turnips. These days farmers are paid a subsidy if they leave a two-metre strip down the side of their fields fallow, to provide corridors for wildlife. Although the strip was untended, the hedge at its side had recently been given a severe haircut by a mechanised strimmer. It must have been a shock for any birds in residence. Bob told me this was classic estate management philosophy: 'What shall we do at this time of year? We'll do a tidy-up.' He was brought up in Lancashire, near the Forest of Bowland. Much of the land rounda-bout there belongs to the Duchy of Lancashire. He remembers the Duchy's estate manager expatiating on the virtues of the winter tidy-up. 'He'd never let a farm to anybody who didn't tidy up,' Bob said. 'He'd go round and tell the farmers they had to maintain all the hedges and the paths and the byways. An orderly looking farm is a well-managed farm. That was his mentality.'

I said I supposed to maintain a hedge as a hedge you do have to keep it trimmed. An abandoned hedge turns into something else, a line of twisted trees, picturesque but not very functional. But perhaps the yearly short back and sides wasn't strictly necessary.

A little further on we crossed a cutting on the dismantled railway that once linked Tweedmouth to Kelso. The cutting was full of rub-bish and there was a sickly sweet smell of decay. Some animal had died and been left to rot. So much for the winter tidy-up.

We followed the stagnant ditch of the Oxendean Burn along its deep cleugh back down to the Tweed. All around were autumn berries – hips, haws, rowans. Bob told me that rowan berries only germinate if they've passed through the bowel of a bird. He is a font of knowledge.

Once again we were above the Tweed, on the high bluffs of

Callerheugh Bank. Bob explained the geomorphology hereabouts was the result of 'postglacial rebound'. Since the melting of the ice-caps at the end of the last Ice Age, he told me, the land in northern Britain, relieved of the burden of the ice, has been gradually rising. As a consequence, rivers like the Tweed have cut back into the land and made deep troughs like the one we now stood above.

What Bob could not explain, however, was the presence, on a narrow shelf by the river one hundred feet below, of an armchair. An elegant, cream-coloured armchair. Perhaps it had been washed down in a flood. Or perhaps some lazy fisherman had dropped it there from the top of the bluff so he could take his ease while casting his fly.

The path gradually made its way down to the river past some small outcrops. The rock here was softer and flakier than the usual Northumbrian sandstone. You'd get a bit of sand under your thumb-nail if you gouged it.

So we found ourselves on Callerheugh itself. A *heugh* is a river-side meadow, while *caller* means fresh, cold, chilly – in the past the fishwives of Newhaven would cry 'Caller herrin! Wha'll buy caller herrin?' It certainly was *caller* on this November day, with a lazy wind blowing. A lazy wind, my father used to explain, can't be bothered to go round you. It cuts straight through you instead.

In the middle of the river – or, presumably, just on the English side of the median line – a ghillie held his boat steady in the current while his client cast a line into Scotland. A white dog sat patiently in the bows. It looked cold. They all looked cold. The boat was a Tweed coble, with its signature flat bottom, sharp prow and broad, straight stern. The fisherman sat hunched on a round swivel stool.

There was a plaintive roar as the ghillie spotted us walking past him on the southern bank. 'Ye cannae come along here,' he shouted. 'Ye got tae go roond the top.' Well, true enough, we were in England and the path wasn't marked as a right of way. Although the ghillie was clearly Scottish, and had lost any right to bawl out walkers on the northern bank, he was black affrontit that anybody should trespass on his master's land on the English side. Quite what harm he thought we might be doing was not clear, but our mere presence as unauthorised human beings was patently offensive.

It was as well we turned back, because the 'private' path would have taken us to a dead end at the tip of the peninsula called Great Haugh – a peninsula that must sometimes, when the Tweed's in spate, become an island. When that happens, the dirty ditch that Bob described as an incipient oxbow lake becomes a fully flowing channel of the river. For now it was dry and jammed full of driftwood. Who knows how far this wood had travelled – from Kelso maybe, or Melrose, or Peebles, or Dawyck or Drumelzier – where, the legend says, the wizard Merlin died, having been chased over the bluffs by who knows what enemies. He fell, they say, among the salmon nets below, which caught him by his feet. Hanging upside down in the water, he drowned.

Just downriver from Great Haugh there are a couple of unnamed islands. The narrow channel between them and the English bank is called the Slap. The name evokes the sound of the river rushing through these narrows, or perhaps the slap a leaping salmon makes when it flops back in the water.

Following the Slap, we came to the roofless Gothic ruins of St Cuthbert's Chapel, standing alone in a field near the mouth of the River Till. Saplings sprout thickly up its nave, reaching up to the light where the roof once was. According to legend it was here that the stone coffin carrying the remains of St Cuthbert came ashore, having floated down the Tweed from Melrose Abbey. Scott refers to the legend in *Marmion*:

> Not there his relics might repose;
> For, wondrous tale to tell!
> A ponderous bark by river tides;
> Yet light as gossamer it glides,
> Downward to Tillmouth cell.

The saint's body was taken on to Durham, but the stone coffin stayed here, close to the Chapel. Centuries later a local farmer put the coffin to use as a cattle trough. Deeply offended, the saint came in the night and smashed it to pieces.*

The seaworthiness of the saint's stone coffin, before it was broken up, was put to the test by later antiquaries. According to William Hutchinson's *History and Antiquities of the County Palatine of Durham* (Vol. III, 1794), 'By some hydrostatical experiments whilst it was intire, we are informed it was proved that it might float with the remains of the saint.'†

The mouth of the River Till barred further progress along the south bank of the Tweed, but a few hundred yards up the Till there's an old railway viaduct you can walk across. The wind was bitter up there, but the views down the Till were worth it, with St Cuthbert's Chapel on one bank and the yellows and bronzes of lime and beech on the other.

Compared to the Tweed, the Till is a sluggish river. It rises on the flanks of the Cheviot, and then takes a leisurely course eastward, then northward and finally northwestward before joining the Tweed. The Till has a sinister reputation, as attested by the following rhyme from the seventeenth century:

> Says Tweed to Till –
> 'Wha gars ye run sae still?'
> Says Till to Tweed –
> 'Though ye run wi' speed,
> And I rin slaw,
> For ae man that ye droon
> I droon twa.'‡

---

* It turns out that this part of the legend was probably concocted by a certain Reverend Lambe, one-time vicar of Norham.

† Why a story pertaining to Tillmouth should be recounted in a book about County Durham is explained by the fact that until 1844 'Norhamshire' was an exclave of County Durham, rather than part of Northumberland.

‡ The Tweed's own reputation for swiftness may be reflected in its name. Toponymists believe 'Tweed' comes from a Brythonic or pre-Celtic word, possibly meaning 'powerful one'. It may be related to a widespread Indo-European word that in Sanskrit appears as *tavás*, 'to surge'.

Beyond Tillmouth it's a pleasant enough tramp along the bank of the Tweed past crumbling sandstone outcrops. There are signs warning of rockfalls and collapsing riverbanks. Bob suggested that some of this eroding English land might end up deposited on the Scottish side. In which case, I wondered, would it become Scottish territory, or form an exclave of England?

Further downriver we came to the scrub-covered flats of Dreeper and Kippie Islands. These actually form a single island, but the former is entirely in England and the latter entirely in Scotland. On the west side of Dreeper the Border follows the conventional median line down the main channel of the Tweed, but then it makes a sharp right turn across the island and then follows the narrow minor channel on the east side of Kippie. Once past Kippie, the Border resumes its customary course in the middle of the main stream. Quite why this little diversion came about is unclear. There is a story that the border between Northern Ireland and the Republic near Derry/Londonderry was decided by floating a barrel down the River Foyle; whatever course the barrel took, it is said, determined the Border line. Maybe something similar happened in this section of the Tweed.

As the river opened out again, dozens of goosanders flew fast and low upriver, their white wing bars flashing. Goosanders are saw-toothed, fish-eating ducks, more elongated and elegant than, say, a mallard. They reminded me of attack jets flying low and mean beneath the enemy's radar.

There were others after the river's fish. As we left the Tillmouth Beat and entered that of West Newbiggin, we met a couple of anglers, one from Haydon Bridge, the other from Hexham. They were just setting up their rods for the day. Normally, they said, they fished the Tyne.

'Nice place to be, intit?' said one. He looked out over the river. 'There's a sea trout across there.'

'Best kept secret, the Border counties,' said the other.

'We've lived here all oor lives,' said the first Geordie. 'I wouldn't move. It's probably work that's the biggest problem. My car up there, it never heads south. North or west. Never south, never south. It's got 125,000 miles on it, and not one of those miles will have been further south than Durham. Always north. Every year. Borders, way up north of Inverness. Ah, beautiful.'

'When we're independent,' said Bob, 'you'll be lobbying to come and join us.'

'Why not? We live in northern England anyway, Northumbria. Depends which way you look at it. The Border used to be the Roman Wall.'

'Some people think that independence would be good for northern England,' said Bob.

'I love the Scots and all the rest of it, but I think they'd be foolhardy to do it.' There's a pause. 'If I was Scottish, I might have a different opinion.'

'I don't get the vote,' I said, 'so I don't have that difficult decision.'

'I've not made my mind up,' said Bob.

'Where do you draw the line in this independence thing?' asked the first Geordie. 'I cannot see that happening. Crazy. As long as you can walk from one place to another.'

The conversation went back to the fish. 'If that water temperature is warmer than the air temperature, they'll not come,' he said. 'That's fisherman's talk. *Probably* true.' He chuckled.

We said our farewells and strode out for Norham. It was getting on for dusk when we got there, so we had no time to linger if we were to make Horncliffe before dark. Fortunately I'd visited the place in August, when I'd been up with Joyce for the Flodden commemorations. Walking round its mighty Border fortress, now an impressive ruin, I'd overheard a little girl ask her mother, 'What were they fighting about?'

'Oh, all sorts of things,' her mother said.

'Was it the reds and the whites?' the little girl asked.

'Hm,' the mother said. 'That and other things.'

After the castle, we'd walked back into the village to buy bacon rolls for lunch. I'd seen a sign advertising them outside the butcher, alongside the sign

R.G. Forman & Son
Established 1840

Mr Forman told us the firm had been founded by his great-great grandfather, Robert George Forman. The present Mr Forman is a man of many parts. It turned out he was the custodian of Norham Castle, and had a sideline selling fishing flies and other tackle.

He also stocked some fine-looking wines and chutneys. I couldn't resist, filled my basket. It turned out Mr Forman sourced all his meat locally. The beef came from a herd that lived just behind his house, about a hundred and fifty yards away from his shop. And the lamb came from Ladykirk, just across the river in Scotland. The church in Ladykirk, he told me, is famous for the fact that it was originally built entirely in stone – even the pews were stone – so the building could never be burnt to the ground, a constant danger in these war-ravaged parts.

'There's a Scottish tenner, and an English one,' I said when it came time to pay.

'We take anything here,' Mr Forman said, laughing. His accent was more Scottish than English, but every now and again there was a suggestion of Geordie.

'Are you from this side?' I asked.

'Aye,' he said. 'Berwick.'

I asked him whether he supported Berwick Rangers, who, strangely enough (or not), play in the Scottish League. He didn't, though he knew many who did. He supported Leeds United. I asked him why such a distant team? It turned out his father came from Leeds; it was his mother who was a Berwicker. But his father didn't support Leeds, he supported Newcastle. I was beginning to find these loyalties, or unloyalties – to place, to parent, to patrimony – confusing.

'Do you describe yourself as a Northumbrian, a Geordie or a Borderer?' I asked.

'Hmm.' He paused for thought.

'Or none of the above?' I asked.

'A Berwicker,' he said.

'The people in Berwick, what are they going to feel when . . .' I didn't have to spell it out.

'I don't know, because a lot of people class themselves as Scottish and a lot class themselves as English. Half and half. It's a divide.'

'Is there a tension?'

'No, not really.'

'But there's an awareness?'

'Exactly.'

It turned out that this Borderer (in the end he *was* prepared to say he was a Borderer, not just a Berwicker) didn't think of himself as English, or at least he felt 'more Scottish than English', as he'd been born in Edinburgh. But he'd only lived on the north side of the Border for half a day, in the Simpson Maternity Pavilion of Edinburgh's Royal Infirmary (incidentally my own place of birth). He'd lived in England since, or at least what is officially designated England. But he had business interests north of the Border, including a shop in Eyemouth. He thought that if Scotland did go for independence there would be an exodus of wealthy Berwickshire farmers heading south over the Border. 'There's already quite a few looking to move,' he told me, and Norham, he believed, offered everything they might need: builders, joiners, bakers, butchers, two pubs, a travelling post office – even a gunmaker.

I'd never been in a gun shop, so I wasn't quite sure what to expect when I visited Castle Gunmakers. The first thing I noticed was a rack of skis for sale. And fishing flies. But then I noticed the guns – rows and rows of shotguns with fine wooden stocks and ornately chased metalwork. I talked to the owners, Sam Wilcox, a gunsmith, and his father Barry, nicknamed 'Gramps', a gunmaker. Gramps, the grandson of a Hampshire gamekeeper, has been working in the gun trade for getting on for sixty years. He'd actually retired, but then when his son decided to set up on his own he couldn't resist joining him.

Sam and Gramps showed me a pair of antique shotguns in for repair. They were valued at £18,000. Gramps could tell they'd been re-stocked, and, from the colour and grain, that the walnut was Turkish. Only walnut will do for a shotgun, he told me. It's a very hard wood, but not brittle. You need wood from the root of a walnut tree for a shotgun stock. There's not enough volume in the trunk. With French walnut almost exhausted, they source theirs from Kurdistan. 'I've been to the place in Turkey it comes from,' Gramps told me, 'and, believe you me, you need an armed guard.' It was not just the political instability in the region. Each 'blank' – the piece of wood from which a single shotgun stock is made – is worth a lot of money. 'You've got to take cash,' he said.

They'd had someone turn up a few weeks before with a carful of walnut blanks from Azerbaijan, obviously hoping to make a killing. 'Beautiful, beautiful blanks. Cut correctly, I would have paid him well in excess of a thousand pound a blank. But it hadn't been cut right. It needs to be quarter sawn. He'd cut it all wrong, he'd planked it. I said, You've just got a carful of rubbish. Logs for the fire. He said, Noooo, I don't believe you. I said, I'm afraid so.'

Castle Gunmakers is well situated for all those wealthy Berwickshire farmers and Border landowners. It seems that there has long been more wealth on the north side of the Tweed. This imbalance was remarked upon three centuries ago by the Scottish-born novelist Tobias Smollett, in *The Expedition of Humphry Clinker* (1771):

> Northumberland is a fine county, extending to the Tweed, which is a pleasant pastoral stream; but you will be surprised when I tell you that the English side of that river is neither so well cultivated nor so populous as the other. The farms are thinly scattered, the lands uninclosed, and scarce a gentleman's seat is to be seen in some miles from the Tweed; whereas the Scots are advanced in crowds to the very brink of the river, so that you may reckon above thirty good houses, in the compass of a few miles, belonging to proprietors whose ancestors had fortified castles in the same situations, a circumstance that shews what dangerous neighbours the Scots must have formerly been to the northern counties of England.

It is still the case that there are many more fine old mansions on the Scottish bank, from Lennel House near Coldstream, where Burns was entertained, to Ladykirk House across the river from Norham, and Paxton House near Berwick, to name but a few. So plenty of people with enough money to buy a hand-tailored shotgun.

Beyond Norham, with the light fast fading, we dodged a great curve of the Tweed by cutting a corner across Hangman's Land and past the Iron Age hillfort on Green Hill. It was the time of day that the French call *entre chien et loup* ('between dog and wolf'), a time when the light plays tricks and nothing is certain. Ahead of us there appeared to be a field full of sheep, glimmering white. Then we heard them. They weren't bleating, they were honking. Louder and louder. They looked like geese, but they were white so could not be pink-foot or greylag. Surely no flock of white domestic geese would be so vast? Then they burst into the air around us, first one group, then another, then another, great heavy wingbeats bruising the air.

They were swans, whooper swans, scores of them, hundreds even, uttering deep honks of indignation that we'd disturbed their supper in a field of beets. Only that day, perhaps, they'd made the long flight across the North Sea from Scandinavia, en route from Arctic Russia. We could just make them out as they flew across the Tweed and settled in another field opposite the little village of Horncliffe, no doubt hoping for some uninterrupted R&R.

When we arrived at Horncliffe it was dark, just past five o'clock. Passing through the square we came to the Fishers Arms. There were no lights in the windows, which was deeply depressing, but there was a bench outside. We sat down, put on warm clothes. In the background, across the river, the swans carried on a constant gossip. I rummaged in my rucksack for some food. The sound and the smell of bread and cheese lured a hungry Labrador.

Then the Lab's owner appeared, bid us good evening. We asked when the pub opened. 'Not till six o'clock, I'm afraid,' he said. This was tragic news. It must have shown on our faces. 'You've had a great big long walk from Coldstream,' he said solicitously. 'I've got a can of bitter at home if you'd like it. If you're desperate?' We said thank you, but we're ok. Really.

It wouldn't have done to appear desperate. So we hunkered down on our bench in the cold, folded our arms, nodded our heads under our hoods like a pair of medieval monks, and dreamt of beer instead, lulled by the distant deep murmurs of the swans across the river.

THIRTEEN

ACROSS THE HILL OF PIGS

Horncliffe to the Sea

As we walked over the low hills, we saw that we were in the midst of field after field of free-range pigs.

Day Ten: Saturday, 16th November 2013   We were back in Horncliffe the next morning. The path took us down from the village square past manicured gardens to the bank of the Tweed. There was a sign so old and peeling it was not possible to make out what it was prohibiting, although the last word was 'FISHING'.

A little further on we met a man from Alnwick in his waders, seeing to his rod. His friend was already out in mid-river.

'Wur half-hearted,' he told us. 'It's late in the season but wur going to give it an hour, see what happens. Maybe a couple of hours.'

We told him about the whoopers we'd seen the previous evening. He said there were a lot of feral greylags that'd started to breed in these parts. They didn't bother to migrate any longer – unlike the skeins of wild geese I'd seen flying over my camp at Scotch Knowe at the end of May. And there were kingfishers, he said. One year he'd heard a corncrake for a day or two, before it had flown off up north.

'What are you fishing today?' asked Bob. 'Black and orange?' This was mystery talk to me. The talk was to get even more mysterious, although I loved the incantatory sound of it.

'Aye,' our friend said. 'Water's a nice height. You're running there at about one four four at the minute. You come here like in June, July, when it's down near enough to summer level and it's not a big river here at all. Once you wade out, even with a fly rod you can touch the other side. Ah, it's not a good stretch this, to be honest with you. This is Waltham and Dritness. Opposite Tweed Hill. Just like a private syndicate, this is. It's not a good beat.'

It turned out that even this far upriver from the sea the Tweed was still tidal. Sometimes this is good for the fishermen, sometimes bad. 'If you get like a four point five or a five-metre tide, it just goes all flat,' he said. 'You can't fish it, you know. But in the summer, when it's drought and everywhere else it's not worth throwing in, here you still get fresh fish coming in, because of the tide.' He pointed upriver. 'The pool over there, that's the Squire Pool. It's nearly top of the tide cos it's like slack water goes up past the island, so the fish'll lie in there. I've seen it. You know this year it was alive in there for three months, just waiting to go. But here, November, it's too late really. The fish're pushing through. But like June, July, August, September, when they're hanging around, when it's low, the fact of it being tidal is actually good, y'know. I've come after work when there's been a tide and it's dropping off and then you get new fish. It's like a new day. It can be really good.'

As if to prove his point, he invited us into the little fisherman's hut behind where we stood. The inside was cosy, with sofas and a pot-bellied stove and rows of photographs on the walls of pleased-looking fishermen holding their catches. He himself had landed a thirty-five-pounder in the summer. So the fishing on the Waltham and Dritness Beat maybe wasn't so bad.

I think our friend would have made us a nice cup of tea if we hadn't been in a hurry. I could sense he was in no rush to plunge into the chilly waters of the Tweed. But we had miles to go before we slept, so stepped on . . .

Our intention to make fast progress was upended by a small Border terrier called Bella. She was shortly joined by her human, a smart-looking, smiling woman with smooth rosy cheeks. It turned out she was a lawyer called Tabitha Bell, a name surely out of Beatrix Potter. Tabitha asked us how the path had been from Norham. She'd been along there in the summer and thought in the wet of November it might be a bit tricky. I told her the trees had kept it quite dry, the butterbur had died back, but the loose earth was slippy here and there.

I wanted to take Tabitha's photograph, but she'd only let me snap the dog. And Bella would only consent to be snapped if Bob held her collar. Even then she looked none too pleased. 'She's been down a mole hole,' said Tabitha, as if this explained something.

'So you're from the other side of the river?' I asked. 'Judging from your accent.' She had what those who care about such things would call an 'educated Scottish accent'; in other words, she had probably attended one of Edinburgh's posher schools.

'No, I'm from Horncliffe,' Tabitha replied, somewhat to my surprise. 'I used to live on the other side of the river, but I'm from Horncliffe.'

'So would you say you're Scottish or . . .?'

'Oh, tricky subject,' she said somewhat guardedly. 'Are you asking in terms of the independence debate?'

'No, not really,' I said. 'I'm just interested in people's sense of their own identity. Border people don't seem to identify themselves as either Scottish or English. Do you see yourself as a Borderer?'

'Yes. I think there's a specific trait. People on either side, whether you're an English person or a Scottish person, I think there's a particular trait. I certainly don't regard myself as English, not out of any antipathy about being English, because I think there's northern English and southern English. I do associate myself with north of the Border and all the issues that that brings. I don't think anyone in London gives a toss what happens north of the Border.'

But she was worried that the Border might become a deeper divide. 'It doesn't mean good things to us. It's the artificiality of it. When you think about the implications it's going to have for all of us who live here. Even basic things. We've got the choice of going to Borders General Hospital, which is in Scotland, if we get sick, or we go south, and they're equidistant. For everything we're equidistant here. So even just those basic things are going to be a real issue for us.'

'And does your dog agree?' I asked.

Tabitha laughed. 'My dog is a terrier from the Durham hunt,' she said proudly. 'My dog's got a Geordie flat cap.'

Tabitha had strong views about the respective merits of English and Scottish law. 'Scottish law is better,' she said unequivocally. Then she told us of an interesting anomaly. The Tweed being tidal at this point, seals quite often come this far inland. The anglers don't like it. 'On this side you can shoot the seals,' she said, 'but on the other side you can't.' She obviously had sympathy with the seals, and the Scots who didn't begrudge them the odd fish. 'They just come up on the tide,' she said. She told us that in the Middle Ages hundreds of thousands of salmon were landed every season on the Tweed. The anglers long ago bought off the net-fishermen, but some still resent the seals taking a few.

Not much further on we came to the Union Bridge, the last bridge over the Border. Up to this point, all of our walk from Coldstream had been on the English side of the Tweed. Now we were to cross back into Scotland. When it was built in 1820, the Union Bridge was the longest iron suspension bridge in the world. This elegant structure was not the work of an engineer but of a naval man, Captain Samuel Brown RN, and only took a year to build, at the modest cost of £5,000.

When the day of its opening arrived, thousands of people gathered to witness the ceremony. First of all Captain Brown rode across in his tandem, followed by twelve double-horse carts loaded with stones. The strength and safety of the structure thus having been demonstrated, it was opened to the public, who queued up enthusiastically to pay their tolls.

The name of the bridge is clearly a political statement, reinforced by a plaque bearing the motto *Vis Unita Fortior*, which means something like 'Stronger Strength in Unity'. Ironically, a sign warns that the Union Bridge is a 'WEAK BRIDGE', with a weight limit of two tons and capable of bearing only one vehicle at a time. A second sign says, 'No Waiting on Bridge'. A third sign warns:

DANGER
Strong current
do not jump
off bridge

The Union Bridge: a bridge that you're not allowed to linger on or jump off; a bridge that can only bear the lightest of burdens.

Just over the Union Bridge into Scotland there's a path alongside the Tweed through the grounds of Paxton House, a fine mid-eighteenth-century Adam mansion built for Patrick Home of Billie. Home apparently hoped such an elegant structure would prove irresistible to Mademoiselle Sophie de Brandt, the Prussian heiress he'd fallen in love with on his Grand Tour. He'd met her at the court of Frederick the Great, where she was a lady-in-waiting. For her part, as a token of her affection she gave Home a pair of her gloves (still on display in the house). However, both families opposed the match. Subsequently, Home fell for a certain Jane Graham, whom he'd met in France. He married her, but she turned out to be of unsound mind, and so when Home returned to Scotland, he returned alone.

Our way did not take us past the house, so we were unable to pay tribute to the East Wing, added in the early nineteenth century by another Robert Reid. This Robert Reid was rather grander than the site engineer for the bridge at Coldstream, for this Robert Reid was none other than the King's Architect and Surveyor for Scotland.

The path along the Tweed here is a delight. Cherries, beeches and larches are succeeded by parallel lines of poplars along the riverside, giving the scene the appearance of something out of Monet. Only the winter bareness of the trees and the cold grey of the river, with its rafts of goosanders, suggests you are somewhere more northerly.

There are well-preserved memories of the salmon netting that used to be so important here. In the past, so Sir Walter Scott tells us in *Old Mortality*,

> . . . salmon was caught in such plenty in the considerable rivers of Scotland, that instead of being accounted a delicacy, it was generally applied to feed the servants, who are said sometimes to have stipulated that they should not be required to eat a food so luscious and surfeiting in its quality above five times a week.

Just back from the river there was a curious structure built into an earthen bank above the path. It was stone-built, with a semicircular roof, a strong iron door and two grills let into the front wall. It looked like an ice house but it turns out it was a fish house. There used to be scores of these along the Tweed. Their cool, damp interiors enabled fishermen to keep their catch for some days before it was loaded onto a boat and taken to market in Berwick. There it would be salted and packed in barrels, and transported as far south as Billingsgate fish market in London.

Next to the fish house there was a boat house, a two-storey structure set well back from the river – presumably to keep it dry when the river rose. Inside there was a small museum devoted to salmon netting. A series of photographs from the 1920s and 1930s showed how the fishermen rowed their coble out into the river to 'lay the shot'. This involved unwinding the net from the stern of the boat, the other end being held on the bank. Once the coble and the net reached close to the opposite bank, the coble and the bank crew moved downriver, towing the net with them. When the coble crew saw the net floats shimmer, indicating the presence of salmon, they would quickly row the boat to close the open mouth of the net. Then the bank crew would haul in the net as fast as they could, sometimes with the aid of a powered winch. They needed to keep it moving before the salmon – which prefer to swim near the surface – realised they could escape underneath the shallow net by diving down. Thus the fish ended up trapped between the net and the gravel at the water's edge.

An older print shows that in earlier centuries the fishermen's technique was more basic: one man wading through the water would hold one end of the net, while a second man held the other. When they had encircled some fish, they would stumble for the shore, pulling the U-shaped net behind them.

Various other netting techniques developed. These were so effective and so widely deployed that few salmon could make it further upriver, prompting Parliament to pass a law in 1830 banning bag nets, bob nets, T-nets and other such ingenious devices.

Beyond the boat house there was a curious wooden structure, a bit like a sentry box on stilts. This was a fording tower. When the look-out stationed here spotted the telltale V-shaped wake of the salmon as they swam up the Tweed, he would raise the alarm. The crew would quickly row their coble out into the river upstream of the fish to lay a shot. It must have been a bit like war: long periods of tense, tedious waiting, interrupted by bouts of frenzied action.

All that's in the past now. The anglers bought out the netters many years ago. The salmon still swim up the Tweed, but in nothing like the numbers that they once did.

Up the bank from us, among the trees, a roe deer ran parallel to the river, rustling through the fallen leaves.

The riverside through the grounds of Paxton House is manicured and well curated, as befits a key component of the Border heritage industry. Beyond the estate boundary the path peters out and things become a bit more feral. I heard a thwack thwack thwack in the woods. It sounded like the Mad Axeman was at work. It turned out to be a couple of wee boys whacking a log with a stick.

'Hiya,' I said.

'Hellaw,' they said.

'I thought you were giving something a right beating there,' I said. 'Hahahaha.'

They sensibly declined to continue the conversation. I plunged down a steep slope, crashing and crunching through the brashings, before the boys could get their bigger brothers on the mobile.

Back on the riverside stood an abandoned fisherman's hut. It was a far cry from the smart cottage-like huts we'd seen further upriver, with BMWs, Audis and four-by-fours parked up outside. Some of them had even had satellite TV. This one wasn't stone-built or even wood-built. It had corrugated iron walls and a panelled door. Someone had kicked the panels in. Inside there were more battered wooden panels, graffiti scratched everywhere, and a load of empty beer cans. It must have been a great place for the wee boys to make a den, and for their bigger brothers and their girlfriends to grow up in. It would have done us for the night had we had the need. But it wasn't even lunchtime.

A little further on the Border leaves the midline of the Tweed and makes a right-angled turn to the north. If nothing else, this is an aesthetic aberration, as the Border from here follows a succession of tracks, minor roads and higgledy-piggledy field boundaries, skirting the northern bounds of the burgh of Berwick-upon-Tweed. It would be so much more dignified, Bob and I agreed, and easier on our feet, if the Border continued down the middle of the river to the sea.

This is exactly what the Border did do at various points in its history. In the Middle Ages the town of Berwick changed hands thirteen times, finally ending up in England in 1482, where it has languished ever since. However, it has continued to have a somewhat ambivalent status. It was declared a free burgh by a treaty between Edward VI and Mary, Queen of Scots, and remained as such until 1885, when it was formally incorporated into Northumberland. Prior to this 'Berwick-upon-Tweed' was added onto various official documents alongside 'Great Britain and Ireland'. According to an apocryphal but frequently pedalled story, Berwick is still at war with Russia: at the onset of the Crimean War in 1853, so it's said, Berwick was included in the declaration of hostilities, but failed to put its mark against the peace treaty of 1856.

The town's impressive artillery-proof walls and fortifications – reminiscent of the massive First World War French fortresses at Verdun – were built in the reign of Elizabeth I, after the last formal wars between the two kingdoms were over. Presumably no one could be sure of that at the time, though the Reformation was bringing both countries closer together, in common cause against Catholic Europe. It was certainly a time of political uncertainty, not to mention – as we have seen on more than one occasion – endemic if informal violence along the Border. As it turned out, the mighty bastions Elizabeth built at Berwick never saw action, although their gun emplacements were still in use until shortly before the First World War, successfully deterring foreign invasion.

Berwick's fortunes have been mixed. Despite the many battles over its possession, in the Middle Ages the town was such a prosperous trading port that it was known as the Second Alexandria. By 1603, when James VI and I came this way on his route to London to be crowned as monarch of his second kingdom, he called it 'the little door to the wide House of England'. In the early eighteenth century its fortunes had declined, Daniel Defoe describing it as 'old, decayed, and neither populous nor rich'.

Today Berwick is bustling enough, with its light industries, its retail park and its high street full of chains – W.H. Smith, Clarks, Boots, Cafe Nero, Superdrug, Burton, Holland and Barratt, Edinburgh Woollen Mill, O2, Phones for You, Clinton's Cards. When I'd wandered round the battlements in August, I'd spotted a single Union Jack flapping disconsolately in the back garden of a terrace overlooking the mouth of the Tweed. A poll conducted by a local paper in 2008 found that seventy-nine per cent of Berwickers would prefer to be governed from Edinburgh than from London. After all, Edinburgh is only forty minutes away by train. Berwickers appear to be looked at as 'other' by people on either side of the Border: a study carried out in 2000 found that inhabitants of Alnwick, thirty miles to the south, considered the Berwick accent to be Scottish, while those of Eyemouth, nine miles north of Berwick, thought the accent was Geordie.

Constrained as we were to follow the Border line on this, the last day of my Border walk, we gave Berwick a wide berth. Instead, we pondered the mystery of the track that emerges out of the River Tweed, bringing the Border onto the north bank from the middle of the river. Might there once have been a ford here? Or was it just a place to launch boats?

Just up the Border track from the river there was, bizarrely, a little roundabout. I supposed that if you changed your mind about crossing the Border, you could turn round here. A man at the wheel of a white van was parked up, eating his lunch. Perhaps he was thinking about which side he was on.

We weren't too clear ourselves as we walked up the lane, known as the Bound Road. You couldn't tell from the map whether the Border ran up one or other side of the carriageway, or along the strip of grass in the middle. The latter appears to be the case, as Logan Mack records that the road's upkeep 'forms a joint charge on the rates of the Counties of Berwick and Northumberland'. There were beech trees on one side, hawthorns on the other. Then there was a field full of what would be neeps or turnips in Scotland, and swedes in England. I jumped from side to side of the strip of grass in the middle of the Bound Road. 'Neeps!' I shouted, then jumped to the other side. 'Swedes!' I shouted. Jump. 'Neeps!' Jump. 'Swedes!' Jump. 'Neeps!' Jump. 'Swedes!' Jump. Bob looked the other way. I quietened down after a while.

Crossing the B6461 at Paxton Toll House, we continued up the track to the Whiteadder Water, one of the main tributaries of the Tweed. Whiteadder is pronounced 'whittidder' (and spelt Whittiter in old documents). The *adder* element in the name is from a Brythonic or pre-Celtic word possibly meaning 'flowing one'; the *white* element serves to distinguish this river from its tributary, the Blackadder (or Blackitter?). Neither are either white or black – just as the Green Needle and the Black Needle had both belied their names.

Along the course of the Whiteadder the toponymy is both poetical and mysterious. We were to pass close to Witches Cleuch, a place you'd be advised not to slither into. Further upriver you'll find Swallow Heugh, Pear Bank, Bite-about Wood, Willie's Hole, Paradise and, strangest of all, a water meadow called Anger My Heart. Perhaps there is a story linking these places, a story of passion and heartbreak. There's also, where the Blackadder joins the Whiteadder, a sewage works.

The leaves of the willows on the far side of the river flickered silver in the breeze. Beyond, there was a wood filled with deep-red haws. It was clear that we wouldn't be able to wade across to follow the Border. The Flowing One was in full flow. The water would have been up to our waists, possibly over our heads. A couple of hundred yards downriver I'd seen marked on the map a double line across the Whiteadder, ambiguously marked both 'Weir' and 'FB'. When we got there, the double lines turned out to represent the weir, not the footbridge, which was little more than a plank across a mill stream on the far side. We contemplated trying to balance across the top of the weir, but we didn't have our walking poles with us to keep us steady, the current was strong, and wet boots – let alone wet clothes – for the last few miles of the walk did not appeal. Not in November. Our only consolation was the sight of a white egret (or 'whittigrit'?), presumably lured this far north by climate change.

So we continued another half mile downriver to cross Whiteadder Bridge, a fine modern structure supported on inverted wedges of concrete.

On the far side was a pub. The sign said:

CORPORATION'S ARMS
ERECTED 1881
JOHN BERTRAM ORDE ESQ
MAYOR

The sad thing was, although it was lunchtime, the pub was closed. Largely because it was no longer a pub. We were doomed to stay dry. The mayors of Berwick seem to have had considerable commercial interests hereabouts, as the fine old mill house a little further on bore a sign on its gable end stating:

REBUILT 1873
JAMES PURVES ESQ
MA OR

On the front façade, another inscription simply said:

HENRY HODGSON ESQ MAYOR 1767

We rejoined the Border west of Low Cocklaw and followed a minor road some way northward, crossing the A6105. Just short of the little settlement called Clappers, the Border sets off on another course, following a field edge and Bailies' Burn towards the northeast. The latter is little more than a sheuch or ditch. To the south the very summit of the Cheviot was shrouded by a big lenticular, but to the west of it we could make out Auchope Cairn and the Schil, over which I'd walked in glorious July sunshine.

We were on the English side of the Border, so in the absence of a marked right of way we had no right to walk there. Our incipient flicker of paranoia was kindled further when we realised there was a pheasant shoot taking place in the field just across the Border from where we walked. We could hear the beaters beating through the wood on the far side of the field, clattering and clanging. Waiting on this side of the wood for things to fly out was a scattering of shooters. The first thing to fly out was a duck. No one took a shot.

'They're not going to turn around and shoot this way?' I asked Bob rather nervously.

'No,' said Bob, donning his metaphorical Barber jacket and flat cap. 'They're not meant to turn more than ninety degrees.'

'That's a relief,' I said. 'Not much coming out of the wood.'

'Not yet,' said Bob.

'There's a rabbit,' I squeaked. 'And there's a pheasant.' There were a couple of cracks from a shotgun, but the bird flew on. Another pheasant burst from cover. No one seemed to notice it.

Then the shoot started to walk our way. I wasn't keen to argue the finer points of access and trespass on either side of the Border. Nor was I anxious to become an inadvertent target. So we dived into a thick conifer plantation and then leapt over a wall into a field. The field turned out to be full of free-range pigs.

I quite like pigs, but when you see them gathering together in pink grunty clusters and trotting towards you with a purposeful look in their beady eyes, it's good to have a Plan B. I offered a commentary to my Dictaphone: *A pig if it's cross with you will pin you against a wall and knock you down, trample on you, and then it'll bite yer ba's off and work its way gradually through the rest. Even the contents of your bowels are not safe from indignity.*

Plan B involved getting ourselves to the corner of the field as quickly as possible, at least before the pigs did, and leaping over another wall. Into another field. Which was also full of pigs, who may or may not have been pleased to see us. Happily, there was an electric fence at shin height between the pigs and the wall, leaving us a yard-wide strip to try to feel safe in. The last thing we wanted to become was a pig's breakfast. Or afternoon tea.

This part of the Border has long had a porcine flavour. Logan Mack mentions, in perhaps his only attempt at levity, that in his day there was a pigsty near here that straddled both countries. It was, Logan Mack, says, 'so arranged that its occupant sleeps in England and has his meals in the adjacent country'.

Apparently the Berwickshire County Authorities considered the sty in Scotland, as about ten years ago its owner bought a pig at Marshall Meadows Farm half a mile away on the English side, and brought it home, and was forthwith prosecuted for having introduced it to Scotland without a licence, and accordingly fined £5 for so doing.

I dare say this tale had them all cracking up around the Senior Common Room.

As we walked over the low hills, we saw that we were in the midst of field after field of free-range pigs. There must have been thousands of them, glowing pink and plump in the late afternoon light. In every field we entered a flurry of pigs rushed up to say hello, only prevented from making our closer acquaintance by the unconvincingly low electric fence. Pigs can't jump, I told myself. Can they?

They were definitely interested in us. We hoped they hoped we'd brought them treats. And not that we *were* the treats. They frisked about clumsily, grunting, belching, keeping their cards close to their chests. There is something reptilian in the unreadability of a pig's eye.

I thought of the Gadarene swine, into whose bodies Jesus confined all the devils of hell till they rushed off a cliff and drowned in the Sea of Galilee. Or Ulysses' shipmates changed into boars by the sorceress Circe on some island in the Mediterranean. Just over the horizon we could see our own sea, the North Sea, shifting, shapeless, uncertain. Nothing can be counted on when the light begins to fade – dogs might become wolves, pigs become devils, or sailors, or eaters of men. There is mutability in the light at dusk; in water at any time.

We were on the broad crest of an undulating ridge. To the north lay Witches Knowe, to the south Halidon Hill. Pigs and pig huts stretched as far as the eye could see. In the midst of all the piggery there was a big brash heritage sign. It had a *Look and Learn*-style colour painting of an armoured knight carrying a sword and shield with a heart and three stars on it. Above him flew a pennant bearing the words 'Scottish Position'. This was the starting point, it transpired, for the doomed Scottish advance at the Battle of Halidon Hill, fought here on 19th July 1333, two centuries before Flodden. As at the Battle of Otterburn, the commander of the Scottish army was a Douglas – Sir Archibald Douglas, Guardian of Scotland. And, as at Otterburn, the Douglas commander was killed. But on this occasion a dead man did not win a fight.

The commander on the English side was none other than Edward III. In the Michael Gove / *Look and Learn* school of English historiography, Edward III is the epitome of English chivalry, the victor of Crécy, the founder of the Order of the Garter, the reviver of the Arthurian ideal of the perfect gentle knight. Even a twenty-first-century English military historian, writing about Halidon Hill, is taken in by the myths of martial glory surrounding Edward: 'At a stroke he avenged Bannockburn,' writes Richard Brooks in *Battlefields of Britain and Ireland* (2005), 'and laid the tactical foundations for immortal successes in France.'

'Infamous depredations in France' might be more like it. It was Edward III above anyone else who was responsible for the Hundred Years War. This was a century of unmitigated calamity for France, initiated by a French-speaking English king who had no better claim to the French throne than the incumbent, Philip VI. Edward and his young followers had been brought up on the romances of chivalry. But if war in France was the path to glory, it was also the means to acquire booty, land and wealth. For the people of France, the war brought famine, disease and devastation. By the end of it, the population had been reduced by a half. And it wasn't just the Black Death that was to blame.

Before turning his unwanted attention on France, Edward looked northward. After the death of Robert the Bruce, the English king was determined to have a say in who ruled Scotland. He backed Edward Balliol, the son of John Balliol, Edward I's puppet. For the English the 1328 Treaty of Northampton, recognising Scottish independence, had been 'the Shameful Peace'. Edward wanted none of it, and led his army north in support of Balliol, whose forces were besieging Berwick. Balliol himself had plenty of supporters in Scotland – the so-called 'Disinherited', who had lost their lands after throwing in their lot with Bruce's defeated rivals.

Archibald Douglas, who was acting as Guardian of Scotland on behalf of Bruce's nine-year-old son, David II, led an army southeast from Duns to relieve Berwick. There is only a narrow approach to Berwick from the north between the Whiteadder and the sea, and to block it Edward took a commanding position on Halidon Hill, a mile west of the present-day A1 and the farm called Conundrum. The Scottish army, coming from the north, took their position on Witches Knowe.

Most of the Scottish knights dismounted to join the infantry. The English knights did likewise. The Scots began their advance late in the afternoon, descending their own slope into marshy ground, and then climbing slowly towards the English. They were met with showers of arrows 'as thick as motes in the sun's beam'. There was no shelter, no defence, no escape from English longbowmen, who could not fail to miss the dense formations of Scottish spearmen, known as *schiltrons*. According to the English *Lanercost Chronicle*:

. . . the Scots who marched in the front were so wounded in the face and blinded by the multitude of English arrows that they could not help themselves, and soon began to turn their faces away from the blows of the arrows and fall.

When the Scots did make contact with the English lines, they had lost all order and momentum, and fell easy prey to the English men at arms. Panic set in, then flight. The English knights remounted and set off in pursuit, felling all in their path for a distance of five miles. Among the thousands of Scottish dead lay Douglas, five earls and a host of notables. The contemporary English poet Laurence Minot exulted over the victory, and the surrender of Berwick the following day:

> A little fro that foresaid toune
> Halydon-hill that es the name
> Thaire was crakked many a crowne
> Of wild Scottes, and alls of tame;
> Thaire was thaire banner born all doune.

Another glorious defeat . . . Fortunately for Scotland, if not for France, four years later Edward turned his attentions across the Channel.

We too needed to flee north out of England, to avoid the attentions of another herd of frisky pigs – perhaps the reincarnations of Edward's vengeful knights. So we clambered over a drystone dike and an electric fence and dropped into Scotland. We found ourselves in a quiet pasture, looking east in the low light. Here and there the dark sea was streaked with pale blue mist. Then over a near horizon there appeared a flock of sheep, advancing purposefully. I offered a commentary to my Dictaphone: *And now the sheep are charging towards us like mad bastards. What the fuck? [laughs] What did I ever do to you? These are very brave sheep. I think there's something about when the low light comes, they change from sheep into lions.*

The sheep turned out to be placid enough. The same could not be said of the heifers in the next field. They were distinctly hostile, obliging us to hop over an electric fence, a barbed-wire fence and a wall back into England. We strode on down to the burbling of a sheuch and the distant roar of the A1. An Eddie Stobart lorry sped south across the Border. A flock of starlings heading for their night-time roost began to swirl about and swarm.

The hedgerow on the side of the A1 lay-by at the Border was full of shit and litter – toilet paper, cans, plastic bags, empty food trays. Dodging the human waste we then had to dodge the traffic across the dual carriageway. On the far side there's a stretch of Border wall, specially built for the tourists. Bob sat astride it for the camera, as no doubt thousands have before him. I dutifully snapped.

On the east side of the wall the Border continues down a hedgerow, but the way is blocked by a fierce fence and barbed-wire entangle-ment. It's clear the farmer does not welcome visitors. Even if you did make your way across unscathed, you'd shortly be confronted by an even trickier obstacle: the main East Coast Line. The penalty, as I understand it, for attempting to cross a railway line is a £1,000 fine, possibly preceded by electrocution.

Fortunately we already had an alternative plan up our sleeves. We'd arranged to meet my sister Tricia and her husband Jem here, and they gave us a lift a few hundred yards down the A1 to the little road that cuts down to Marshall Meadows Farm, then across a bridge over the railway to a caravan park on the top of the cliffs overlooking the sea. There's also, this being the English side, a marked right of way.

We drove down to Marshall Meadows Farm and parked in a large expanse of empty tarmac. A man emerged from the house.

'This is a private road,' he said. He had a Scottish accent.

'Oh, is it?' I said, playing the daft laddie. 'Sorry. We didn't see a sign.'

'There's a sign.'

'Oh. Could we possibly park here? We're walking the length of the Border, and we couldn't get along it further up because of the railway.'

He stared at us as if he'd never heard such nonsense.

'Most people who come and ask to park here I tell 'em to get lost.'

'Oh. Oh dear.'

Then something must have softened in his steely soul. 'Just park over at the other side there by that thing,' he said, exasperated. 'Just park there and on you go.'

'Thanks very much. Cheers.'

'Nae bother,' he said, although I fear this concession may have cost him dearly.

The way across the bridge over the railway line is blocked by a barrier, striped in red and white, just as if it was an actual border post. It could have been Checkpoint Charlie. We didn't need our host to lift it, though, as we could walk round the side. And so we came to an edge above the sea. Sheer cliffs of soft red sandstone dropped down onto steep slopes of grass and bracken. At their foot stretched a boulder-strewn beach.

We joined the coastal path and followed it north through a gate into Berwickshire. There was a Welcome to Scotland sign with a Saltire that lit up in the flash of Bob's camera. Fàilte gu Alba, it said.

Having rejoined the Border, we were now faced with something of a problem. There was a steep cliff between the path and the shore. I'd brought along a rope and harness, thinking we might have to abseil. But, though the light was fast fading, it looked like there might be a steep grassy gully offering us a way down between the cliffs on either side. We investigated, cautiously stepping from tussock to tussock, from rabbit hole to rabbit hole, down the steep muddy slope. Further progress was barred by a cliff beneath our feet. But there was a ledge that led southward under a massive sandstone overhang. We made our way carefully along this, hoping there might be a route. It was becoming difficult to make out any detail as darkness fell. The ledge came to an end. Below us there was a steep nettle-covered slope. Then it seemed to stop. There must have been a drop, a cliff of maybe twenty or thirty feet blocking the way to the shore. If there'd been light and time, we might have rigged up an abseil, or walked three fields north where there was rumoured to be some kind of path down to the shore. But when we got back up to the cliff top there was only one decision to be made. The very end of the Border, now shrouded in darkness, would have to remain untrodden.

There was no swell. The sea was calm. We could just make out the white foam of low waves as they lapped the shore. To the south the lights of the castle on Holy Island stood out against the darkness. Beyond it, the lighthouse on Inner Farne gave an occasional flash. To the west, just above the horizon, was the planet Venus. Eclipsing all else, though, to the east a full moon rose above the sea through bands of grey and pink cloud into the darkening blue above.

I'd always thought that the west coast was the place for endings. After all, the west is where the sun goes down, offering the promise of a brighter, other world beyond the horizon.

But coming eastward to the North Sea – the Septentrionalis Oceanus of the ancients, the German Ocean as we used to call it, the Nordzee, the Nordsøen, la mer du Nord – turned out to be a fitting end to this Border walk.

The moon was at the full and spread before us a path of beaten gold and silver. People across different borders might be looking at the same moon, and to each person the moon would extend the same path.

So, as we gazed out towards where vision ends and imagination begins, a path of beaten gold and silver shimmered before us, shimmered across the boundless, blue-grey borderless sea.

That was a Saturday night in mid-November. By Monday the wind had turned to the northwest and the first snows were falling over the Highlands, spreading south. It was time to go home.

Where was home? It was complicated. It wasn't a war zone, a shanty town, a refugee camp, an overcrowded room. Was it the city or the hills? Edinburgh or London? Scotland or England? Past, present or future? In waking or in dreams?

Perhaps home lay between places, dodging definition. Perhaps home is not a house, a piece of land, a sovereign territory. Perhaps we carry home with us wherever we go, like a tent and a sack on our backs; or inside us, in our minds and memories, wherever the heart is. Perhaps home is wherever you're made welcome, wherever they look you in the eye and offer you a smile.

INDEX